Modern Scottish Painting

J.D. FERGUSSON

Edited, introduced and annotated by
ALEXANDER MOFFAT and ALAN RIACH

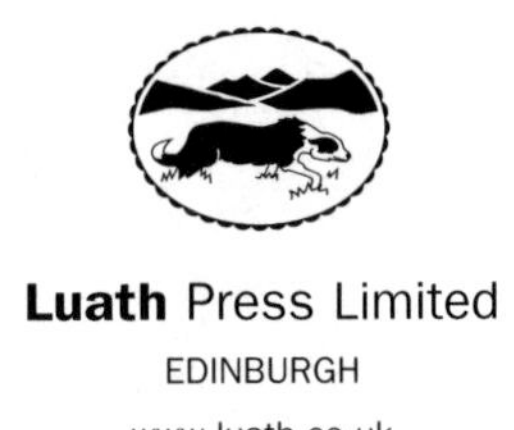

Luath Press Limited

EDINBURGH

www.luath.co.uk

First published 1943 by William MacLellan & Co. Ltd., Glasgow
This edition published by Luath Press 2015
Reprinted 2016, 2017, 2020, 2024, 2026

ISBN (PB): 978-1-910021-88-0
ISBN (HB): 978-1-910021-89-7

The paper used in this book is recyclable. It is made from low chlorine pulps
produced in a low energy, low emissions manner from renewable forests.

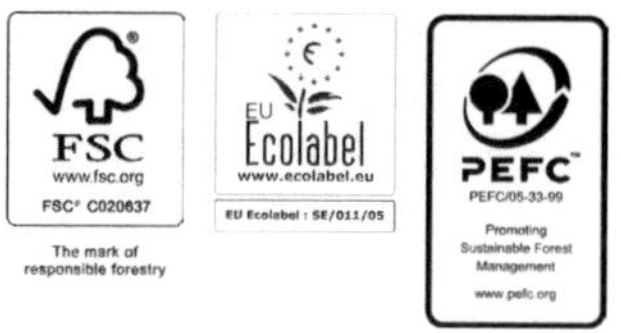

Printed and bound by Robertson Printers, Forfar

Typeset in 11 point Sabon by 3btype.com

Illustrations reproduced by permission of The Fergusson Gallery.

JD FERGUSSON, born in Leith in 1874, was one of the four artists collectively known as the 'Scottish Colourists'. He lived in Paris from 1907 until 1913 where, more than any other of his Scottish contemporaries, he embraced and developed the latest advances in French painting by artists such as Matisse and Picasso. On the outbreak of the Second World War, Fergusson returned to Glasgow with his life-long partner, the dance pioneer Margaret Morris, where they did much to galvanise the Scottish arts scene. Fergusson died in 1961.

ALEXANDER (SANDY) MOFFAT RSA is an artist and teacher. Many of his paintings grace the walls of Scotland's National Portrait Gallery, including the well-known Poet's Pub and other portraits of significant Scottish writers. Born in Dunfermline in 1943, he studied painting at Edinburgh College of Art. He was the Director of New 57 Gallery of Edinburgh 1968–78, later joining the staff of Glasgow School of Art, where he became Head of Painting 1992–2005.

ALAN RIACH is a poet and the Professor of Scottish Literature at the University of Glasgow. He was born in Airdrie in 1957 and studied English at Cambridge University 1976–79. He completed his PhD in the Department of Scottish Literature at Glasgow University in 1986. His academic career has included positions as a post-doctoral research fellow, senior lecturer and Associate Professor at the University of Waikato, New Zealand 1986–2000 and he has been a visiting lecturer or keynote speaker at universities around the world. His most recent book of poems is *Homecoming* (2009).

Also by Alexander Moffat and Alan Riach:

Arts of Resistance: Poets, Portraits and Landscapes of Modern Scotland
(Luath Press, 2008)

Arts of Independence: The Cultural Argument and Why it Matters Most
(Luath Press, 2014)

*Paintings as Arguments: Five Decades of Cultural & Political Change
in Scotland* (Peacock Visual Arts, 2014)

Also by Alan Riach:

Poetry

This Folding Map (Auckland University Press, 1990)

An Open Return (Untold Books, 1991)

First and Last Songs (Auckland University Press, 1995)

Clearances (Scottish Cultural Press, 2001)

Homecoming (Luath Press, 2009)

Wild Blue: Selected Poems (Wydawnictwo Maski, 2014)

Criticism

Hugh MacDiarmid's Epic Poetry (Edinburgh University Press, 1991)

The Poetry of Hugh MacDiarmid (Association for Scottish Literary Studies,
1999)

*Representing Scotland in Literature, Iconography and Popular Culture:
The Masks of the Modern Nation* (Palgrave Macmillan, 2005)

Contents

Acknowledgements

We are very grateful to the trustees of the J.D. Fergusson Art Foundation for their generous contribution towards the publication of this book; to Jenny Kinnear, Collections Manager, Perth and Kinross Council; to Amy Waugh, Art Officer, The Fergusson Gallery, Perth; to Professor Angela Smith and Jane Cameron of the University of Stirling; to Roger Billcliffe, of the Billcliffe Gallery, who kindly reviewed the introduction and timeline; and Ian Riffell of the Department of Greek and Classical Studies, University of Glasgow, who provided the notes for the Greek phrases used by Douglas Young in his letter in Appendix II. We are particularly indebted to Alice Strang, Senior Curator at the Scottish National Gallery of Modern Art for her help in sourcing Fergusson's paintings and to Lord MacFarlane of Bearsden for giving us permission to reproduce works from his personal collection. We should also like to thank Duncan R. Miller, Fine Arts, London for providing colour transparencies of Fergusson's paintings.

Illustrations

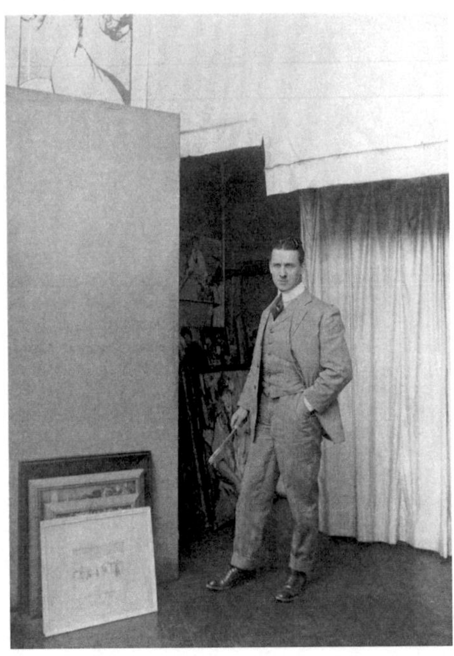

'For me, considering myself a revolutionary, this was a very great honour – and being based on the Glasgow School, it had the effect of confirming my feeling of independence, the greatest thing in the world, not merely in art, but in everything.'

J.D. FERGUSSON, on his election as a *sociétaire* of the Salon d'Automne in 1909

Modern Scottish Painting:
An Introduction

ALEXANDER MOFFAT AND ALAN RIACH

The Year of the Manifesto: 1943

J.D. Fergusson's *Modern Scottish Painting* appeared in the same year as Hugh MacDiarmid's autobiography *Lucky Poet: A Self-Study in Literature and Political Ideas* and the major breakthrough volume of modern Gaelic poetry, Sorley Maclean's *Dàin do Eimhir*. Taken together, these three key books signal the co-ordinate points by which a new Scotland was to be created, and Fergusson, MacDiarmid and MacLean might be seen together as artists whose shared vision of what Scotland could be has inspired the nation's cultural and political regeneration, from the dark times in the middle of the Second World War, to the early decades of the 21st century.

Each book in its way is an artist's manifesto. What each of these books mean enhances our understanding of them taken together. At this moment in the war, no victory could be predicted. Each man was writing a testament of faith in the arts that would maintain a currency of value beyond their present moment. The depth of their commitment and conviction must not be underestimated.

The physical books themselves, when you hold them and feel and see the quality of paper and print, speak of the era of their publication. Each appeared in the context of wartime restrictions. *Dàin do Eimhir* and *Modern Scottish Painting* were both published in Glasgow by William MacLellan.

Modern Scottish Painting was a pocket-sized hardback, prefaced by an 'Author's Note' from Fergusson's address, 4 Clouston Street, Glasgow, NW, and dated 28 April 1943:

> In February, 1939, a Scottish firm of publishers in London commissioned me to do a book on *Modern Scottish Painting*, fully illustrated. The war made this impossible, so it has been decided to publish this book without

illustrations meantime, and later to do an edition with reproductions, as many as possible in colour.

We hope the present edition fulfils Fergusson's intentions at last.

William MacLellan (1919–96) was the major Scottish publisher of his time. Alasdair Gray, in an obituary tribute (*The Herald*, 19 October 1996), noted that he should have 'a place in any thorough history of Scottish letters'. In the 1940s and '50s, he published many of the significant Scottish poets then writing, including Douglas Young, W.S. Graham, Sydney Goodsir Smith and George Campbell Hay, as well as novels and short stories by Fionn MacColla, J.F. Hendry and Fred Urquhart, plays by Ewan MacColl and Robert McLellan, music scores by Erik Chisholm and *Memoirs* by Frederic Lamond, books on folklore by F. Marian MacNeill and periodicals such as *Million*, *The New Scot*, *Scottish Journal* and *Scottish Arts and Letters* (five issues, 1944–50, co-edited by Hugh MacDiarmid and Fergusson himself). At the back of the first edition of *Modern Scottish Painting*, there is the publisher's manifesto, a one-page essay entitled 'The Scottish Cultural Revival', written by MacLellan:

In Scotland today there is a growing sense of identity, a realisation of a regional sense of community, which is partly a reaction to the mal effects of over-centralisation. There always has been a strong patriotic spirit, even at the time of the Roman forays into Scotland, but for the last 200 years the preoccupation of building an Empire has had the effect of diffusing this love of soil and awareness of environment.

The days of Empires and exploitation are, we hope, numbered, and it is now the primary concern of communities to organise themselves into the natural units which environment, climate and geography have forged on the human species. These units, recognisable as nations, have as their basis a culture, a way of doing things, which is in the very soul and spirit of man in action. This is one of the important elements in human nature, this is the quality which leads man to a fuller life, stimulates the individual to creative activity and nullifies the tendency to mechanical collective action, Auden's 'unrehearsed response'.

In Scotland we are today well served politically with two virile nationalist movements. In the cultural sphere we hope that our publishing organisation will become the focal centre for creative activity that recognises a Scottish

MODERN SCOTTISH PAINTING

tradition and way of life which is unique, distinct from surrounding cultures, has elements worth preserving and developing, and has a distinctive colour which can be harmoniously woven into the tartan of world culture.

Our list of publications overleaf demonstrates how far we have succeeded in our aim. We invite writers, artists and musicians to submit their work, which will receive sympathetic consideration. We ask the Scottish people to buy our publications and then talk about them.

The publications listed included books of poems, anthologies, novels, plays, history and music books, pamphlets and an opera libretto. The price of *Modern Scottish Painting* was 8/6 (45 pence) and MacLean's *Dàin do Eimhir* was 10/6 (55 pence). In 1955, MacLellan was to publish Hugh MacDiarmid's epic *In Memoriam James Joyce*, with illustrations by Fergusson, making a definitive intervention in modern literature with a major work that radically altered the possibilities of what poetry could do to an extent that has not been fully taken into account, half a century after its production. We shall return to this work later.

In the early 21st century, 100 years since John Duncan Fergusson was engaged in his most radical work, it is high time his achievement was comprehensively reassessed in the context of art and literature, political self-determination and educational understanding. By looking at *Modern Scottish Painting* together with the books published in the same year by MacDiarmid and MacLean, by considering the ways in which poetry and paintings work their magic and deliver their insights, we can open up the appreciation of any sympathetic reader, viewer and thinking person, to enhance the self awareness and self-confidence that arises from critical and self-critical experience. As all three writers insisted, this is explicitly a matter of the utmost consequence in both cultural and political arenas of action.

Modernism was slow to be appreciated in Scotland, as it was almost everywhere. It was resisted. Yet Modernism in Scotland was prefigured in the late 19th century by such major figures as J.D. Fergusson himself, Charles Rennie Mackintosh, Patrick Geddes and Robert Louis Stevenson. However, the breakthrough work in painting, architecture and literature was relegated after the turn of the century, in the second decade of the 20th century. It all had to be rediscovered and reinterpreted by the writers and artists coming after the First World War. At the heart of the matter are questions of politics and education. In Scotland, the idea of an independent, multi-faceted cultural identity already existed, but its political corollary was drastically disadvantaged by the status of the country in the context of the British Empire. Parliamentary bills pushing for home rule were put forward through the turn of the century, but were dismissed or held back at Westminster, so the imperial 'North British' identity was maintained, at the expense of cultural self-confidence and educational commitment. In schools and universities, Scottish writers might be encountered across Britain – Burns and Scott were as familiar to some as Shakespeare – but they were considered as British authors and the uniquely Scottish traditions they inherited and developed were largely ignored or consigned to positions of inferior significance. In terms of the state-sponsored education curriculum, the distinctive qualities of Scottish artists and writers were neglected. This is taken up by Fergusson in *Modern Scottish Painting* and is a major theme running through the entire book.

Fergusson: Four Key Points

There are four key points to keep in mind when thinking about J.D. Fergusson.

First, he was a Scottish artist working in Paris in a revolutionary period in politics and art, 1907–1914. At this time, he was on the front line of the cultural and political 20th-century avant-garde. One of his sketchbooks includes a portrait drawing of someone who looks remarkably like Lenin. As neighbours in Montparnasse, he was in Lenin's company in his first extended residence in Paris (Lenin spent four years there, 1909–12, when Fergusson was living in the same neighbourhood).

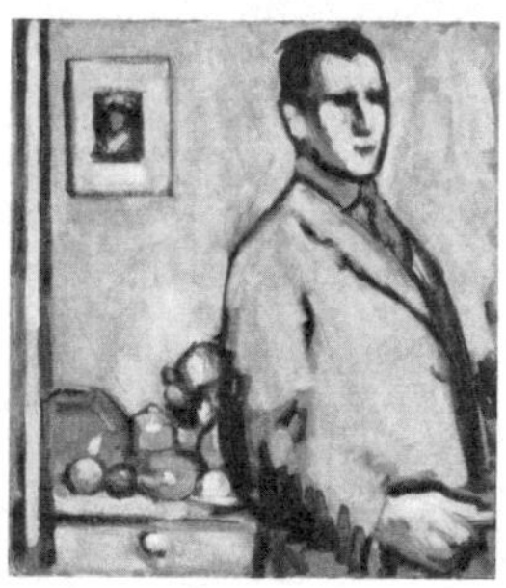
Self-Portrait, 1907

Second, he embraces Modernist conceptions of painting, what new art might do, beginning with what he experiences in France, then introducing this to his sense of what Scottish art might be. He is not an artist who works in 19th-century genres in an unbroken line of Scottish tradition, reconfirming conventions and appealing to established structures of appreciation and the market. Rather, he is committed to new forms and deep refreshment, a regeneration of vision.

Third: after 1909, his central subject matter is the female nude. Always keen to promote sexuality in art, his nudes, large in scale, make a major contribution to modern painting. They are grand statements, clearly laying down a challenge to all of the leading artists in Paris. More importantly, they represent the first successful manifestations of his vision of a Celtic arcadia. These beautiful and strong women might well be pagan goddesses from a mythical Celtic past, 'a place of unlimited happiness, feasting and lovemaking'.[1] They also represent Fergusson's open confrontation with what he deemed the joyless puritan ethos of Calvinism.

The fourth main thing is that he writes a book, a manifesto, this book: *Modern Scottish Painting*. This is a declaration of practice, of painting, as national intent. Unlike any of his Scottish artist contemporaries, Fergusson gathers his thoughts, beliefs and commitments about art and politics in this book. He begins by defining his terms and spelling out clearly what he intends to do, then he elaborates his ideas in ever-expanding, sometimes repetitive or rambling fashion. His specific topics in chapter titles are prompts for variations on the central theme of painting and freedom – freedom from the tyranny of academic authority in taste, practice and artistic social priorities, and equally and increasingly, freedom from the coercive pressures to conform politically in British imperialism, as opposed to distinctively Scottish national art. His political nationalism and repeated call for Scotland's independence is unmistakable, loud and clear, yet it has frequently been passed over in silence or only given muted acknowledgement by most of his commentators.

His book distinguishes him among the company of international artists. Other writings by significant contemporaries of Fergusson would include: Amédée Ozenfant's *The Foundations of Modern Art* (France 1928; English 1931), *Matisse on Art: Writings, Interviews and Broadcasts* by Henri Matisse (1869–1954) and edited by Jack D. Flam (1973) and *Functions of Painting: Essays 1913–1954* by Fernand Léger (1881–1955) (France 1965; English, 1973). The Russian Wassily Kandinsky (1866–1944) writes about the aesthetic, non-representational, psychological aspects of painting in his book, *Concerning the Spiritual in Art* (1911), the Russian-French-Jewish Marc Chagall (1887–1985) writes an intensely personal autobiography, *My Life* (written 1921–22), and various statements are gathered in *A Picasso Anthology: Documents, Criticism, Reminiscences*, edited by Marilyn McCully (1981), which collects writings not only by Picasso but also by André Breton, Guillaume Apollinaire, Georges Braque, Jean Cocteau, Carl Jung, Salvador Dalí, Wyndham Lewis and Tristan Tzara. However, the artist closest to Fergusson in writing of the kind in *Modern Scottish Painting* was the Mexican social realist David Alfaro Siqueiros (1896–1974) in the essays collected in *Art and Revolution* (London: Lawrence and Wishart, 1975), dating mainly from the 1930s, '40s and '50s. Here we find declarations of the social, political and aesthetic principles of the far left. The far right equivalent is to be found in the futurism of Filippo Tommaso Marinetti (1876–1944), whose *Futurist Manifesto* was published in 1909, clearly predicting Italian fascism. Article 10 is: 'We want to demolish museums and libraries, fight morality, feminism and all opportunist and utilitarian cowardice.' This is at the opposite end of the spectrum from what Fergusson is leading us towards. Fergusson refuses the political fanaticism of his time. His own independence as an artist is too important for that. So *Modern Scottish Painting* is the manifesto of a major working artist, expressing his belief in, and commitment to, what modern Scottish art is for, could be, and should be. It is also a critical appraisal of how art in the modern world has developed and reached the point at which it has arrived.[2]

The artists who have written their own manifesto or set down their own theoretical considerations on art and society, who have committed themselves to political ideals, are, however, relatively few. Marinetti is perhaps the most infamous – and dangerous – of them. In his manifesto, like Marinetti, Fergusson is talking not only about art and especially painting, but also about politics and education. But unlike Marinetti, whose drive was towards destruction, militarism and war, Fergusson is a humanitarian, pacifist and Scottish nationalist. He places himself and his life's work fully in the international context of society and people in all their diversity, and he centres his political and creative thinking in the national condition and potential of Scotland. He addresses the religious context, the oppression of Calvinist Scotland and its antagonism to sensual expressiveness in art and life, and he attacks that oppressiveness vigorously. The book is constantly and consistently engaged, actively taking part in

MODERN SCOTTISH PAINTING

a conversation with its readers about how Scotland might be made better through the work of artists and social change. As Roger Billcliffe says in his introduction to the catalogue for the exhibitions in London, Glasgow and Edinburgh in 1974, 'Fergusson was a leader, not a follower'.

Bécheron: Where the Book Begins

The questions raised by Fergusson in his little book are always vital and valid. When Scotland becomes an independent country once again, they will still be with us. The book begins on the eve of the First World War, with reference to Jo Davidson's sculpture of the great poet of American democracy, Walt Whitman (1819–92). Jo Davidson (1883–1952) and Fergusson, living and working in France, were hardly artists in ivory towers. They were all too aware of the world around them and what the coming war would mean. Davidson's sculpture of Whitman shows the great poet purposefully striding out, the world yet to be discovered. The example of Whitman's practice is always relevant: starting from where you are, to go out into the world and see what it is. By such methodology we come to understand how people still neglect the most important things. The future in September 1938 was not predictable, nor easy to be complacent about. What meanings Whitman's poetry, Davidson's sculpture and Fergusson's art and book convey are as vital now as they were in the 19th century. In the first chapter, we read:

> Then Jo said, 'About time for the news,' so we went to the dining room and listened to the latest news on the wireless. Suddenly we were thrown into a complete mess of everything that was wrong with the world, where everyone was anxious, worried, afraid, bluffing or attempting to dis-entangle from a mass of rumour and information, something to help or interest his side.

And towards the end of the book, in Chapter 11, there is this:

> Although I am aware that at the moment art doesn't seem to be the thing of the first importance, that ARP [Air Raid Precaution] is the thing to think about, I am hoping that the use of the preparations for war will be that they will bring about conditions of peace, and that art will be taken more seriously as part of the life of the person who will have time and a

desire to think of other things than defence. And I think 'we've got to be prepared' for peace as well as for war. Starting to think about art only when we are quite certain that war can't happen, seems to me to be a hopeless state, for *everyone* to be in.

Anyone who has devoted his life to the arts of peace should not be expected to throw everything aside until he is sure that peace has come for good. At the moment the problem is 'how to make a living' when only war is in everybody's mind, and all the money is being spent on war preparations.

The pressure on the artist to become commercial is daily increasing, and research in art or science must be immediately applicable to the needs of the moment rather than attempting to develop people capable of making better conditions for the future.

The book is written in dark times, but Fergusson insists that we should be thinking about a future where art will really count for something valuable. In that spirit, knowing what he wants to endorse, Fergusson starts writing his book. It is not published until five years later, by which time he is back in Scotland, in Glasgow. The war is making the whole western world uncertain of its future. The need to say clearly what art is for, beyond all military contexts, is crucial. Every paragraph is made to activate awareness of what Fergusson's commitment is to, and where it might lead.

It begins like a Modernist novel. Who is being referred to? Who is the narrator? What is going on here? Fergusson and Jo are listening to the radio, getting the latest news. Then the book takes us in, and the arguments begin, the questions take us through the context of its origin and open out the territory of Scotland, the worst aspects of the nation's history and its best, and the matter of art, beginning from the fundamentals of reality. Each chapter is an elaboration of variations on the main theme proposed by each chapter's title. This is most evident in Chapter Four, 'Art and Engineering', where the title and subject are repeated about eight times in order to remind us – and presumably Fergusson, writing it – what he's supposed to be talking about. It's an engaging way of writing, the opposite of academic, far removed from jargon-drenched analysis or exposition. We are in the company of a living human being.

The style of the book is erratic. We have pretty much left this as it is in the first edition. Occasionally we have corrected errors so glaring they could only be distractions to new readers (such as 'MacKintosh' for 'Mackintosh'). Font and spacing have been revised, but we wanted to keep the book as pocket-sized and handy as it was when it first appeared. Read it at a sitting. Then, act.

Fergusson's Early Life: Sunshine in Leith

John Duncan Fergusson grew up in Leith, near, but not part of, Edinburgh. Leith is and was a port and in Fergusson's youth it was a town quite distinct from the polite establishment ethos of Edinburgh. It ran downhill from the respectable 18th-century New Town, and faced east, out to the Firth of Forth, the estuary and the sea. It was a centre for trade and the focal point for sailors of all sorts, ships' crews and officers of all nationalities. Fergusson grew up with one eye looking at a world that opened out internationally, and the other looking at what was no longer the capital city of an independent nation.

He must have been impressed from an early age by the contrast between the austerities of Calvinism, Kirk elders dressed in black, and the colour of the port of Leith. The contrast he would have experienced was also linguistic. His parents were Gaelic speakers from Perthshire. He would have heard rich Edinburgh Scots spoken in the streets around him as a boy, and a range of other languages spoken by the seamen, and he would have been familiar with the polite, genteel English of the Edinburgh bourgeoisie. It must have been a rich mélange. After attending the Royal High School in Edinburgh, he enrolled at Edinburgh University as a medical student, becoming familiar with the shapes and structures of bodily form, and perhaps with the idea that he might go to sea as a ship's surgeon in the company of the sailors who frequented the Leith of his boyhood, as the Scottish novelist Tobias Smollett (1721–1771) had done in the 18th century. Afterwards, he briefly attended classes at the Trustees' Academy, but he spent little time in any formal academic pursuits. He walked away from them as quickly as he could.

Fergusson positioned himself as a modern and independent artist from the beginning, acquiring a studio in Picardy Place at the top of Leith Walk in 1894. He began visiting Paris on a regular basis from 1897 onwards.

The subject matter and style of his early paintings show him exploring possibilities and attitudes to social realities around him. Fergusson clearly learned from the work of James Abbott McNeill Whistler (1834–1903), the American-born, British-based artist who emphatically asserted his Scottish pedigree as a McNeill. Whistler's *Arrangement in Grey and Black No.1* (1871), popularly known as 'Whistler's Mother', had shown what might be done with subtle dark shades, while *Nocturne: Blue and Gold – Old Battersea Bridge* (1872) and *Nocturne in Black and Gold: The Falling Rocket* (1877) seem to foreshadow Fergusson's paintings *The Trocadéro, Paris* (c.1902) and *Dieppe, 14 July 1905: Night* (1905), though in the latter, Fergusson characteristically erupts into the tranquil nocturne with the dazzle of fireworks more explosive than Whistler's and depicts a carefully-posed onlooking man, the artist Sam Peploe, Fergusson's fellow-Colourist who was accompanying him in France at this time, whose whole attitude seems sceptically and sensually engaged by what he sees.

He comprehensively rejected Victorian academicism and the legitimacy academic qualification would have conferred upon him. In Chapter Five, 'Art and Philosophy', he writes that the academic discipline:

> …is a thing *arreté*, fixed and defined absolutely. Once learned or acquired further thinking or examining or awareness is quite unnecessary and undesirable. All that is necessary is to apply it and keep on applying it till it can be done automatically, and the *métier*, the trade is mastered.

As opposed to this, Fergusson insists upon the absolute requirement of artistic freedom, 'free or liberated art' and he refers to the *Declaration of Arbroath* to evoke this spirit of freedom. For Fergusson, academic painting was simply a lie. The task of the artist was to create, not to imitate: 'Craftsmanship has generally a dehumanised accuracy.' Also in Chapter Five of *Modern Scottish Painting*, he goes further:

> To earn the name artist it seems clear that one must *create* something, must make something, be a '*makar*'. The modern movement has stood for that, and that's the difference between the modern movement and the academic craftsmanship, which enables people to pass examinations on accepted academic lines, what is called a *thorough artistic training*.

MODERN SCOTTISH PAINTING

From the Glasgow School to Modernism

Fergusson was looking for Modernism in Scotland and the Glasgow School seemed to him to fit the bill. He says in Chapter Three, 'The Glasgow School':

> The modern movement in art was an attempt to get down to truths, to fundamentals, and start afresh to create a free art, or an art freed from the academic imbecilities which at that time dominated the world.

He argues that the Glasgow School was an attempt to do the same thing in Scotland, and it started about 1880, nearly 20 years before he began his search: 'By started I mean took definite form. If there was any considerable progressive art in Scotland before the Glasgow School I didn't see it or hear of it.' However, later in the book, Fergusson qualifies this: 'But at that time [the 1890s] the Glasgow School was not merely starting but *established*, and was a most inspiring lead to any young Scots painter.' So for Fergusson, the Glasgow School was exemplary in being both modern and distinctively Scottish, but, as he explains, ultimately the Glasgow School failed the test – it was to fade out as a force for a Scottish tradition in painting because it gave in to academic conservatism:

> While they were Scots they could not be academic. When they aimed at the Royal Academy and the Royal Scottish Academy, then the Bougereau, Gèrôme, Jean Paul Laurens influence was a help of course. *It was just what was wanted*, and the homespun was shed for the 'Braidclaith' which 'gie's folks an unco heese', makes for 'respectability' and conformity.

> I feel really depressed as I think of it. Here were twenty-five men, all *painters*, probably fourteen whose good work will stand anywhere to-day. Twenty-five men, independents, who established themselves without any official recognition; who even trained a public to accept their work in spite of it having been at first received with ridicule; who were recognised and bought all over the Continent. Twenty-five men who were *not* conscious of the tremendous contribution they had made in founding a first class tradition of Scottish painting. Twenty-five men who mostly preferred academic honours and success to the Wallace and Bruce example of patriotism, of fighting to the last for Scottish Independence.

He elaborates on this:

This perhaps is the truth about the psychology of the Glasgow School. Their weakness was their feeling of inferiority in face of the alleged culture of their time. This alleged and accepted culture was represented by Lord Leighton who was a Lord, the President of the Royal Academy, and a painter of classical figure subjects, so what more could anyone ask.

Fergusson's disgust at the priorities of this kind of academicism, allied to the imperial status of London, is escalated by his disappointment at the failed potential he sees in the best of their work:

> This is still the awe-inspiring combination for the bourgeois artist, and this brings us to something that for a long time I couldn't understand. It is, that these men, even Melville who had complete freedom in landscape, seemed generally to become paralysed when dealing with a portrait or figure subject, apparently quite terrified that he might 'go over the edges' of accuracy, meaning by accuracy not emotional accuracy, but photographic or anatomically exact measurements. Paint was used freely and fully in dealing with anything but flesh. Liberties could be taken with landscape, but to paint figures you had to have a discipline that could only come of what's called a *sound academic training*, such as that of Leighton, Bougereau, Gèrôme & Co., the super 'pompiers', expert extinguishers of the youthful fire of inspiration and free expression.

> So now we come to realise that the Glasgow School's achievement was wonderful, and if they weakened they did so on account of an atmosphere in which it was impossible or nearly impossible to carry on.

Reading this today, it might seem that Fergusson was much too obsessed by academic art, but we should remember the battle that had raged, especially in France, between the radicals, from Millet and Courbet onwards, and the conservative upholders of academic art. We should also remind ourselves of the enormous power and authority wielded by the Royal Academy in the early years of the 20th century, which persisted until the 1950s. The Picasso/Matisse exhibition organised by the British Council in 1945–46 as a gesture of renewed cultural co-operation after the ravages of the Second World War was met with a hostile reception from the then President of the Royal Academy, Sir Alfred Munnings. In a notorious radio broadcast, he attacked Modernism and Picasso in particular for 'corrupting' art. The RSA in Scotland was similarly backward looking. As Fergusson says in Chapter Three, 'The Glasgow School': 'The Scottish Academy at that time was hopeless, had nothing to do with progressive art. It was just the RA of Scotland, which is all right for people who like that sort of thing.' It took considerable courage to stand apart from the established academic institutions as he did throughout his long life, never wavering from his central belief that painting and sculpture should never be seen as mere craft, 'but as a means of expressing human reactions to life'.

Paris: 1907–1914

Fergusson moved to Paris in 1907, after a series of summer trips to France with Peploe from 1904. In Chapter Four, 'Art and Engineering', Fergusson tells us:

> Paris is simply a place of freedom. Geographically central, it has *always* been a centre of light and learning and research. It is a place that has always been difficult to dominate by mere deadweight of stupidity. It will be very difficult for anyone to show that it is not still the home of freedom for ideas; a place where people like to hear ideas presented and discussed; where an artist of any sort is just a human being like a doctor or a plumber, and not a freak or madman, and where he doesn't need to look fantastic. After going there over thirty years ago I have some right to speak – *Salut!* to Paris. It allowed me to be Scots as I understand it, and has *made* me so Scots that I am leaving it and coming home. I wish it was to the Highlands, but I'm not strong enough to cut myself off completely.

He established a studio in Montparnasse, at 18 Boulevard Edgar Quinet, and began his relationship with the American painter Anne Estelle Rice. In Paris, Fergusson eagerly embraced all the new discoveries being made in painting by Cézanne, the Fauves and the Cubists. His ideas were now thoroughly steeped in this new wave of French Modernism. It was a time of great optimism, an optimism almost tangible in all his work of this period. Also in Chapter Four, he says this:

> [A]bout 1909 or 1910 Picasso and Braque simultaneously they say, realised the possibilities, or became intrigued in, the idea of compositions of forms; forms that were quite representational, and resembling objects or

things as definite as roofs of houses, boats or trees, but not necessarily in the juxtaposition as they were in nature, but in the juxtaposition that seemed to them good in the composition of forms they were presenting. *At a stroke* these two liberated the world of art from the slavery of trying to make things fit the ordinary accuracy of position according to recognised conventional measurements, topographical, anatomical, or otherwise.

This was what John Berger called 'The Moment of Cubism'. In his 1969 essay of that title, he compares the significance of Cubism with that of the Renaissance, noting that while the Renaissance lasted for over half a century, Cubism lasted about six years. Yet the similarity of the depth in understanding and perception is comparable, just as the changes enacted in one 'moment' and then in the other were similarly profound. Both signalled 'moments' in which the potential of the world was changing human perception of what the future might be, and the imagination was working to propose a future that would be utterly different from the past: 'Cubism changed the nature of the relationship between the painted image and reality, and by so doing it expressed a new relationship between man and reality.' This is Fergusson's definition of modern painting:

> And that is the point about modern painting. I mean the *modern movement of the last thirty or forty years*. It was an attempt to get back to fundamentals, and it succeeded. It couldn't possibly resemble academic painting which never is concerned with anything fundamental, so it naturally resembles any other art but the academic, and by that I mean the academic ancient or modern. So there's nothing *out of order* about really modern painting resembling really ancient painting, which was in its time of course really modern, and there's no reason to feel clever at having seen a resemblance, or to be astonished or to be sure that the artist has merely copied it from something in a museum.

Although influenced by Picasso and Braque, Fergusson was never a Cubist. He was too much in love with strong colour, decoration and all manner of sensual subject matter, and much less so with construction. But later, in the years after the First World War, he became as Josef Herman noted, 'Britain's leading Cézanne-ist'. The journey towards this Cézanne-ist position that saw him move forward from the influences of Whistler and Manet was a shared one with Peploe, who lived in France from 1910 to

MODERN SCOTTISH PAINTING

1912. During this period the two friends worked closely together, often outdoors, painting rapidly and spontaneously as their paintings took on a new Fauvist simplicity. All of the major 'advances' of early modern art were the result of group efforts, and never the work of lone individuals. In this sense Fergusson and Peploe were well-matched collaborators, encouraging each other to explore new paths and take new risks.

When Fergusson was working in Paris from 1907, he was in the company of Picasso, Léger, Matisse, Ezra Pound, James Joyce, Apollinaire, Stravinsky, Ravel, Fauré, Lenin, Trotsky, and others at the forefront of revolution in the arts, literature, music and politics. The Fergusson archive in Perth contains letters from Picasso that clearly reveal the depth of affinity, affection and professional respect they had for one other. We do Fergusson a grave disservice not to contextualise him fully among his great Modernist contemporaries.

In a letter to Hugh MacDiarmid by Donald Bain, dated 6 December 1961, there are vivid depictions of Fergusson in Paris and the significance of the experience of Paris in this era of political and artistic revolution:

> The ignorance of art authorities in the UK regarding the contribution Fergus made to the modern movement in Europe is appalling. London takes the view that there are no artists in Scotland. People like [Alan] Davie who have become Londonised and sooked in with certain authorities just don't count, all such painters are able to do is to exploit fashionable trends, they are quite incapable of making a statement of their own. No one was more aware of this than Fergus, he lived long enough in London to know what goes on there. And I can say that he wasn't very happy about living there... When in France he knew Guillaume Apollinaire and many other writers, Francis Carco in particular, who experienced great emotion from the work of Fergusson.

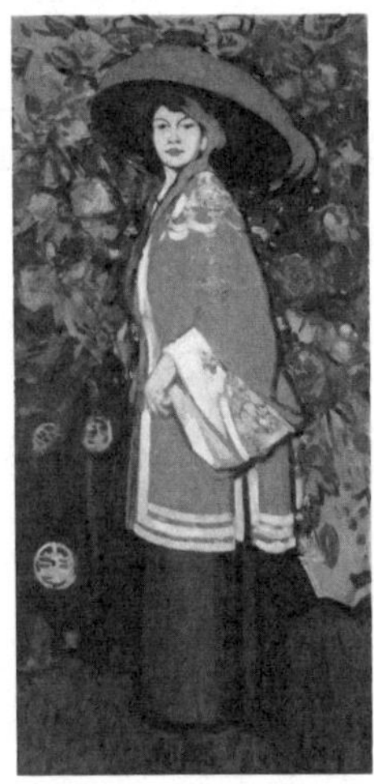

Le Manteau Chinois,
1909

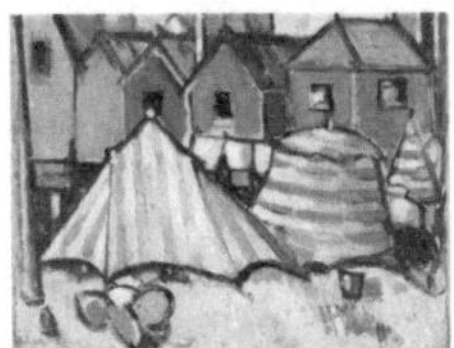

Bathing Boxes and Tents at St Palais, 1910

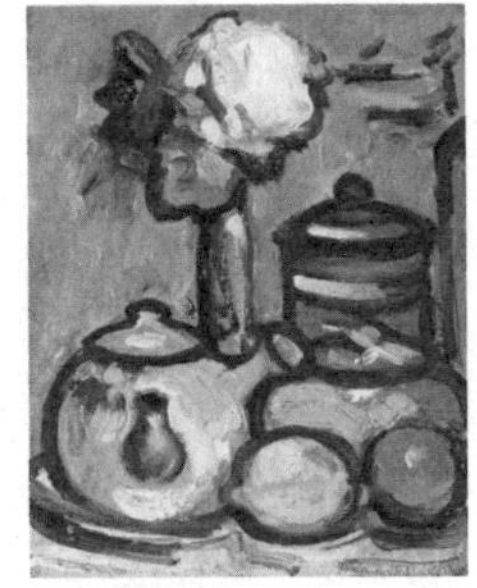

Still Life, Teapot with Fruit and Flowers, 1912

I remember Fergus telling me of being in a Paris café at a time when the leading Russians of the Revolution were making their plans, and that it was interesting to Fergus because the painters had already started their revolution, and the Irish too were in the same café. Outwardly everything calm, no one would have guessed the implications. Fergus used to say, 'Only in Paris could this happen'.

He told me that he saw some of Picasso's early, and at that time, revolutionary works. The beginnings of the latter's Cubist period. Fergus was very much for Picasso, and never got tired of saying so.[3]

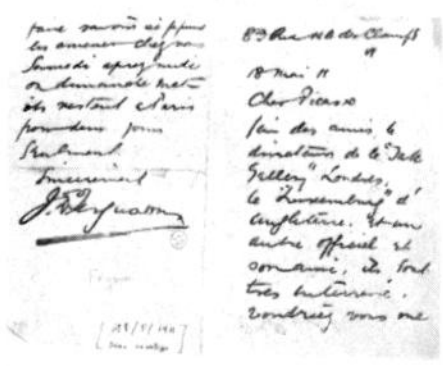

Letter to Picasso

It's clear from Bain's letter that Fergusson thought the artists were ahead of the political revolutionaries. Liberty and freedom were sadly never delivered by men like Lenin and Trotsky, but liberty and freedom are precisely what the paintings of Fergusson offer Scotland.

Fergusson's most radical work was done during this period beginning in 1907 in Paris. His subject matter was carefully selected – beach huts, still lifes emphasising his new-found love of colour – but, as Duncan MacMillan has noted, women were his real subject, his lifelong preoccupation. This is borne out in his great series of female nudes: *La Force* (1910), *At My Studio Window* (1910), *Torse de Femme* (c.1911) and *Rhythm* (1911). All seem to point forward to his most ambitious and largest painting, *Les Eus* (c.1913).[4]

Fergusson and the Nude

In Chapter Four, 'Art and Engineering', Fergusson hits out against prevailing attitudes towards the nude: 'To the Calvinist, of course, any sign of breasts or other necessary functional parts is indecent and immoral. That's what is really distressing about Scotland.' He continues in Chapter Nine, 'Art Schools and Directors':

Who started this poisonous unnatural idea, and how has it come about that a nation claiming to be an independent and thinking nation, has allowed such a perverted and unwholesome point of view to come to be considered by other nations *one of its outstanding characteristics* and not just pathetic hypocrisy. Is it because the Scots are not interested in nudes?

MODERN SCOTTISH PAINTING

Let's hope not. Let's hope it's pure hypocrisy. But what has this to do with Modern Scottish Painting? It has to do with freedom of thought, and consequently with modern painting everywhere, for one of the chief characteristics of modern painting is free thinking and free expression, and Calvinism has produced a state of mind in Scotland that makes the Scots artist afraid to paint a nude.

Fergusson arrived in Paris in the early years of the 20th century, during a period of experimentation and ferment that traced its origins back to the French Revolution and the contest between Classicism and Romanticism that defined French art throughout the entire 19th century. This was a contest which all painters and sculptors were involved in, both within and without the academy, and where the nude remained an important subject for every aspiring artist, because it was the centre of academic discipline. In the official Salon, idealised neoclassical figures set in the ancient worlds of Greece and Rome predominated. They were placed within a moralistic narrative that tacitly identified with the ruling classes. In this context the nude figure was deemed respectable, noble even, a model of refined taste and chastity.

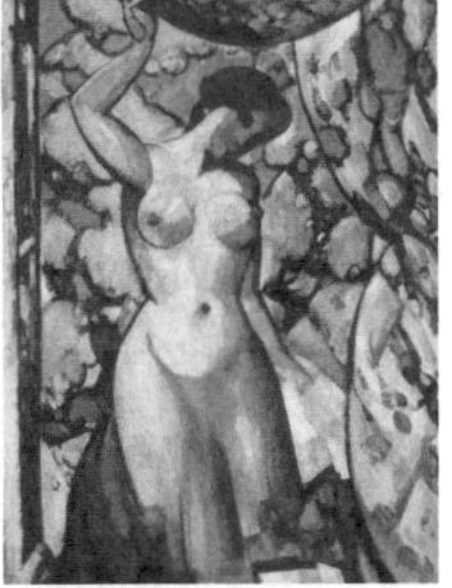

At My Studio Window,
1910

But an altogether different concept of the nude preoccupied the great radical painters and sculptors from the Revolutionary period onwards: Géricault, Delacroix, Courbet, Manet, Renoir, Degas, Rodin, Maillol, Cézanne, Seurat and Gauguin all formed part of an ongoing vanguard, a vanguard that not only set itself against the academy, but was political in the widest sense, challenging both the assumptions and certainties of bourgeois art and society. Their mission was to make a living art, as opposed to the falsified productions of the Salon.

Émile Zola thought that Delacroix, Ingres and Courbet were the three great artists of the 19th century and if we are to take his claim seriously – there is no reason not to – the centrality of Gustave Courbet is worth closer investigation. He was a socialist who referred to the solidarity of the workers and the dignity of art and can actually lay claims to being the first independent artist – he was certainly the first to stage a one-man exhibition of his work in his own pavilion of Realism in 1855, setting out his stall, as it were, with the intention of addressing as large a public as possible.

Courbet's preference for modern themes not only meant an affiliation with modern political thought, but also frequently involved a significant personal identification with the model and with the natural environment. These issues are often ignored in critiques of artists such as Courbet, Manet and Degas, contending that their images of female nudes in particular conform to a stereotype that reduces the subject to little more than a voyeuristic illustration of an unclothed woman. It is highly unlikely that any western art can entirely escape the masculinist norms of western culture, but such criticism, which carries an inbuilt ideological bias, is inadequate and largely contradicted by art-historical sources and the evidence of the paintings themselves. The art historian Sarah Faunce in an essay entitled 'Courbet: Feminist in spite of Himself', tells us that Courbet painted a number of especially erotic compositions, but also:

> In the process of achieving his Realist project he created a number of powerful, memorable images of women, images that were noticeably at odds with the gender conventions of his time, just as they were at odds with the stylistic conventions which so effectively encoded those gender messages.

> We are not in an exotic world, nor in a library of reliable poses, but thrust into the reality of the here and now, and of the sexual energies of the female body as observed and constructed with a fresh eye. Courbet's life-long battle for painting's engagement with reality makes it possible for him to paint flesh that is erotic in the actual, not the voyeuristic sense of the term. These are women with blood vessels, muscles and nerve endings, who are capable of being motivated by desire, and whose flesh can experience passion. Whatever the role of the 'male gaze' here, it does not exclude the female viewer, because these are figures that provide an image of the subjectivity of passionate women. Such an image takes its place among the varied number of paintings by Courbet in which, as he worked to forge a new kind of art, he demonstrated the depth of his respect for a new kind of woman.[5]

With Cézanne and Matisse, we have other matters to consider. Cézanne's rejection of Impressionism and his desire to make a modern painting that was as solidly constructed as the great 17th-century French classicists Poussin and Claude, set painting on a new path. For Cézanne, especially in his late paintings of female nudes (The Bathers Series, 1900–1905), painting was an intellectual construction where issues of form and content were paramount. On the other hand, Matisse's search was for a vocabulary of expression that would allow things to be presented in their most primal form, undistorted by received opinions and interpretations. In considering his *Blue Nude* of 1907 we should note that the painting is not only a representation of a woman's body, but a dialogue with the new perceptions of space that Cézanne had opened up, a dialogue with African tribal art and a struggle to use colour rather than traditional tonal values in defining the formal aspects of the composition. 'There are two ways of expressing things,' Matisse wrote in 1908, 'one is to show them crudely, the other is to evoke them through art.' Crude accusations that Matisse was simply a painter of male pleasures minimise the transformative qualities of painting, including its ability to mean, simultaneously, more than a single thing. As the disting-uished Matisse scholar John Elderfield points out:

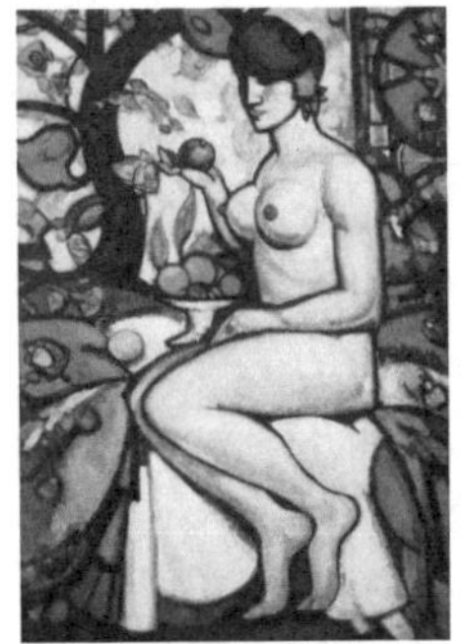

Rhythm, 1911

> Sensuous art by its very nature seems to require candour, yet a kind of candour that can never slip into the overtly erotic. Overtly erotic art is inescapably illustrative and therefore intrudes something between form and subject. Nudity, and decorated femininity in the paintings of Matisse, along with the other great sensualists of modern French art – Renoir and Bonnard, has the appearance of being a completely natural state because these women are representatives of the natural, amoral, pastoral world. They live, in effect, in a pastoral garden, with a wall around it like paradise.[6]

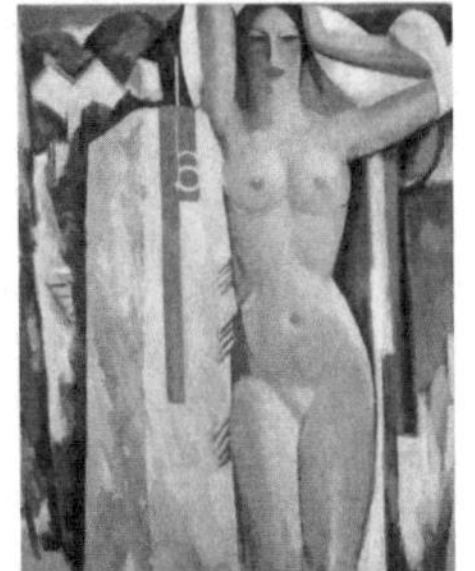

Megalithic, 1911

This was the world of modern painting Fergusson entered on his arrival in Paris in 1907. Making grand paintings of the nude was something he knew he would have to attempt if he was to successfully demonstrate his Modernist credentials. If Modernism was to be a return to fundamentals, then the nude, linked as it was to the most elementary concepts of order and design, was an obvious starting point – not the old academic version, but a nude that deployed the revolutionary language of modern painting, derived from Cézanne, Picasso and Matisse. For Fergusson, the female nude represented several important ideas: firstly, a nude woman was a thing of beauty, natural and paintable as he repeatedly states, and in doing so he could directly confront the fear and prudery he found in Scotland. As a result his nudes project an unashamed eroticism that speaks of a new openness in sexual relations between men and women. And secondly, with his growing interest in Celtic mythology and his belief in a feminine Celtic spirit, the nude provided a subject that allowed him to fulfil his vision of a Celtic arcadia. This was a vision where women are the agents of a creative energy that would lead to a rebirth of the Celtic world he passionately

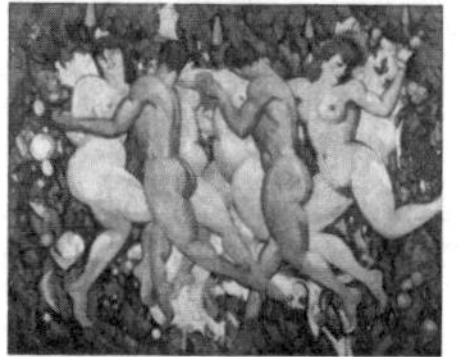

believed in. All of this is realised in his great masterwork, *Les Eus*.[7]

Les Eus, 1913

Although painted in 1913, and thus directly connected historically with Stravinsky's ballet *Le Sacre du Printemps* (*The Rite of Spring*), the painting was not seen from 1914 until after Fergusson's death in 1961. *The Rite of Spring* caused a riot. Not only the music, but the Russian peasant costumes of the ballet dancers – Stravinsky's sub-title was 'Pictures of Pagan Russia' – profoundly shocked the Parisian aristocracy. A few years later, Sergei Prokofiev (1891–1953) conducted the first performance of his *Scythian Suite*, which premiered (January 1916) in St. Petersburg, Russia. As with the climactic 'Sacrificial Dance' in *The Rite of Spring*, the 'The Evil God and the Dance of the Demons of Darkness' in the *Scythian Suite* is a cataclysmic orchestral evocation of the exhilarations, pleasures and mortal dangers brought upon human beings by the spirit of the god Dionysos, the awakenings of spring in human creaturality. Too vigorous a dance, too lusty a sacrifice, too self-indulgent a ritual leads to death and destruction, limbs torn apart by drunkenness and demonic possession. There is warning in the music of both composers. And the warning is implicit in the fact that, politically, pleasure can serve any purpose and there are both fascist and communist aspects to the idea of youth and health. The socialist film *Kuhle Wampe, oder: Wem gehört die Welt?* or *Kuhle Wampe: Who Owns the World?* (1932), written by Bertolt Brecht (1898–1956) with music by Hanns Eisler (1898–1962) shows young men and women in youth camps in delighted expression of physical wellbeing that augurs well for socialism. But youth camps were also the provenance

MODERN SCOTTISH PAINTING

of the Hitlerjugend, which was active from 1922–1945. Fergusson's painting, however, repudiates both extremes of political commitment. If the figures are riskily susceptible to the invasion of any political dogma, that openness itself is a rejection of political determination. They represent a humanity that will not be disfigured or dictated to by any politics. Fergusson's independence as an artist was too important, too deep, too vital and too vibrant to allow that. For him, this is what dance means.

So why was the painting not exhibited more widely? Was *Les Eus* too risky for Fergusson to show? Might we infer from the foliage around the dancers that this festive physicality is taking place in France? Or might we think of a sunny afternoon in Perthshire? The hypocrisy of Calvinism, the Scottish self-suppression of sensuality, the tendency of so many Scots to go to the furthest extreme *away from* the ideals of health, dancing, happiness, shared sexual joy and pleasure in rhythmic movement, is still with us in the 21st century. The popular novelist John Buchan (1875–1940), in what he deemed his favourite among his own works, *Witch Wood* (1927), addresses the ambiguities of the oppressions of puritanism and the liberations offered in the nocturnal activities of a coven of witches in the Scottish Borders in the 1640s. Fergusson's great painting is the antidote.

During the first decade of the 20th century, dance was associated with intellectual and social concerns. The influence of Nietzsche was especially strong, in particular his notion of the dance as a liberating embodiment of the Dionysian principle. This is articulated in a famous passage from *The Birth of Tragedy*:

> In song and in dance man expresses himself as a member of a higher community; he has forgotten how to walk and speak and is on the way toward flying into the air, dancing. He feels himself a god, he himself now walks about enchanted, in ecstasy, like the gods he saw walking about in his dreams.[8]

Dance was also linked to physical, social and moral wellbeing. As we've noted, in Germany dancing was associated with sport and physical discipline – likewise in France it was held up as an activity that would benefit the French public in its political and economic competition with Germany.

There is no mention of Henri Matisse in *Modern Scottish Painting*. This is surprising, given that Matisse exhibited regularly at both the Salon d'Automne and the Salon des Indépendants between 1907 and 1912. It's even more surprising considering what Matisse was doing at that time appears to have had a direct influence on Fergusson's work.

Dance had been the theme of Matisse's first great mural commission, *La Danse* and *La Musique* (1909–1910), for the Moscow home of Sergei Shchukin. Matisse associated the theme of the dance with vitality and rejuvenation: 'Dance is an extraordinary thing – life and rhythm,' and throughout his life he associated the dance with a kind of primitive potency. There are two versions of *La Danse* and the Ballet Russes may well have inspired him to treat the second version with greater vigour and physicality. Even the most cursory examination of *La Danse* suggests there are unmistakable connections between it and *Les Eus*.

That *Les Eus* is a response to the challenge *La Danse* represented seems entirely plausible. *La Danse* was an enormous canvas measuring three metres by four metres. *Les Eus* was Fergusson's largest work, measuring over two metres by three metres. The simplification of the circling figures in *La Danse*, the suspended animation of the dancers, the emphasis on decorative pattern, the non-perspectival space and indeed the primal intention of Matisse's great picture are all there in *Les Eus*. There are a number of vivid eye-witness accounts of Matisse actually painting *La Danse*, climbing up and down the step-ladder, making change after change to the drawing of the figures, Bonnard asking why he had eliminated all the tones and shadows. The first public showing of *La Danse* and *La Musique* was in Paris in the Autumn Salon of 1910, when both paintings were savagely attacked. As Hilary Spurling says in *Matisse the Master* (2005):

The response was immediate and devastating. Crowds collected, jeering, catcalling and shouting insults in front of the two panels as they had done for three years running at the height of the Fauve upheaval. Old friends were dismayed by the new works, fellow artists were outraged.

One wonders if Fergusson anticipated a similar reaction to *Les Eus*. It would have been illuminating to hear Fergusson's own story of how he conceived his most ambitious composition, and how it was initially received

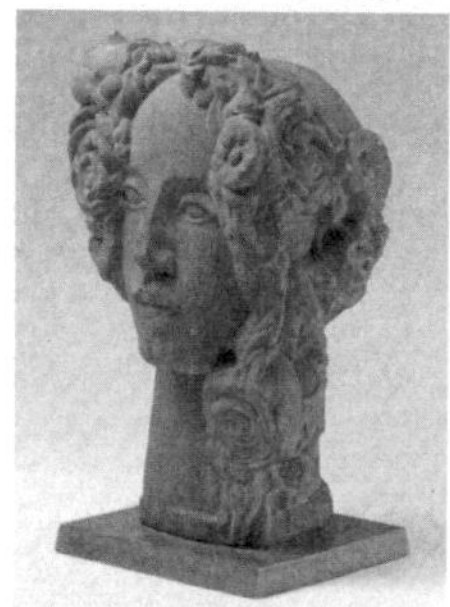

Head of a Woman,
1916

MODERN SCOTTISH PAINTING

by the public and his artist friends, but there is no mention of any of this in his text.

The title was something he invented himself, meaning simply 'The Healthy'. The painting is a depiction of dance as a signal and enactment of health. He had met Margaret Morris (1891–1980) in the same year, 1913, and her new conception of dance had been inspired by Isadora Duncan. After studying with Duncan's brother Raymond, who taught Morris the six Classical Greek positions, Morris developed her own system of dance and movement, which was known as the Margaret Morris Movement. Interestingly, many of the leading innovators of the new dance were women and champions of female emancipation. Apart from Duncan, there was Mary Wigman in Germany, who created a form of Expressionist dance that inspired the painter Emil Nolde. In Paris, Ida Rubinstein, after defecting from the Ballet Russes, formed her own company, commissioning works from Debussy, Ravel and Stravinsky. And Morris herself made a unique contribution as a choreographer and teacher of dance in the UK. Strikingly attractive, she possessed a true bohemian spirit and there was an immediate attraction between her and Fergusson. They formed a formidable partnership from the beginning, with Fergusson taking on the role of artistic director of her summer schools where painting and design became an important part of the curriculum.

His relationship and collaboration with Margaret Morris confirms his belief in the independent authority of women. This is an important difference from the prevalent patriarchal attitude of men towards women in the period. There is a famous – or notorious – letter dated 19 December 1901 by Gustav Mahler to his wife Alma in which he defends his primacy as the artist-creator in their relationship. He asks her to imagine their lives if they were both dedicated to composing: 'Have you any idea how ridiculous and, in time, how degrading for both of us such a peculiarly competitive relationship would inevitably become?' He elaborates on this, and tries to excuse himself or rationalise his attitude:

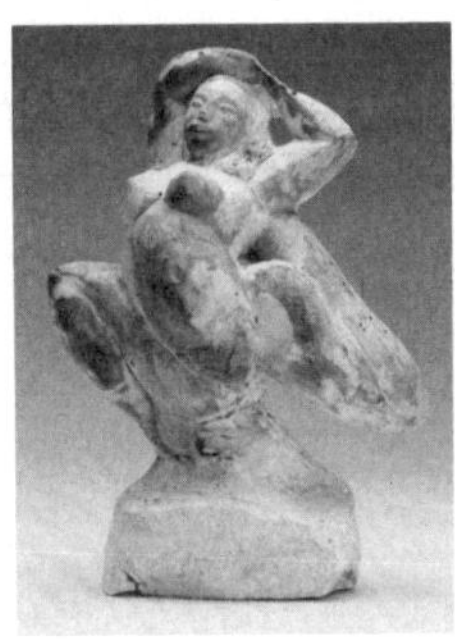

Female Dancer,
c.1920

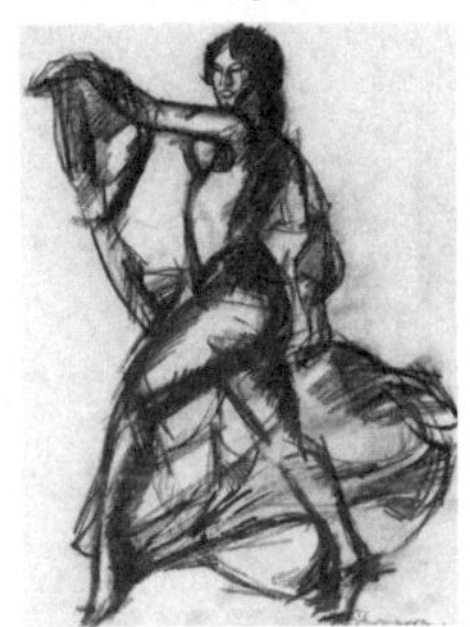

Margaret Morris
Dancing, 1913

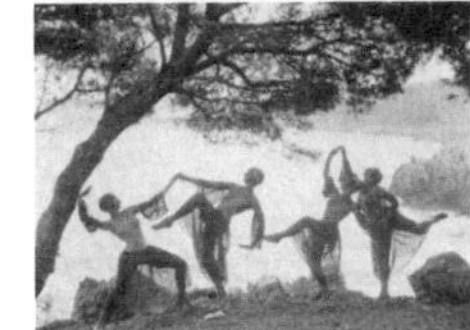

Photograph of
Margaret Morris and
her dancers in Antibes

Don't misunderstand me and start imagining that I hold the bourgeois view of the relationship between husband and wife, which regards the latter as a sort of plaything for her husband and, at the same time, as his housekeeper. Surely you would never suspect me of feeling and thinking that way, would you? But one thing is certain and it is that you must become 'what I need' if we are to be happy together, i.e. my wife, not my colleague. Would it mean the destruction of your life and would you feel you were having to forego an indispensable highlight of your existence if you were to give up *your* music entirely in order to possess and also be mine instead?[9]

In this regard, both Fergusson and Charles Rennie Mackintosh are at the opposite end of the spectrum of social and personal attitude from Mahler, great composer as he was. Both respected, admired and championed the art of the women they loved. Both were committed believers in the significance of the relations between the artistic self-expression of women, the independent thinking on any subject any woman might bring to social and artistic articulation, and the help that might be in bringing about social change and a better society. One might ask, though, what if Morris had been a 'rival' painter? Before 1914, few women would enter an art school. The artistic provenance of women would have been mainly confined to crafts subjects, embroidery, weaving and jewellery. These were the 'suitable subjects' for women, or more particularly, 'young ladies'. During this period, the Glasgow School of Art was ahead of the game, thanks to the enlightened rectorship of Henry Francis (Fra) Newbery, with the Macdonald sisters, for example, enrolling in 1893.

It is essential to understand the central significance of Fergusson's nudes, and most of all the greatness of *Les Eus*, as part of the artistic and social revolution to which he was committed, and not merely as an extension of the conventions of the patriarchy or the academy. Equally essential is our understanding of his commitment to national regeneration or rejuvenation in Scotland.

Hugh MacDiarmid, in the long poem, *A Drunk Man Looks at the Thistle* (1926), looks back on the revolutionary optimism of the years before the First World War and asks, 'Whaur's Isadora Duncan dauncin' noo?' – as if to record his ironic dismay at the failure of the post-war world to live up to the aspirations of pre-war optimism. Yet this too is a measure and acknowledgement of that optimism, and MacDiarmid more than any writer in Scotland in the 1920s begins to recapture and rejuvenate the nation's political and cultural purpose and drive. He takes account of what had apparently been destroyed in order to help bring about this new regeneration. This is the meaning of what he called the Scottish literary and cultural Renaissance of the 1920s. He took the word from Patrick Geddes, who had used it in the 1890s, and he met Geddes and Fergusson, understanding their greatness and dedicating himself to the development of the vision they had for Scotland before the First World War. That sense of continuity, picking up the traces after the devastation, is vitally important in any understanding of Scotland in the 20th century, and of Fergusson's place in that story.

Art and Nationality

Fergusson declared that his experience of France and Paris led him to a deeper understanding of his own nationality, his apprehension of his own capabilities as a Scottish artist. In Chapter One, 'Bécheron', he asks, 'What do we mean by "Scottish painting"?' And he answers:

> The first thing is easy. It must be painting produced by Scotsmen or Scots-women, not necessarily in Scotland or of Scotland. I mean of Scottish subjects; but it must have the essentials of the Scottish character, and not merely the Scottish character at this moment or of recent years, but some-thing that we feel is and has been inherent in the Scots character all through its history. Something that 'time but th'impression deeper makes' would be a heartening feeling, and we would like something that is as true as the geological fault that divides Scotland, or the road to the Isles which is the natural track for both pilgrims and dealers in ponies. Can we find it? Again perhaps not *absolutely*, but nearly enough to let us get on with the job. A working meaning of what we call Scotch or Scottish, that brings us to art and nationality.

Two key paintings that deliver this sense of a national Scottish landscape art in the context of Modernism are *A Puff of Smoke Near Milngavie* (1922) and *Storm around Ben Ledi* (1922). They are contrasting scenes: one is of cultivated fields, farmland, a small town or village in the fore-ground with the outlines of buildings, a church spire, homes, shops, schools perhaps, implied; a road runs into an avenue of trees leading to the village, coming into the painting from the lower edge of the frame. The hills are in sunshine, three big white clouds are passing in the blue sky, the puff of smoke looks benign, also white, perhaps from a passing train? Leaves on branches hang down from the upper edge of the frame, almost visibly swaying in the breeze. It is joyful but realistic. Seasons will cross this landscape, farmers and their workers will be on this land in the course of those seasons. The commerce of the small town will be what it is. The trees viewed from above in the foreground are leaning, their shape formed by prevailing winds. Weather and climate are present but unromanticised. The address of the landscape – how people who live there might experience it, how it might affect the experience of people who live there – is in the painting itself. It invites the viewers' consideration of this. It is not merely a pretty picture.

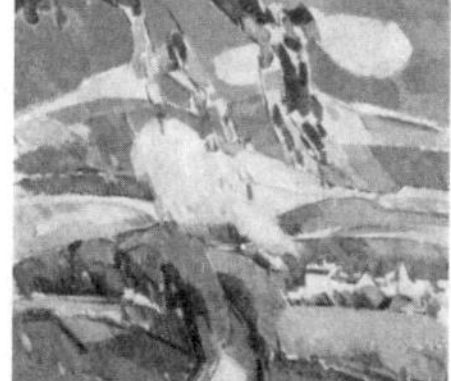

A Puff of Smoke near Milngavie, 1922

This involvement with the vision of the inhabitants of a place takes the work into alignment with the great literary works of Modernism, especially in Scotland. One of the key characteristics of Modernism was the repudiation of the security of the master narrative, the reliable voice of the author or secure sense of where we are standing when we look at what is visualised before us. In classic realist fiction of the 19th century, the hierarchy of author and characters is secure. In Scotland, generally, the authorial language is English, the characters speak Scots. In the 1920s and 1930s, pre-eminently Hugh MacDiarmid in poetry and Lewis Grassic Gibbon in novels and stories, use the Scots language. Gibbon creates a linguistic idiom that is attuned with the language of his characters. The hierarchy is gone. The authority of judgement must be created out of the experience of life which the work of art brings into form. This is as true of F.G. Scott (1880–1958) in music, MacDiarmid and Gibbon in literature, and in painting William Crozier (1893–1930), William McCance (1894–1970), William Johnstone (1897–1981) and William Gillies (1898–1973). They all build on Fergusson's example.

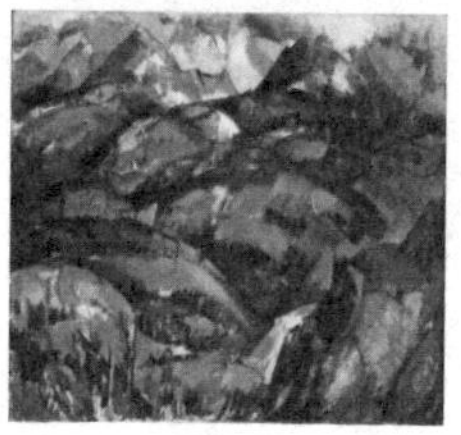

Storm around Ben Ledi, 1922

Even less of a 'merely' pretty picture, and even more impressive, perhaps, is *Storm around Ben Ledi*. The dark greens of the forests and the disrupting

MODERN SCOTTISH PAINTING

shapes of the mountains; the storm clouds; greys and blues of rain and wind, the dark blue loch in the foreground, the trees standing resistant against the weather's onslaught, all create a wilderness that is more attentive to geological and topographical reality than romantic encounter. The perspective is disconcerting, taking your gaze vertiginously down into the glens, through and over the woods, and up to the summits, across curved, sheer, steep and convoluted surfaces: impressive but uninviting, exhilarating but not easy. The permanence of the mountains seems secure, the promise of eternal movement in the rivers and rainfall equally promises an eternity of change. Looking at these paintings, the answer you might give to the question, 'What sort of place is this, Scotland?' would be very different from what could be imagined were you looking at a painting by any more conventional 19th-century landscape artist.

Both these works were painted in the same year as the publication of James Joyce's *Ulysses* and T.S. Eliot's *The Waste Land*, and the year in which the name Hugh MacDiarmid first appeared in print as the author of poems in the Scots language. They might best be considered in such company. Fergusson's work must be seen in this international context, but with equal emphasis, he addresses the question of Scotland and nationality specifically. In Chapter Two of *Modern Scottish Painting*, he says this:

Why should we say that one art is more representative of a country or of a race than another? I know Scotland and Scotsmen pretty well, and I've never met anyone that put Holy Wullie as more representative of Scotland than William Wallace, Bruce or Robert Burns. I've certainly come across people who were ashamed of Robert Burns. In fact the generation I had the misfortune to be born into *were* for the most part ignorant or ashamed of Burns and only associated him with drink. But supposing that the worthy Scot admires Wallace and Bruce and the spirit of the Arbroath Manifesto then he should admire painting of the same spirit. Does any sane person suggest that the average painting expresses the courage and independence of Wallace, Bruce, Knox or Burns? Has *any* painting? Certainly. The Glasgow School from the *Galloway Landscape*, Hornel and Henry at their best, Melville till the last, Guthrie's *Garden Party* and his portrait of Ned Martin, Lavery's Miss Burrel in Kelvingrove Gallery, Crawhall; in fact the whole school at their best had the Scots characteristic of independence, and vigor, colour and particularly quality of paint, which means paint that is living and not merely a coat of any sort of paint placed between containing lines like a map. Theirs was paint that expressed the envelopment of things in light, low tone or bright, and their own people backed them.

At the same time, McTaggart, *not* Glasgow School, was producing without official recognition work that is thoroughly Scottish. I find it very difficult to believe that anyone has painted the sea better than McTaggart. I've seen a lot of painting. I've never seen any as good.

Fergusson here is signalling that the greatest Scottish artist of the late 19th century, William McTaggart, was given limited recognition: he was Scottish, and therefore beyond the interest of metropolitan commerce and appraisal. And yet, in the whole trajectory of British art in the 19th century, it would be fair to describe McTaggart as the major painter after Turner and Constable, far exceeding in creative brilliance the Pre-Raphaelites who were his immediate contemporaries. It is perhaps only because of the failure of a working infrastructure of art criticism and appreciation within Scotland, and the inadequacy of Scotland's national art establishment to promote the country's greatest artists, that McTaggart is not internationally familiar. Fergusson says as much in Chapter Nine, 'The Master':

> The Scot is perhaps justified in thinking that a free art should naturally be produced in a free nation. That seems quite right, but it's the survival after its birth that the nation should be concerned about. It certainly is the artist's affair to start a free art, that is to say, to express himself freely and honestly, but if the nation is against or negligent of free and honest art expression, the artist cannot exist in that atmosphere, climate or surroundings, and must stay and die, or move to a more hospitable surrounding.

For Fergusson, McTaggart was one of three exemplary figures along with Whistler and Charles Rennie Mackintosh. In Chapter Three, 'The Glasgow School', he says:

> One man that did stick to his point of view till the end was Charles Rennie Mackintosh. Though this book is about painting I'll take the opportunity to say that Scotland, and particularly Glasgow, ought to be ashamed of their neglect of Charles Rennie Mackintosh, undoubtedly one of the best architects of the world in modern times.

Apparently they could not stand his honesty and independence, and bamboozled by buildings and pretentious imbecility couldn't see that his simplicity had the dignity of the traditional architecture of Scotland.

He thoroughly established a style of architecture and interior design which did not copy existing buildings or bits of buildings, Scottish or foreign, but created something new and Scottish. Had it been carried on it would have made Scotland one of the leading schools of architecture of the world.

Mackintosh's work was recognised and taken up on the continent and made use of everywhere except in Scotland.

I think the Glasgow Art School designed by Mackintosh to the smallest detail of wood and ironwork, inside and out, is a masterpiece of constructional integrity.

Most Glasgow people haven't noticed it, haven't even heard of Mackintosh, and I don't think a book on his work has been done in Scotland, although he may be considered the father of modern architecture.

He told me that as people didn't want architecture as he wanted to do it, he preferred to give it up, and he took to painting and did very good water colours which have the same constructional integrity as his architecture.

Both Mackintosh and his wife Margaret MacDonald always insisted on their great indebtedness to the director of the Glasgow Art School, Francis Newbery and his wife for their wonderful sympathy, understanding and encouragement, without which they said they did not think they could have got a start, so all respect and good wishes to the Newberys.

Like McTaggart and Patrick Geddes before him, and along with his close friends S.J. Peploe and Charles Rennie Mackintosh, Fergusson had a vision for Scotland. 'It is quite possible to turn Scotland into one of the most wonderful and vital countries in the world, but it has to be done by Scots.' This vision, Fergusson understood, had to be realised by means of literature and art, architecture and design, hence his rallying call in Chapter Six, 'Scotland and Colour':

It seems reasonable to suppose that in Scotland's great times the black suit (the now accepted 'stan' o' black') was not the idea of a gala dress. Then where does this black and gloom and grey come from? Who or what caused it? Is it really in the soul of the Scot?

> ...Glasgow free from dirt would be a beautiful city. So all Scots should refuse to have anything to do with black, dirty, drab colours. *It is the duty of* artists, architects, decorators and designers to give a lead to make a brighter Scotland.

His vision was far-reaching and continues to inspire and instruct. That is the real legacy of *Modern Scottish Painting*. His love of country and his desire for independence was recognised by all of his friends and fellow artists, including Pablo Picasso. In her biography, *The Art of J.D. Fergusson,* Margaret Morris remembers Antibes in the summer of 1924:

> One day we met Picasso at Eden Roc and we walked back to the hotel together. He said, 'You do not fit into this place,' and picked a sprig of bog-myrtle from a bush and handed it to Fergus, saying, 'This is you'.

Independent Art

'À Nous La Liberté' is the key theme throughout. It is a statement of intent and desire that can be heard throughout history, in many different languages. In Chapter Seven, 'Independent Art', Fergusson states his case most boldly:

> Scotland should have an independent art. No one has a right to decide for others what *is* art and what isn't. The public has a right to decide for itself, and to like what is considered to be bad art if they choose. Any intelligent person ought to be able to see that in any properly composed community art is an important social asset.

> I can hardly imagine that any intelligent person thinks that art is not part of education, or that art can develop without research. Research demands free thinking. Therefore there ought to be encouragement for free thinking or free *feeling* in art.

> ...Why should the restraint and discipline of the academies and academic art schools be accused of keeping back the artists or thinkers? They are not keeping them back in the *academic* sense. The student is perfectly free to do what the academies think he should do. They encourage him, give him prizes and scholarships, but it is very evident that the academic suc-

cesses have hardly ever, I should say never, been the *research men* and the *explorers*, inventors and discoverers.

Independence in politics, art and literature is at the heart of Fergusson's book. In Chapter Five, 'Art and Philosophy', he spells it out:

> Since the union with England perhaps, and the industrial boom, his [the Scot's] conduct has been that of a person content most of the time with the results that came from material things that he could prove to his own satisfaction to be workable. His *conduct* has been that, but there is something deeper than conduct, and he has at times shown, as at the Glasgow School period, that there was deeper down a feeling for art, for most of the time submerged, and the belief that this still exists makes it worthwhile to try to get the Scot to apply his reasoning powers to the examination of art and its place, value and contribution to the social condition of a free nation.

This 'free nation' is nothing less than an independent Scotland where the arts can flourish and people have the dignity and self-esteem that is their most vital human property. Fergusson saw how this could work, in France and elsewhere, and knew what it meant to the innate capacity of women and men to live in a world not given to the destructions of war and commercialisation. This is his distinction between freedom and slavery:

> I say to a *free* nation, for to a *slave* nation freedom of thought, invention and creative ideas in any form are not necessary. A slave nation can always steal, and exploit by cheap slave labour, the ideas and inventions of a free nation.

In other words, it is not only the problem of Scotland bound to the priorities of British imperialism, but rather the people of a nation bound to the practices of theft and exploitation, the worst excesses of capitalism and everything they bring. For Fergusson, prophetically, the answer was to liberate Scotland from both forms of oppression at once, for: 'What is art and what makes it? Independent art is created by an independent people. Is that saying too much? Well, gaze around in this year of grace.'

Fergusson places great importance on how one becomes an artist, or better still, an independent artist. His reason for writing *Modern Scottish Painting* was his desire to 'try to give the young Scottish artist the help he himself wasn't even offered', and his main premise is that an art school is not the only way to train an artist: 'I object to people (and especially arts students) being under the impression that [the art school] is the only education possible if you want to become an artist'. Instead, he advises that the aspiring young artist:

> If he is intelligent and honest with himself, he will realise that he has more chance of becoming an artist by working in human conditions from still life, his people or friends as models (they need not be nude), or street scenes, landscape and the endless subjects of human interest instead of the set model in the set light.

Pressing home his argument, he concludes:

> If the student realises this and wants what is to be got by it he will then not go near an art school, and if he has got there he will be glad to leave it. If he wants to work in a group and share expenses of a room to work in where each can work in his own way. His group can have an exhibition… and hang their works in their own way. In short, have freedom. But he won't have everything provided for him in a school. He'll have to pay for this freedom, do without things, make sacrifices. Certainly it's not easy. It merely depends on what is wanted.

What Fergusson says here about self-help and sharing studio space is now commonly accepted as the most practical model for many young artists, a model that has been increasingly adopted across Scotland in the last decades of the 20th, and into the 21st centuries.

In Chapter 11, 'Responsibility of Art Schools and Directors', he states clearly what he thinks is the real purpose and proper function of an art school:

> I have heard that it has been frankly said that in an Art School the main thing is to turn out people fit to make a living. *That should not be the main thing.* That should be a *by-product.* The making of a living should be the result of having created or produced something.

Fergusson insists that art can never be about examinations and tests, nor can it be about mere craft, which academic methods prioritise. In Chapter Eight, 'The Journeyman Artist', he attempts to explain the difference between an artist and a craftsman, pointing out that the journeyman mechanic, 'say in wireless, has not invented wireless' and that a doctor's degree simply proves his ability to pass exams: 'It does not prove that he is able to invent anything'. Invention is crucial for Fergusson: 'The research man needs no degree, the only excuse for using the name artist is to mean a *creator or inventor*.' Indeed:

> The idea that the artist is a supercraftsman and that there is a technique of painting that can be *completely* acquired by study, application or *a thorough artistic training* (I suppose in anatomy, etc.) simply means that there is an apprenticeship and that by examinations or tests it can be decided that the apprentice at a certain point becomes a journeyman, what the French call a 'patented plumber', or gets a degree like a doctor. What could be more confusing. Further, that if he proves exceptional ability he can become a professor. Then his work and opinions on art are not to be questioned by the ordinary man or the student or unrecognised artist.

The academic notion of technical expertise is also highly suspect in Fergusson's view:

> It makes me wonder what people mean when they say that *technically* a work of art is wonderful, meaning, I suppose that there is something called '*technique*' that can be separated from the work of art.

He counters this kind of admiration for technical skill by pointing out that:

> It is pretty clear that most people have not even thought of *quality* of paint, and that many think that quantity of paint is quality. Quality of paint like quality of line or quality of tone is not a thing that can be fixed. It is the artist's statement in paint of his reaction to form created by the play of light, and is poor or full according to the painter's sensibility and experience of life.

In Chapter Nine, 'The Master' his thoughts are particularly illuminating where he articulates the dilemma that every creative artist has to face:

> One of the great mistakes of the artist is to desire to become a master, that is 'to be called Rabbi' – master of one's destiny, 'master of one's medium', 'cher maître' and all that. The word master and artist seem contradictory. Can any real artist be a master? A great craftsman should be a master of his medium, or his trade, which only seems to mean that he can put the final polish on his productions.

The artist, I think, is not concerned with final polish but with ultimate truth, and no one worthy of the name artist can really believe he can reach the ultimate truth.

To the real artist life is continuous defeats, some less discouraging than others, some that for a *moment* almost *look like* successes, but never even for *a moment*, success. The artist to live, must go on.

In addition, he fully understands that success cannot be predicted or guaranteed:

But how are we going to know who is the artist deserving of support if we have not the guide of academic success or approval? Well! You can't know. *You must take a chance on it!* Use your judgement.

His low opinion of art schools was of course based on his experiences of the academic methods of training students on offer in the 1890s. That art schools had responded to the challenge of Modernism thanks to enlightened educators like Fra Newbury is unacknowledged. The far-reaching reforms William Johnstone put in place during his period as Principal of Camberwell from 1938–1945 and then as Principal of the Central School of Arts and Crafts in London from 1947–1960, when he engaged Alan Davie and Eduardo Paolozzi as teachers, would surely have softened Fergusson's hard-line stance. One also imagines the inspired teaching of William Gillies (who had studied in Paris with the Cubist, André Lhote) during his period as Head of the Painting Department at Edinburgh College of Art from 1945–1960 would almost certainly have been recognised by Fergusson as a step in the right direction.

When he states that what the Modern movement refused to admit was a knowledge of anatomy, architecture, perspective, chemistry of colour and the history of art, he may well be closing down his options rather than expanding them. A basic knowledge of anatomy, for instance, has never really harmed any painter and no less a thinker than David Hume proposed that the two professions best acquainted with the human body were anatomists and artists and the knowledge held by the anatomist might be very useful for the artist. The trouble here is the polarisation of 'academic' and 'independent': the question is how can they best enable each other? Picasso and Matisse, for example, equipped themselves with a working knowledge of anatomy, architecture and the history of art, and perhaps it was that knowledge that enabled them to keep exploring new territories and make so many discoveries throughout their long creative lives.

Few would argue, however, with Fergusson placing vision, imagination, independence of spirit, invention and creative power above anatomy and the chemistry of colour, and there was a period when art schools finally adopted most of Fergusson's ideas and abolished the academic curriculum – no more systematic study of the human figure, no anatomy, no drawing from the antique casts. But what has been put in place begs many questions. The wholesale removal of artist-teachers and an increasing emphasis on academic qualifications, an insistence on professionalism (craft in disguise?), a lack of independence and compliance with central authority has diminished the creative ethos that artist-educators like William Johnstone fought so hard to establish.

Fergusson was surely right in thinking that an art school, no matter how liberal, would tend to produce conformism in students rather than encourage them to be independent and fearless. An uncritical acceptance of contemporary art suggests his worst fears have come to pass. As Fergusson himself says in the Foreword, 'painting and sculpture' are 'a means of expressing human reactions to life'. It is not good enough, as he says in Chapter Four, merely to be 'adding clever gadgets' or 'using fashionable stunts'. Fergusson's distinction between the truly modern and the merely contemporary ('Up-to-date generally means with all the latest gadgets') seems remarkably prescient given the current state of 21st-century Kulchur.

The emergence in the past few years of a number of alternative art schools in London, driven by the rise in fees and a growing disillusionment with university art education, suggests that Fergusson's views on art schools, artists' co-operatives and how artists might be supported retain their relevance. In his chapter on 'Independent Art', he describes how in London (with the help of Charles Rennie Mackintosh, who was to design the exhibiting spaces), he attempted to organise an Independent Art exhibition in Hyde Park, 'but we were told that the parks belonged to the King and that was impossible'. He was always of the view that artists should fight for their rights and take the initiative themselves in terms of presenting their work, something now taken for granted amongst young artists and a distinguishing feature of Glasgow's early 21st-century art scene.

For Fergusson, the independence of the artist remained a crucial ideal throughout his life. Free from the dead hand of regulation, the independent artist could only be on one side of the dividing line between the academic and the modern, the conventional and the new, the fabricated and the real. The independent artist would be an outlaw to the establishment, a pioneer without prediction, a figure unconstrained by tradition, privilege or class prejudice.

The two greatest painters of the 20th century, Picasso and Matisse, regarded themselves as independent artists, seemingly totally opposed to any form of academicism. At the time when France was collapsing in the face of the German army, in June 1940, they met by chance in Paris and Picasso immediately exclaimed, '*C'est l'Ecole des Beaux Arts!*' This summed up their feelings. The 'Beaux Arts' mentality: the authority of the fixed and static had been replicated in the planning of the French military top brass. The failure was all around them. France had fallen because of a failure of imagination. There is also the legendary radio broadcast Matisse made in 'Vichy' France in early 1942, where he said that the instruction given at the Beaux Arts is deadly for young artists because:

> Deprived of their instinct, their curiosity, the poor artists are turned into chronic invalids at a period of their lives, between 15 and 25 years, which determines their future. On the whole the milieu of the Beaux-Arts Prix de Rome is a mutual aid society out of which nothing lasting has ever come. The management of the Beaux Arts has never been interested in independent artists.

But – and it's a big but – both Matisse and Picasso emerged from the academic tradition they seemed so eager to demolish. Both spent a full decade or more under the influence of traditional methods of painting. Both retained a great respect for the necessity of technical proficiency and a belief in the study of nature as a means of arriving at the truth. This provided firm roots in the traditions of the 19th century and gave both painters the confidence and ability which would serve as a source of liberation from the very tradition that had nurtured them.

While in general agreement with Fergusson's main ideas, their views on Modernism take different directions. For instance, in 1923 Picasso says:

> Cubism is no different from any other school of painting. The same prin-
> ciples and the same elements are common to all. The fact that for a long

                                        MODERN SCOTTISH PAINTING

time Cubism has not been understood means nothing. Cubism has kept within the limits and limitations of painting, never pretending to go beyond it. Drawing, design and colour are understood and practised in Cubism in the spirit and manner that they are understood and practised in all other schools. Our subjects might be different as we have introduced into painting objects and forms that were formerly ignored.[10]

Matisse, too, believed in the continuity of European painting. In his 1935 statement 'On Modernism and Tradition', he says this:

As for me, having left the Beaux-Arts, I spent my time in the Louvre copying and submitting myself to the influence of such undoubted masters such as Raphael, Poussin, Chardin, and the Flemish. I felt that the methods of the Impressionists were not for me. I wanted to see beyond their subtle gradations of tone and continual experiments. In short, I wanted to understand myself.

As T.J. Clark writes in *Picasso and Truth* (Princeton University Press, 2013):

Perhaps this view of Picasso and Braque's achievement will strike some readers as paradoxical – but only because we are so used to the notion that modern art is always, at defining moments, an arrow pointing to the future. This seems to me an article of faith (maybe borrowed from Modernism's original cheerleaders) and largely counterfactual. It leaves us with little or nothing to say about the vision of history underlying many of the early 20th century's key works – *The Waste Land* and the *Cantos*, for instance, or the regressive semiconsciousness of *Finnegans Wake*; Proust's effort of memory or Kafka's rewriting of the quest; Matisse's pastoral; Bartok's Beethoven and Schoenberg's Brahms. Modernism, as I see it was just as backward-looking as any other art form, and most often not to its detriment.

Of course it may be easier for us in the early 21st century to reach a different kind of understanding and overview of the art of the early 20th century, an overview denied to Fergusson because he was right there in the thick of it all, believing at all times in the revolutionary potential of his work and ideas. We can see too that his uncompromising stance may well have contributed to the limitations of his art – certainly in comparison with Picasso and Matisse – in terms of both subject matter, formal exploration and sheer painterly expertise. But these limitations should not be used to present Fergusson as an artist of little consequence. On the contrary, his contribution alongside that of his fellow Colourists has been expertly summed up by Michael Fry in his book *A New Race of Men: Scotland 1815–1914*:

> Considering what Matisse was doing at the time… let alone what Picasso was doing in his Blue Period and his Rose Period, the Scottish Colourists indeed remained a trifle tame. But once they were home again after 1918, they showed that what they had learned in the paradisal, pre-war Paris might be transformed into a distinctly Scottish idiom. While they could be confident and vibrant in the use of strong colour, it was still a generally timid range of subjects they chose in comparison with their French and other continental counterparts: insular landscapes, domestic interiors, fashionable models. And they never ventured into the seamy side of life, as the French Impressionists had once been happy to do: no can-can, no absinthe here.
>
> All the same, the Colourists transformed the pictorial traditions of Scotland. Each in his own style, they redefined the qualities of light and colour in one medium and another. Alas, they could not in Scotland count on much of a sympathetic public to encourage them and buy their paintings: they had difficulty earning a living. Yet the Colourists made a promising start to the Scottish art of the 20th century. They were the first Scots to see themselves as modern European painters. Just as important, their example of dedication and independence helped the succeeding generations in their own country to find a way forward in a new world of art without signposts but with a journey possible in almost any direction.

Something of that sense of continuity and change can be seen in *Summer 1914* (1934). This painting depicts a woman lying on a hammock surrounded by leaves and perhaps fig trees, where the fruit is becoming so ripe it might drop into her hands. Her arms are raised round her head as she sleeps. She is clothed in an elegant but comfortable blue dress. Another woman stands further away, dressed in soft red. They are framed by green foliage. It is a vision of Eden. The potential or promise of sexuality is present but so is languorous ease, recalling Milton's Adam and Eve in a garden unbroken by error or violence:

Under a tuft of shade that on a green
Stood whispering soft, by a fresh Fountain side
They sat them down, and after no more toil
Of thir sweet Gardning labour than suffic'd
To recommend cool *Zephyr*, and made ease
More easie, wholsom thirst and appetite
More grateful, to their Supper Fruits they fell,
Nectarine Fruits which the compliant boughes
Yielded them, side-long as they sat recline
On the soft downie bank damaskt with flowrs:
The savorie pulp they chew, and in the rinde
Still as they thirsted scoop the brimming stream...[11]

The poignancy of the date in the title and the date of the work's composition create pathos. When you look long and longingly at what Fergusson has shown, realise what was to follow and what, in the act of creating the painting, the artist was fortunate enough to be able to look back over, through time, it is a far more powerful, poignant, resonant work, in the context of an era of war, than *Damaged Destroyer* (1918) or *Portsmouth Docks* (1918), which were in fact painted towards the end of the First World War. These works show oblique perspectives and forms in bright, unblemished colour. They are without stain, despite their subjects. It is as if Fergusson was choosing not to directly depict scenes that would confront the destruction of war.

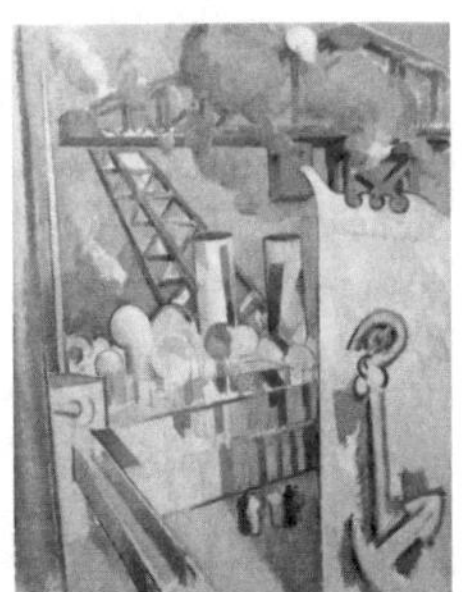

Portsmouth Docks,
1918

Yet, considering the power of *Summer, 1914*, it is impossible to deny his sense of what is at stake, and what the cost would be. The poignancy and power of *Summer 1914* is increased first by our sense of what it shows, knowing that the First World War commenced on 4 August of that year, and then by our own understanding as we look at the painting of what was about to happen in the years after its completion, after 1934, the gathering forces

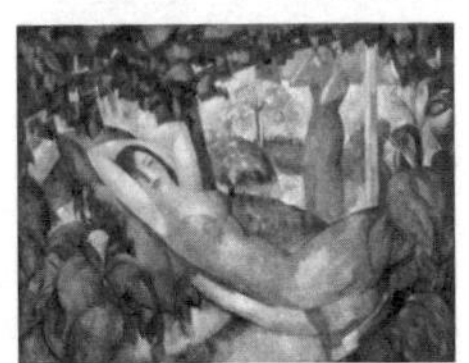

Summer, 1914,
1934

of fascism that were to become unavoidable after the outbreak of the Spanish Civil War in 1936, and then the Second World War, and in the destructions that have followed, into our own time. Fergusson is giving us a vision of health and human happiness, a moment of repletion without satiety, fulfilment without excess, almost as if it were rest after the dance of *Les Eus*, a permanent ideal that has emphatic specific reference in the dates, but has relevance much further back than Milton, and much further forward than the 20th century.

The Final Period: Glasgow

Fergusson chose to return to Glasgow in 1939 because, he said, it was the most Highland city in Scotland. He was a galvanising force, and as soon as he arrived he set about invigorating Glasgow's art scene. Dissatisfied with the existing Glasgow Art Club because it would not admit women, he established the New Art Club in 1940. He was the founder-member of the New Scottish Group, holding annual exhibitions from 1943–48, and again in 1951, 1953 and 1956. There was no jury selection, basing this procedure on his experience of the Salon des Indépendents in Paris. This openness encouraged influential European refugees such as Josef Herman and Jankel Adler as well as non-conformists like Ian Hamilton Finlay and William Crosbie to exhibit and participate actively. Alongside Fergusson's activities, Margaret Morris formed the Celtic Ballet in 1947, and in 1960, the Scottish National Ballet.

The major affinity and collaborative work with Hugh MacDiarmid begins at this time. MacDiarmid wrote to Fergusson on receiving a copy of *Modern Scottish Painting* (see Appendix 2), and Fergusson replied affectionately to him (8 February 1944) to thank him 'for your most sympathetic letter about my book... I appreciate your letter which makes me feel with you in what you have fought so courageously for, that we don't see each other often isn't so bad if we're in sympathy.'

Danu, Mother of the Gods, 1952–53

MacDiarmid and Fergusson were respectively the literary and artistic editors of the periodical *Scottish Art and Letters*, which was published by MacLellan from Glasgow and ran to five issues, from 1944 to 1950. MacDiarmid reviewed Fergusson's exhibition at the Annan Gallery in Glasgow in the journal in 1949, applauding the fact that having lived in France for so long, having known all the great modern artists before they became famous, and having secured his own achievement, Fergusson had now come home to devote his 'life-long experience and hard-won mastery to his own country and the encouragement of young artists in Glasgow and throughout Scotland generally.'

This sense of resurgence was characteristic. *Scottish Art and Letters* represented a reconfiguration of Celticism at the end of, and immediately after, the Second World War, linking back to and coming forward from ideas about Celtic identity that had been familiar in Scotland and Ireland in the 1890s. A new Celticism was in play now, drawing on certain qualities that had been present in the prophetic call for a Scottish Renaissance made by Patrick Geddes in the late 19th century, but opening out into an international constituency that could not have been predicted. The 1940s and 1950s was the period in which Fergusson paints *Danu, Mother of the Gods* (1952) and designs the 'decorations' that embellish the first and second editions of MacDiarmid's *In Memoriam James Joyce: From A Vision of World Language* (1955). Rejuvenation and renaissance were conjoined with a global accommodation of the history of cultural creation, and a sense of the vastness of human potential.

The book-length poem that constitutes *In Memoriam James Joyce* (1955), which is further extended in *The Kind of Poetry I Want* (1961) and other passages that had been published in part since at least the 1940s, was being worked on right through to its publication. This work was an attempt to take into account as many of all the languages and artforms of the world by referring to human creativity in all its aspects, as far as MacDiarmid could find out about them, through his own experience, through talking with others, through correspondence in letters, through his reading of books and reviews of books in magazines. He pillaged everywhere and transformed his thefts into verse, amassing page upon page of information about subjects you would never encounter anywhere else between the same covers, turning from a Finnish dialect idiom to the dancing of Fred Astaire, from ancient epic literature in manuscripts dating from five centuries before Shakespeare to *Tarzan of the Apes*. His collaboration with Fergusson was appropriate, as the literary work MacDiarmid produced was joined with the visual work Fergusson provided, both evoking and representing the musical component of language and human creativity as equally essential. Literary, visual and musical forms were all understood to be vital. As Louise Annand says in her book, *J.D. Fergusson in Glasgow* (2003):

> Fergusson wanted his decorations to be in sympathy with 'the kind of thing Joyce was trying to do' and deployed Ogam, a system using straight lines related to a central horizontal line to represent letters or more usually sounds. The lines are vertical or slanted above, below or through the horizontal base in groups of up to five. Fergusson made a note that Ogma was the Celtic god of literature and eloquence and Ogam the indigenous script of Ireland.

In John Purser's words:

> In Fergusson's frontispiece illustration, we see a female – perhaps the Celtic goddess Danu and quite possibly modelled on Margaret Morris herself. She is, in any event, created substantially out of Celtic, pre-Celtic and musical symbolism. Her breasts and ovaries are spirals, a form which was carried through from the stone age into early Celtic Christian art; her pubic hair is the letter R – its name in Ogam is *Ruis*, meaning the elder tree. Her hips are nudged by shamrocks. Treble clefs (incorporating the spiral form) accompany her and the letter I – Iogh in Ogam – leads from her breastbone to her navel and also makes a stitched gash in her thigh – Iogh stands for J and also for Y and means the yew tree that was one of the noble woods and used for making musical instruments. Intermingled with these is the conventional Roman letter J, on one side of her hip incorporated in a shamrock and harp motif. The whole thing is a kind of *jeu-d'esprit* in which letter and image become inextricably intertwined, and for which the most obvious precedent is the *Book of Kells* and others such as the *Book of Durrow*.[12]

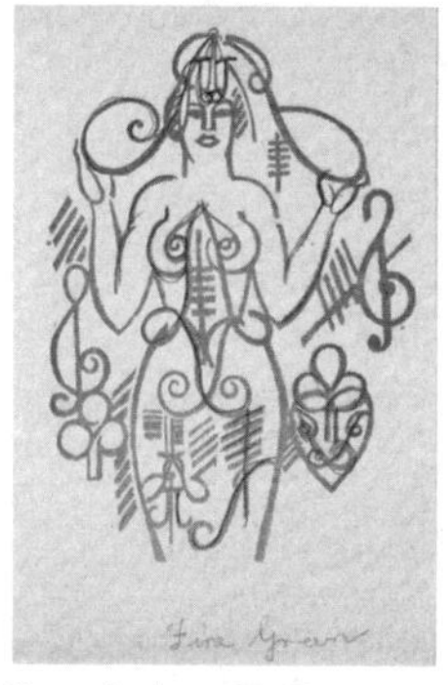

Frontispiece for *In Memoriam James Joyce*, 1955

MacDiarmid wrote the Foreword to *The Art of J.D. Fergusson: A Biased Biography* (1974) by Margaret Morris, at Morris's request. She invited him to do so, she said, because she believed that Fergusson would have wanted MacDiarmid more than anyone else to write the Foreword. Here, MacDiarmid says: 'There has never been more need of art than today.' His recognition of Fergusson's significance is to endorse the work he created in answer to that need, both in the paintings and sculptures, and in this book, *Modern Scottish Painting*.

MODERN SCOTTISH PAINTING

Notes to Introduction

[1] Sheila McGregor, '*L'Esprit Gaulois*: Fergusson's Celtic Nationalism' in *J.D. Fergusson* (Edinburgh: National Galleries of Scotland, 2013).

[2] In its own quirky way, *Modern Scottish Painting* is a history of modern Scottish art, and as such, a rarity. Its immediate precursor was John Tonge's *The Arts of Scotland* (1938) but other than that, there was almost nothing in the way of historical, critical accounts of Scottish art for any young artist to use as an introduction to the subject. The British Council published Ian Finlay's booklet *Scottish Art* (1945; reprinted 1946), but this ran to a mere 42 pages. Its bibliography informs us: 'The standard book on Scottish painting is Sir James L. Caw's *Scottish Painting Past and Present* (Edinburgh, 1908) already almost 40 years behind the times; and there is also W.D. Mackay's *The Scottish School of Painting* (London, 1906).' There is reference to Robert Brydall's *History of Art in Scotland* (1889), M.P. Ramsay's *Calvin and Art* (1938), described as 'a scholarly defence of the Reformed Religion's attitude to culture' and a Saltire Society booklet, *The Arts and Future of Scotland* (1942) by Agnes Muir Mackenzie. And that's it. The Orcadian artist Stanley Cursiter (1887-1976), director of the Scottish National Galleries (1930–48), wrote as a labour of love a study of Fergusson's fellow Colourist, *Peploe: An Intimate Memoir* (1947), but this was another rarity. Comprehensive historical accounts of Scottish art remained almost unknown until Duncan MacMillan's *Scottish Art 1460–1990* (1990; revised edition, 2000), William Hardie's *Scottish Painting 1837 to the Present* (1990), Murdo Macdonald's *Scottish Art* (2000) and John Morrison's *Painting the Nation: Identity and Nationalism in Scottish Painting*, 1800–1920 (2003). Fergusson in his book, as much as in his painting, was breaking new ground.

[3] *Dear Grieve: Letters to Hugh MacDiarmid (C.M. Grieve)*, edited by John Manson (Glasgow: Kennedy & Boyd, 2011), pp. 455–456.

[4] In fact, John Middleton Murry took the title of the periodical he founded, *Rhythm*, from Fergusson; it was the artist's gift to him. Murry was a young single Englishman adventuring in the

intellectualism and sensualities with which Paris was resplendent, and determined to start a publication that would bring something of their excitement from Montparnasse to London. The first issue in 1911 carried Fergusson's nude woman holding an apple on its cover, and contributors included Picasso, Anne Estelle Rice and Fergusson himself. It ran to 14 issues, folding in 1913. Fergusson assisted Murry as art editor and the New Zealand writer Katherine Mansfield was assistant editor from February 1913. But Fergusson's paintings of this period were his major work, and *Les Eus* remains his masterpiece.

[5] Sarah Faunce, 'Courbet: Feminist in Spite of Himself', in *Body* (Sydney: The Art Gallery of New South Wales, 1997).

[6] John Elderfield, *Pleasuring Painting: Matisse's Feminine Representations*, (London: Thames & Hudson, 1995).

[7] Although the entire idea of the nude in art has changed utterly since 1914, when charges of indecency and obscenity were regularly brought against depictions of nudity in all forms of modern art, a long struggle was to lie ahead – a struggle that took until the social liberalisation and sexual revolution of the 1960s to bring about the openness and tolerance that Fergusson had worked and hoped for. Today, in the early 21st century, film and television, magazines, advertisements and the internet are saturated with images of naked or virtually naked bodies while the invention of the digital camera has encouraged almost everyone to make their own naked images – a phenomenon, which at the very least, Fergusson would surely have found intriguing. Within the art world the nude has become 'The Body' with considerable focus on discoveries made by medical science. Photography, finally accepted as a fully-fledged artform, has led the way, but, most notably in late 20th-century London, painters such as Bacon, Freud, Hockney, Kitaj and Auerbach found extraordinary things to say about the nude, and now, in the early 21st century, two of the most prominent painters of the female body are women: Gwen Hardie and Jenny Saville, whose intensely personal identification with the subject began in the Life Classes of Edinburgh College of Art and Glasgow School of Art in the 1980s.

[8] Friedrich Nietzsche, *The Birth of Tragedy and the Case of Wagner*, translated by Walter Kaufmann (New York: Vintage Books, 1967), p. 37.

                                    MODERN SCOTTISH PAINTING

[9]   Gustav Mahler quoted in Peter Franklin, *The Life of Mahler* (Cambridge University Press, 1997). p. 141.

[10]   Dore Ashton, editor, *Picasso on Art: A Selecton of Views* (Boston: Da Capo Press, 1972). The statement was made in Spanish to Marius de Zayas. Picasso approved De Zayas' manuscript before it was translated into English and published in *The Arts* (New York, May 1923), under the title 'Picasso Speaks'.

[11]   John Milton, *Paradise Lost*, Book IV, lines 325–336, in *The Complete Poems*, ed. B.A. Wright, introduction and notes by Gordon Campbell (London: J.M. Dent, 1980), p. 223.

[12]   John Purser, 'The Celtic Ballet: Ballet, Baton and Brush in Search of Peace in Time of War', *Journal of the Scottish Society for Art History* (Vol 13, 2008–09).

J.D. Fergusson:
A Biographical Timeline

After the year, events in Fergusson's life are noted, followed by major events in history and significant publications, performances, exhibitions, works of literature, music and art.

Leith and Edinburgh, Scotland, 1874–1907

1874   Born 9 March at 7 Crown Street, Leith, son of John Fergusson or Ferguson, whose father had been a farmer in Perthshire; his mother's maiden name was also Fergusson. His name was registered with one 's' but on his father's birth certificate there are two. Both parents are Gaelic-speakers. / Wagner, *Götterdamerung*

1877   Whistler, *Nocturne in Black and Gold: The Falling Rocket*

1881   Foundation of University College, Dundee

1882   Battle of the Braes in Skye

1883   Napier Commission on the Highlands; founding of the Highland Land League

1883   His mother encourages him to draw and takes him to the National Gallery of Scotland and the Royal Scottish Museum; he is given his first box of oil paints. / Stevenson, *Treasure Island*

1883–84   Nietzsche, *Thus Spake Zarathustra*

1884   Twain, *Huckleberry Finn*

1886   Family home now 77 Ferry Road, Leith. J.D. enrols at the Royal High School, Edinburgh. / Scottish Home Rule Association founded; Marx, *Das Capital, English translation, volume* 1

1887   Scottish office established in Whitehall

1888   Founding of the Scottish Labour Party

1889   Leaves the Royal High School and goes to Blair Lodge, near Linlithgow, where he is encouraged in his studies of art and French. / Stevenson, *The Master of Ballantrae*; Barrie, *A Window in Thrums*

1890	Whistler, *The Gentle Art of Making Enemies*; Frazer, *The Golden Bough*; Wilde, *The Picture of Dorian Grey*
c.1891	Leaves school and decides to become a naval surgeon, says that he spends time in Edinburgh preparing for the entrance examinations but does not matriculate at the University or the Royal College of Surgeons. / Conan Doyle, Sherlock Holmes stories begin in the *Strand Magazine*
1893	McEwen, *String Quartet in F Major*
c.1894	Gives up on medicine and focuses on art. Takes a studio in north Edinburgh, painting watercolours; prompted by Alexander Roche to turn to oil painting. / Munch, *Madonna*; Kipling, *The Jungle Book*; MacCunn, *Land of the Mountain and the Flood*
1895	McTaggart, *St Columba's First Sermon* and *The Sailing of the Emigrant Ship*; Wells *The Time Machine*
c.1896/7	Possibly first visit to Paris. / Chekhov, *The Seagull*.
1896	Opening of the Glasgow underground; Jarry, *Ubu Roi*
1897	Gauguin, *Where do we come from? What are we? Where are we going?*; Stoker, *Dracula*
c.1898	Paris again: is impressed by Bonington in the Louvre and the Impressionists in the Salle Caillebotte in the Luxembourg and Durand Ruel's Gallery. Possibly attends classes at Atelier Colarossi. / The Curies discover radium
1898	Cézanne, *Mont Sainte-Victoire paintings*
1899	Visits Morocco, possibly also Spain. First exhibits at the Royal Society of British Artists. / Anglo-Boer war begins; Elgar, Enigma Variations; Havelock, *Studies in the Psychology of Sex*
1899–1902	Boer War, South Africa
1900	Visits Paris again and sees the art sections of the Exposition Universelle. / Mackintosh exhibits at the Vienna Secession; Bonnard, *Man and Woman*; Scottish Workers' Parliamentary Committee formed; Carnegie, *The*

Gospel of Wealth; Cunninghame Graham, *Thirteen Stories*; Joseph Conrad, *Heart of Darkness*; Freud, *The Interpretation of Dreams*; Planck begins thinking about quantum physics

1901   Visits Spain. Elected member of the Royal Society of British Artists. / Douglas Brown, *The House with the Green Shutters*; death of Queen Victoria, accession of Edward VII; Freud, *Psychopathology of Everyday Life*; Second Glasgow International Exhibition

1902   Painting in the Scottish Borders, near Peebles. Also painting cityscapes and landscapes in Paris, London, Edinburgh, Fife and Islay. / James, *The Varieties of Religious Experience*

1903   Gaudi begins work on 'Sagrada Familia, Barcelona'

1905   Visits Dieppe. First solo exhibition in London, at the Baillie Gallery, May–June (56 oils). / Einstein formulates first theory of relativity; Freud, *Three Essays on the Theory of Sexuality*; Weber, *The Protestant Ethic and the Spirit of Capitalism*

1906   Summer: Visits Paris-Plage (Le Touquet). / Bone, *The Great Gantry, Charing Cross* (etching); Scottish Federation of Women's Suffrage formed; Founding of Labour Party (formerly the Scottish Labour Party, then the Independent Labour Party)

Paris, France, 1907–1914

1907   Moves to France, Hotel de la Haute-Loire, Paris. Exhibits at the Salon d'Automne for the first time. Summer: visits the Normandy coast. Teaches at the Académie de la Palette; meets Segonzac. / Picasso, *Les Demoiselles d'Avignon*

1908   Moves to 18 Boulevard Edgar Quinet. Works on sculpture. Moves to 83 rue Notre-Dame-des-Champs. In October, he exhibits once again at the Baillie Gallery, London, in *Some Modern Painters* (36 oils).

1908–13   Fergusson's relationship with Anne Estelle Rice in this

                                   MODERN SCOTTISH PAINTING

period is vital in his development. Research into Rice's work as an artist suggests that her influence on him as a painter was highly significant and that in some respects they became reliant upon each other, mutually supportive and inspiring. Fergusson did not enjoy unflattering comparisons with other artists and his split with Rice, which was extremely brusque on his part, may have been triggered by the state of their joint development as artists, as well as his meeting Margaret Morris in 1913, who was considerably younger than he was. / Grahame, *The Wind in the Willows*

1909	Is elected to the Sociétaire of the Salon d'Automne. / Completion of the Glasgow School of Art designed by Rennie Mackintosh; Ford's 'Model T' car; McEwan, orchestral tone poem *Grey Galloway*; Kennedy-Fraser, *Songs of the Hebrides*, volume 1 (volume 2, 1917, volume 3, 1921)
1910	Visits Royan with Peploe. From October teaches in the afternoons in the Atelier Blanche. / Matisse, *Dance & Music*; George V reigns 1910–36
1911	Joins Middleton Murry and Katherine Mansfield to launch the periodical *Rhythm*, of which he becomes Art Editor. Another visit to Royan with Peploe. Becomes a member of, and exhibits in, the Salon des Indépendants. / Churchill speaks in Dundee in favour of a Scottish parliament; Third Glasgow International Exhibition; Mahler, *Das Lied von der Erde*
1912	He exhibits three times at the Stafford Gallery, London: in February (40 drawings); in March, *Pictures by J.D. Fergusson* (30 oils and four works of sculpture); in October, *Pictures by S.J. Peploe, J.D. Fergusson* (six oils). / Founding of Scottish Unionist Party; Schoenberg, *Pierrot Lunaire*
1913	In Paris, meets Margaret Morris, who became his lifelong companion. Visits Cassis with Peploe. With Segonzac and others, illustrates Francis Carco's *Chansons aigres-douces*. Peploe returns to Paris but Fergusson stays on at Frank

Harris's flat in Nice, until finding a house in Antibes. In the autumn, he is in the *Post Impressionist and Futurist Exhibition* at the Doré Galleries, London (4 oils). / Cursiter, *Impression of Crossing Princes Street, Edinburgh*; Renoir begins work on his monumental series of sculptures of nude women; Lawrence, *Sons and Lovers*; Stravinsky, *The Rite of Spring*; McEwen, *String Quartet No. 6 'Biscay' in A Major*; establishment of Chair of Scottish History and Literature at Glasgow University; Proust, *Remembrance of Things Past* begins to be published

1914   Outbreak of war; moves to London. In February, he exhibits at the Doré Galleries, London: *Pictures by John Duncan Fergusson* (47 items, mainly oils but some gouaches). / Oskar Kokoschka, *The Bride of the Wind*; Hay, *Gillespie*

England and France, 1914–1939

1914–18   World War I

1915   Moves to studio at 14 Redcliffe Road, London, sw10. / Working-class rising in Glasgow: Red Clydeside; Buchan, *The Thirty-Nine Steps*; Geddes, *Cities in Evolution*

1915–17   Spends three months each year in Edinburgh with his family.

1916   Easter Rising in Dublin, Ireland; Einstein, *General Theory of Relativity*; Anti-War demonstration on Glasgow Green; Maclean imprisoned for advocating end of hostilities

1917   The Russian Revolution; Jung, *The Subconscious*

1917–21   Goes with his partner Margaret Morris to the Margaret Morris Movement summer schools at Ilfracombe (1917 and 1918), Harlech (1919 and 1921) and Dinard (1920).

1918   Paints a series of war pictures under the aegis of the Royal Navy. In May, he exhibits works of 1914–18 at The Connell Gallery, London: *Painting and Sculpture by J.D. Fergusson* (32 oils; four sculptures). Moves to studio in 15 Callow Street, London, sw3; stays there till 1929. / Maclean appointed Bolshevik Consul in Glasgow and tried for sedition

1919	Strike in Glasgow for 40-hour week, demonstration in George Square, police and military called in; Versailles peace conference; G. Gregory Smith, *Scottish Literature*
1920	First public radio broadcast; Prohibition in USA; Rennie Mackintosh designs theatre for Margaret Morris; Lindsay, *A Voyage to Arcturus*; *Northern Numbers* poetry anthologies edited by Grieve (Hugh MacDiarmid); Carswell, *Open the Door!*
1922	Painting tour of Scottish Highlands and visits Pourville. / BBC founded; Mussolini forms fascist government in Italy; Wittgenstein, *Tractatus Logico-Philosophicus* translated; Eliot, *The Waste Land*; Joyce, *Ulysses*; Mussolini marches into Rome; MacDiarmid, first published poems; McEwen, *A Solway Symphony*; McCance, *Heavy Structures in a Landscape Setting*
1923	At Antibes. First Scottish exhibitions in Edinburgh and Glasgow: in June, *Painting and Sculpture: J.D. Fergusson* at the Scottish Gallery, P.M. Dott, Edinburgh (19 oils; six sculptures); in September, the same works are exhibited in Glasgow: *Painting and Sculpture: J.D. Fergusson* at the Société des Beaux-Arts (Alexander Reid). / Scottish Home Rule Association leads protest march of 30,000 in Glasgow; USSR established; Grieve, *Annals of the Five Senses*
1924	June exhibition in Paris, Galerie Barbazanges: *Les Peintres de l'Ecosse Moderne: F.C.B. Cadell, J.D. Fergusson, Leslie Hunter, S.J. Peploe* (six oils). / First British Labour Government; Scott, *The Eemis Stane*
1925	January: exhibits at the Leicester Galleries, London: *Paintings by S.J. Peploe, Leslie Hunter, F.C.B. Cadell and J.D. Fergusson* (eight oils; three sculptures); December: exhibits at Reid & Lefèvre, London: *Pictures, Sculpture and Pottery by some British Artists of Today* (4 oils; 3 sculptures) / Founding of National Library of Scotland; MacDiarmid, *Sangschaw*; Muir, *First Poems*; Hitler, *Mein Kampf*, Volume 1; McCance, 'The Engineer, His Wife and Family'; Whitehead, *Science and the Modern World*

1926   First American exhibition in New York at the Whitney
        Studio in December: *John Duncan Fergusson* (20 oils;
        10 water-colours; 16 drawings). / General Strike in Britain;
        Schrödinger develops ideas of quantum mechanics; Tory
        Government under Baldwin upgrades Scottish Secretary to
        Secretary of State for Scotland; Logie Baird invents
        television; MacDiarmid, *Penny Wheep, A Drunk Man
        Looks at the Thistle, Contemporary Scottish Studies*;
        Gunn, *The Grey Coast*; Miro *Dog Barking at the Moon*

1927   Heisenberg, the principle of uncertainty; Bohr, the
        principle of complementarity; MacLeod, *The Road to the
        Isles: Poetry, Lore, and Tradition of the Hebrides*; Crozier,
        Edinburgh (from Salisbury Crags)

1928   January: exhibits in the Chester Johnson Gallery, Chicago;
        second exhibition in Chicago, date and place unknown;
        February: *Painting and Sculpture by J.D. Fergusson* at Reid
        & Lefèvre, London (31 oils; six sculptures); March:
        Painting and Sculpture by J.D. Fergusson. Glasgow, Reid
        & Lefèvre, Glasgow (23 oils; nine drawings; four
        sculptures); November: *Paintings and Sculpture by J.D.
        Fergusson*, at C.W. Kraushaar, New York (18 oils; six
        sculptures). / National Party of Scotland founded;
        Shepherd, *The Quarry Wood*; Corrie, *In Time o' Strife*;
        Jung, *The Spiritual Problem of Modern Man*

1929   Leaves London for Paris once again; December, paints his
        first picture in new studio in rue Gazan near the Parc de
        Montsouris. / James Whyte opens gallery in St Andrews
        and starts publishing *The Modern Scot*; Whitehead,
        Process and Reality

1930   Freud, *Civilization and Its Discontents*; Gandhi begins
        civil disobedience campaign in India; St Kilda evacuated

1931   *Les Peintres Ecossais*, exhibition of six Scottish artists:
        Fergusson, Peploe, Cadell, Hunter, Telfer Bear and
        R.O. Dunlop, in the Galerie Georges Petit, Paris, in March
        (10 oils; seven sculptures); French Government buys one
        picture for the Luxembourg. / First exhibition of paintings

by Munch in the UK, in Edinburgh, at the Society of Scottish Artists; Munro, *The Poetry of Neil Munro*; Mitchison, *The Corn King and the Spring Queen*

1932   March: *Painting and Sculpture by J.D. Fergusson* at Reid & Lefèvre, London (31 oils; seven sculptures); April–May: *Paintings by Six Scottish Artists: Peploe, Hunter, Fergusson, Cadell, Bear, Gillies* at Barbizon House, London (eight oils; one sculpture). / Hunger marches in Britain; Roosevelt elected US President; Scottish Party founded; Grassic Gibbon, *Sunset Song*; MacColla, *The Albannach*; Muir, *Poor Tom*; Scott, *Milk-Wort and Bog Cotton*; Beckmann, *Departure* (triptych)

c.1933   Moves to new studio at 6 Place Henri-Delormel. / Hitler comes to power in Germany; Grassic Gibbon, *Cloud Howe*

1934   October–November: exhibits at Pearson & Westergaard, Glasgow. / Founding of Scottish National Party (merging National Party of Scotland and Scottish Party); SS *Queen Mary* launched on the Clyde; Pound, ABC *of Reading*; Grassic Gibbon, *Grey Granite*; Linklater, *Magnus Merriman*; MacDiarmid, *Stony Limits and Other Poems*; Muir, *Variations on a Time Theme*; Gillies, *The Dark Pond*

1936   February: *Paintings and Sculpture by J.D. Fergusson*, at Reid & Lefèvre, London (32 oils; six sculptures); November: *Water-colours by J.D. Fergusson*, at Barbizon House, London (30 water-colours; four sculptures). / Spanish Civil War begins; BBC begins television service; Founding of Saltire Society; Chisholm, *First Piano Concerto: Piobaireachd*; Muir, *Scott and Scotland*

1937   Picasso, *Guernica*; Shostakovich, *Fifth Symphony*; SNP pledges to oppose conscription except by a Scottish government; McLellan, *Jamie the Saxt*

1938   Empire exhibition, Glasgow; Brecht, *Galileo*; Johnstone, *A Point in Time* (painted 1929–38)

1939   Remains in Paris through the 1930s with regular summer visits to the south of France. Becomes President of the Groupe des Artistes Anglo-Américains in Paris. At the

outbreak of the Second World War moves to Glasgow.
February: *Painting and Sculpture by J.D. Fergusson*, at
Reid & Lefèvre, London (29 oils; four sculptures). /
Scottish Office transferred from London to Edinburgh;
Joyce, *Finnegans Wake*; Chisholm, *Second Symphony:
Ossian*

Glasgow, Scotland, 1939–1961

1939–45	World War II; bombing of Hamburg (1943), Dresden and Tokyo (1945); nuclear bombing of Hiroshima and Nagasaki (1945)
1940	With his wife Margaret Morris, takes a studio flat at 4 Clouston Street, Glasgow, where he lives from now on. Founds the New Art Club, from which comes the New Scottish Group of painters, Fergusson as President
1941	The Clydebank Blitz; Japanese bomb Pearl Harbour; Gunn, *The Silver Darlings*
1942	Shostakovich, *Seventh Symphony*; Redpath, 'The Indian Jug'
1943	*Modern Scottish Painting* published. / Russian victory at Stalingrad; Germany surrenders in North Africa; fall of Mussolini; Maclean, *Dàin do Eimhir*; MacDiarmid, *Lucky Poet*; Mondrian, *Broadway Boogie-Woogie*
1945	Founding of The United Nations; 1946–49: Beginning of the Cold War; rise of public television broadcasting; development of electronic digital computers; Bartók, *Third Piano Concerto*; Braque, *The Billiard Table*
1947	First Edinburgh International Festival; Pollock, early abstract drip paintings; Lamont Stewart, *Men Should Weep*; McLellan, *The Flouers o Edinburgh*; Mitchison, *The Bull Calves*; Mackenzie, *Whisky Galore!*; Whyte, *First Symphony*; Nolan, *Ned Kelly*; Colquhoun, *Seated Woman and Cat*
1948	May: *J.D. Fergusson: First Retrospective Exhibition* at the McLellan Galleries, Glasgow (57 oils; 16 sculptures); this exhibition was then shown in a number of other places.

November: *Paintings by Four Scottish Colourists: S.J. Peploe, Leslie Hunter, F.C.B. Cadell, J.D. Fergusson*, at the Annan Gallery, Glasgow (five oils). / Zionist Jews declare State of Israel in Palestine; Chisholm, *Pictures from Dante*; Hay, *Wind on Loch Fyne*; Henderson, *Elegies for the Dead in Cyreneica*; performance of Sir David Lyndsay's *Satyre of the Thrie Estaits*; Goodsir Smith, *Under the Eildon Tree*; Soutar, *Collected Poems*

1949   September–October: *Paintings by J.D. Fergusson*, at the Annan Gallery, Glasgow (41 oils). / Apartheid regime begins in South Africa; de Beauvoir, *The Second Sex*; Scott, *Thirty-Five Scottish Lyrics*; Chisholm, *Second Piano Concerto: The Hindustani*; Mackendrick's film, *Whisky Galore!* released

1950   February–March: *Paintings of France and Scotland by John Duncan Fergusson* at L'Institut Français d'Ecosse, Edinburgh (42 oils). Awarded honorary LLD by Glasgow University. 1950–60: makes annual visits to the south of France. / Removal of the Stone of Scone from Westminster Abbey; Korean War begins; Daiches, *Robert Burns*

1951   School of Scottish Studies established at Edinburgh University; Chisholm, *Night Song of the Bards* (1944–51)

1952   August–September: *Four Scottish Colourists: Peploe, Cadell, Hunter, Fergusson*, at Gladstone's Land, Saltire Society, Edinburgh (20 oils); October–November: *J.D. Fergusson*, at the Hazlitt Gallery London (28 oils) / de Kooning, *Woman I*; de Stael, *The Footballers*

1953   Coronation of Queen Elizabeth II; Watson and Crick discover the structure of DNA; Hillary and Tensing climb Mount Everest; Beckett, *Waiting for Godot*

1954   *Paintings by J.D. Fergusson* (touring exhibition organised by the Arts Council, Scottish Committee (45 oils). / Minelli's film, *Brigadoon* released; Leger, *La Grande Parade*

1955   March: *Paintings by John Duncan Fergusson from 1898–1954* at Reid & Lefèvre, London (31 oils). Illustrates MacDiarmid, *In Memoriam James Joyce*. / Scottish

Television begins broadcasting; de Chardin, *The Phenomenon of Man*; Graham, *The Nightfishing*; MacCaig, *Riding Lights*; Munro, *Para Handy* tales; Eardley, *Children, Port Glasgow*; Davie, *Seascape Erotic*

1956   Suez crisis; Soviet invasion of Hungary; Donegan, 'Rock Island Line'

1957   May–June: *John Duncan Fergusson: Paintings 1898–1957*, at the Annan Gallery, Glasgow (42 oils). / Campaign for Nuclear Disarmament march to Aldermaston; Scottish Nationalist anti-nuclear movement; Chomsky, *Syntactic Structures*; Trocchi, *Young Adam*

1959   Snow, *The Two Cultures*; Mackay Brown, *Loaves and Fishes*; Fleming, *Goldfinger*

1960   Oil discovered in the North Sea; Sharpeville massacre, South Africa; independence in Nigeria; John F. Kennedy elected President in USA; Lawrence, *Lady Chatterley's Lover* goes on trial as an obscene publication at the Old Bailey, London; Hamilton Finlay, *The Dancers Inherit the Party*; Muir, *Collected Poems 1921–1958*; MacCaig, *A Common Grace*; Trocchi, *Cain's Book*; Goodsir Smith, *The Wallace* (performed at Edinburgh Festival and published)

1961   Dies in Glasgow, 30 January. April–May: *J.D. Fergusson: Water-colours and Drawings*, at the Glasgow University Print Room (34 exhibits); October–November: *Scottish Painting*, at the Glasgow Art Gallery (16 oils); November–December: *Memorial Exhibition*, in Edinburgh and on tour for the Arts Council, Scottish Committee (134 oils; 11 sculptures); December: *Paintings by J.D. Fergusson*, at the Scottish Gallery, Aitken Dott & Son, Edinburgh (46 oils; 15 watercolours). / Construction of the Berlin Wall; mass CND rally, London; South Africa withdraws from British Commonwealth; Yuri Gagarin becomes first man in space; Hamilton Finlay, *Glasgow Beasts, and a Burd, Haw, an Insecks, an, Aw, A Fush*; Spark, *The Prime of Miss Jean Brodie*; Crichton Smith, *Thistles and Roses*

Modern Scottish Painting

To
Johnnie and Lily
and
Harry and Jean [1]

Foreword

This book is merely the attempt to state in the ordinary language of informal discussion the impressions, ideas and opinions of a painter who has devoted an ordinary lifetime in trying to understand painting and sculpture, not as a craft, but as a means of expressing human reactions to life. Craftsmanship has generally a dehumanised accuracy. The accuracy of art is the accuracy of statement of human limitations.

This book does not pretend to be *exact*, historically or otherwise. The ideas and opinions it submits for consideration are the result of a lifetime's experience. It is not meant to inform those who know it all already, or to tell those who don't, how to know it all.

The reason for writing it is that the author would have been glad to have had its contents submitted to him when he was starting out on what has been a very long road. His chief desire is to try to give the young Scottish artist the help he himself wasn't even offered.

London, May 28, 1939.[2]

CHAPTER I

Bécheron

A Nous La Liberté [3]

During the crisis of September, 1938, I was staying with Jo Davidson in Touraine.[4] After a long preparation for my London show[5] I was glad to be with Jo in his charming peaceful manoir of Bécheron.[6] Having tea on the front porch under the wonderful *tilleuls*, we looked across the valley to the house where Balzac wrote *The Lily of the Valley*.[7] We talked, as we have always talked since we first met in Lavenue in Montparnasse, about 35 years ago, which was then frequented by Americans, through being made known by Robert Louis Stevenson. Until recently there was a relief of him on the wall outside.

While we talked, my memory went back to Montparnasse in 1898, and the *Hole in the Wall*, not the one on the Grand Boulevard, a small *crémerie* under the Haute Loire Hotel, 114 Boul. Montparnasse, now a stocking shop. We used to lunch and dine there, and I was never more happy than with that band of jovial Americans, painters, sculptors and writers. Rodin's *Balzac*, which has just been placed opposite the Dome about fifty yards from the *Hole in the Wall*, had just been seen, and no one but myself, in the *Hole in the Wall*, could stand it. 'It wasn't sculpture.' 'Just like a snowman.' 'Sculpture was pure form', whatever that meant. I suspect it meant smooth and anatomical form.

Rodin could draw and model; there was the *L'homme qui marche* to prove it. The *Balzac wasn't serious*. I never was impressed by the *L'homme qui marche*, and I was very much impressed by the *Balzac*. The reason was as I see now, that my knowledge of anatomy was what I got as a medical student, and I never thought of it as a means for expressing anything in art.

Then we went to the studio and I saw Jo's new figure of *Walt Whitman*, a subject he had started over 30 years ago. The figure now was more spiritual, less idealised, more real, than the earlier studies. More real because the spirit is the reality of a work of art, and ideal means not real. The ton of clay nine foot high represented Whitman taking to the open road, afoot and light-hearted, and it gave the feeling of freedom and lightness that Kenneth MacLeod gives us when he says, in 'The Road to the Isles', 'as step I with the sunlight for my load'.[8] Compared to the earlier studies, there was in its way the same difference as between *L'homme qui marche* and the *Balzac*. The *Balzac* is not abstract. It is real. The head and the dressing gown are like a head and a dressing gown. Jo's head, coat and trousers of his *Whitman* are head, coat and trousers, but they give the feeling or spirit of Whitman, 'afoot and light-hearted', taking to the open road.

Then Jo said, 'About time for the news,' so we went to the dining room and listened to the latest news on the wireless. Suddenly we were thrown into a complete mess of everything that was wrong with the world, where everyone was anxious, worried, afraid, bluffing or attempting to disentangle from a mass of rumour and information, something to help or interest his side.

Having heard the news, we talked again about the things that we have always been interested in till the next news came on. While 'tuning in' to get the news things came through from all the different countries. A girl sang a very good comic song at a Portsmouth Music Hall. Then there was the Paris café concert, and so on. Then Jo, looking at the programme, said, 'Here's something from Scotland,' so we listened. Two people spoke on different subjects; one made an excellent statement about pigs, but the point was that each speaker before starting said, 'It will be as well before we start to have an idea of what we mean by...' This to me was really Scottish and immediately reminded me of the saying that the Scotsman when asked a question always replies by asking another. It doesn't seem to have occurred to most people that very few people can ask a question, and the Scots habit of saying 'What do you mean by...' merely means that he wants at least a working definition of what you expect to get an answer to.

Well, in this book I'm going to try and give a *working* definition of what I'm trying to talk about, and I mean a *working* and *not* an *absolute* definition.

From the experience of a lifetime of discussion I know that there are people who expect you, if you know your job, to tell them *absolutely* what you mean. Taking art for example: if you've been at it for a lifetime you

                              MODERN SCOTTISH PAINTING

ought to be able to tell them exactly what it is. If not why should they listen to you? I submit that the only reason for listening to someone who has spent his lifetime trying to understand anything is that he may help you to form an opinion of your own about the subject, and *prevent* you from accepting his without very thorough consideration – if at all. That anyway has been the use of discussion to me, and it has been of very great use to me, and really quite necessary for my work. I haven't changed my main idea, but I have amplified and freed it by discussion. So in this book I am not attempting to convince or convert anyone. I am submitting the results of a lifetime's discussion and research, theory and practice, most of it conducted in Paris, which city has certainly for the last 40 years been the art centre of the world.

As I have said in the prologue, the book is not intended for people who already know all about modern painting. It is for the young student and painter, and the people interested in painting who have had neither the time nor the opportunity for being in the heart of things during the modern movement. To a great many people it will seem very long 'about it and about', but if they think for a minute they will see that it has been long for me, much longer than it takes to read this book, and I was *in* the 'nineties' when anyone that didn't deal in epigrams was considered a bore. I know that 'bright' *fin de siècle* side of things, and I don't think it's enough, though it's certainly very useful and entertaining. I remember when Whistler was asked 'What is your opinion on subject matter in art?' He replied, 'Everything but the subject matters in art', a very bright remark and a very good start for examining that subject. 'The fact that a man is a poisoner has nothing to do with his prose.' That won't do. It has, or may have, a lot to do with his prose, but it doesn't make it good or bad prose, and so on.

People who haven't read *The Gentle Art of Making Enemies* should read it if they like or want that sort of thing.[9] It was a great contribution to freedom at a time when the Victorians, *the world's worst people*, dominated Britain by their ponderous imbecility. The curse of their stupidity, lack of taste and sanctimoniousness, still hangs over us, and we still suffer from a sort of suffocation under the hangover of their hypocrisy. So I'll be very glad to think that the students, young artists, and people interested in modern Scottish painting, when reading this book, will be constantly in the state of mind which makes them ask 'What do you mean by...' I'll try to give them a *working* meaning, if not a definition of what I mean to base my statements on, and here I say as clearly as possible and at the beginning, that *I never talk in absolutes, or even imagine I am capable of talking in absolutes.* If the reader will admit this from the start, it will save a lot of misunderstanding. I say this because I have found, after a lifetime of formal and informal discussion, that most people do talk in absolutes, and reply as if the other person was talking in absolutes.

I'd also like to say that after a lifetime's study I don't know what *is* Art and *what isn't*, and that I'm not trying to find out. This must not be mistaken for an apology, for I am quite sure that I know quite a lot about art, enough to know that people don't know, and that the person with the smart definition is the one to trust least.

There is a lot of repetition in this book that is intentional and I think necessary. So now, having I hope made reasonably clear what I intend to try to do, let us start to find some meaning for the words modern painting, and then more particularly for modern Scottish painting.

We know that many people are very much struck by the resemblance of the very latest paintings to Stone Age sculpture, or African bushmen cave painting, and we have, thanks to Frobenius, had a wonderful chance to compare them.[10] Some people apparently have a great satisfaction in being able to say, when they see a picture by one of the youngest painters, classed as modern, that it is not modern at all, but just like something they've seen in a museum. This satisfaction is apparently due to the idea that criticism is a sort of detective business, and that a work of art is original only when it cannot be proved that it resembles any other work of art of any period. So we are back again with the absolutist. The other reason for satisfaction of this sort is apparently the idea that erudition, that is a vast knowledge of all that has gone before, is absolutely essential as a starting point or equipment for criticism; certainly that was the belief in the Victorian times, and evidently has not ceased to exist to-day. It is the 'genius is the capacity for taking infinite pains' idea, and intuition is ruled out, or at least not considered to be worthy of any serious attention unless backed by the 'infinite pains', which means nearly always, infinite *reading* and research in books.

So we are then, according to that idea, put in a position of not being able to come to any decision merely by our own 'honest to God' feelings. If we have any feelings we must compare them with the opinions of the best authorities, and justify them before we allow ourselves to have an opinion. That *was* the Victorian belief, and we are still asked every minute, 'What is your authority?' The asker doesn't seem to think that this state of mind is the worst possible form of '*snobbery*', for a snob is obviously one who has not the guts to have and state an opinion of his own, whether it is on the worth of a person or work of art or anything else. Until he is assured of the support of someone in power he will make no statement, for or against.

Now about this modern or not modern, the resemblances the average person finds in modern painting to ancient painting, I mean Stone Age and that sort of ancientness, the resemblances are resemblances of human functions. It must be evident that even the 'Moustiers' man[11] of some hundred thousand years ago walked by putting one foot before the other, must have eaten with his mouth, and so on. At the beginning, childbearing must have been fairly much as it is for simple women today and so on. When things are brought down or come down to fundamentals they do resemble each other in spite of many thousands or perhaps hundreds of thousands of years of time.

And that is the point about modern painting. I mean the *modern movement of the last 30 or 40 years*. It was an attempt to get back to fundamentals, and it succeeded. It couldn't possibly resemble academic painting, which never is concerned with anything fundamental, so it naturally resembles any other art but the academic, and by that I mean the academic ancient or modern. So there's nothing *out of order* about really modern painting resembling really ancient painting, which was in its time of course really modern, and there's no reason to feel clever at having seen a resemblance, or to be astonished or to be sure that the artist has merely copied it from something in a museum. (This is based on the idea that the artist of to-day is so *much more civilised*. Civilisation may produce the same state in one artist as the lack of it does in another artist.)

One might as well say that he has copied walking or drinking, from something he got from the Stone Age. Drawing is just as natural to some people as dancing is to others, and dancing must be quite an old thing. Legs have been going for a long time, although most people seem to think that dancing started with the Italian ballet, just as they think that sculpture started with the Greeks. The whole confusion seems to start with the idea that to be an artist you must be a scholar, or if scholar only applies to book learning, what corresponds to a scholar in painting and sculpture.

That is what the modern movement refused to admit, knowledge of anatomy, architecture, perspective, chemistry of colour, the history of art. Skill in copying appearances and all that sort of thing did not seem to the modern movement men necessary for an artist. On the contrary, vision, imagination, independence of spirit, rhythm, colour sense, courage, invention and creative power, were essential. Now a child can have vision, imagination, independence of spirit, rhythm, colour sense, courage, invention and creative power. These are not acquired, but they can be developed without academic art schools, and that is the difference between the academic and the independent point of view. But then, if that's art, any child can do it! No! Not *any* child, but *some* children can and do produce works that are more works of art than most grown-up artists produce, and that's not saying too much.

We are fairly accustomed to the idea that child prodigies in the musical work can play better than most grown-up musicians, or professors of music. But that's different! That's pure inspiration! is the reply, meaning, I suppose, that pure inspiration is not possible or allowable in painting. And why not? What is meant is that playing the violin or the piano may be done by feeling, but for painting you must know how to draw, and by that is meant draw anatomically or photographically. Well, then again that's what the modern men don't admit. *Drawing is a matter of expressing form as you feel it*, although the feeling is caused by the impression you get through your eyes, and to see living things anatomically is extremely unnatural and difficult. To find them to be anatomical on examination is quite a different thing, and the idea that we see people we are interested in anatomically is, if we must be careful, at least most unusual, if not entirely unnatural. Does any one claim that without an anatomical knowledge of his parents, a man cannot get any real human impression of them? Well it's just this human impression or feeling about people and things that the artist does get and express, and it does not depend on anatomical or photographic accuracy or exact measurements.

So what it amounts to is that in the modern movement people do not

　　　　　　　　　　　MODERN SCOTTISH PAINTING

allow that their feelings and impressions are to be corrected, justified, or interfered with in any way, by measurements made with instruments of precision, footrules, calipers, anatomical diagrams, photographs plain or coloured, or anything of that sort. Then what is the proof that their work is any good? There isn't any proof. If it gives you nothing, it gives you nothing, that's all. If it gives you something, then there's no need for you to try to prove it does, or to justify your liking or love for it. No need for you to ask for the approval of the expert. There is such a thing as real love, and it applies to works of art. Your mother likes you even if you are not approved of by the best people or the crowd.

And that is my attempt to give you a *working* meaning of what I mean by modern painting.

The next thing to tackle is what we mean by modern Scottish painting. Well, what do we mean by Scottish, which I'd much rather call Scotch, but it appears that that word is not used for painting, so I won't go against the authorities. The first thing is easy. It must be painting produced by Scotsmen or Scotswomen, not necessarily in Scotland or of Scotland. I mean of Scottish subjects; but it must have the essentials of the Scottish character, and not merely the Scottish character at this moment or of recent years, but something that we feel is and has been inherent in the Scots character all through its history. Something that 'time but th'impression deeper makes' would be a heartening feeling, and we would like something that is as true as the geological fault that divides Scotland, or the road to the Isles which is the natural track for both pilgrims and dealers in ponies.[12] Can we find it? Again, perhaps not *absolutely*, but nearly enough to let us get on with the job. A working meaning of what we call Scotch or Scottish, that brings us to art and nationality.

CHAPTER II

Art and Nationality

'Freedom is a Nobil Thing'
Barbour's *Bruce*[13]

When I was leaving Scotland to settle in Paris I told our family lawyer and he said 'So you're going to become a Frenchman'. I said 'No! I hope I'm going to be able to persist in being a Scotsman'. Naturally the reply proved to him what he had suspected; that as I was an artist I was just daft. Well, what did he mean and what did I mean? He meant that anyone of Scots parents registered in Scotland was a Scotsman to him. Of course (the legal position was the only position) legally a Scotsman. Well if I'm not a Scotsman there aren't any.

What did I mean? I meant that I had definitely decided to persist in being what I considered an artist, and a Scots artist, and the art atmosphere and the painting I was surrounded by in Scotland, in my opinion, were not Scots at all, and definitely and clearly not Celtic. I recently met in London a *very interesting* young Scot, an ardent nationalist, and began to, as the Americans would say, 'tell him' what I considered was Scottish, what I prefer to call 'Scotch', a word which the Scots seem to find intolerable. This good young lad, when I began to 'tell' him, said, 'What's your authority?' This was quite a dazing question. It had never occurred to me that I needed an authority for my opinions about my own country, and after a pause from astonishment I said, 'Authority, I don't need an authority. I *am* it.' 'Oh!' he said, 'You are *it*.' I said, 'No, you've got the accent on the wrong word, and you'll never understand.'

This is a point I would like to talk about – this always wanting to justify things by recognised authorities, or anything but one's own existence and feelings, is understandable in a person without a racial or national 'background', but to me quite inexcusable in a Scot. So, of course, the reply is always 'That may be your opinion', and that reply is considered to be completely destroying. What they mean is that in the opinion of some recognised authority they've read, they have superior knowledge, and I'm wrong. What they (I mean a certain type) deal in is what are called facts, and what they call history is fact. You'd think Scotsmen would be less trusting.

But about Art and Nationality? That *is* about it. Well, have we anything that we can call an example of something really National? Yes, and something I think National and Scottish. At the risk of being considered anti-English, which I'm not, here is the Arbroath Manifesto. Put the same thing into painting and you've got what I'd call Scottish painting.

This is *not* included as an attack on England, but a statement about liberty, with which every *real* Englishman (our ancient enemy) will heartily agree. It is not *anti-English* but *anti loss of liberty*, and applies as much to art as to anything.

ANSWER FROM ABROATH TO ROME

SCOTS PARLIAMENT 1320

On the Pope's unwillingness to recognise Bruce
as King of Scotland.

...If this Prince should leave the principles he has so nobly pursued; and consent that we or our Kingdom, be subjected to the King or People of England, we shall immediately endeavour to expel him as our enemy – and as the subverter both of his own and our rights – and will make us a King who will defend our liberties; but as long as there shall but one hundred of us remain alive we will never subject us to the dominion of the English. *It is not glory, it is not riches, neither is it honour, but it is liberty alone that we fight and contend for, which no honest man will lose but with his life!*[14]

Let's return to our family lawyer's point of view, which amounts to saying that you are a Scottish artist if you are legally a Scotsman. Very simple. Anyone can then know what is Scottish painting. The final extension of it is that anyone a member of an officially recognised art body is beyond question; and the more official the more certain. Clearly for any thinking man that won't do, but if we're not to accept authorities how are we to know? Clearly in this matter or all matters of art, *by our feelings*. To 'know what you like' may be limited and it may be entirely right. In any case, the important thing is that it's honest, and not mere snobbery, which means not having the guts to take a decision about people or things on your own feelings, and it certainly is better than to know what so and so, the great recognised authority of the moment says that you should like. Art is what you feel it is, *for you*. You can develop yourself, extend your range of appreciation indefinitely, but it is still *for you*, art is what you feel it is, if it does it for you whether it's a grocer's calendar or the most modern painting, it's your affair. The people who have devoted their lives to any job are worth listening to and can probably extend your field of appreciation, but what you like is still your own affair, and no apologies or attempts at justification are necessary.

The Scots have been dazed for generations by education, which they have accepted as a royal road to understanding everything, and they think that appreciation of art is something that belongs to the educated in the sense of what the French call 'instructed', 'The man o' independent mind, he bears the gree for a' that'.'[15]

A distinguished R.A. in his diary of a tour of Scotland to meet everyone of importance, after no end of stuff about all the distinguished cultured people he met, dismissed Burns in a few lines by saying he was dressed like a workman and had no Latin or Greek.[16] Poor Burns, what could *he* have understood about art.

In these days all MPs started their speeches with a Greek or Latin quotation, and frequent classical quotations in their speeches proved they were a cultured people. Burns, they say, got a hearing because they thought his work was by some nobleman writing as a ploughman. When they found it wasn't, everybody but Moore dropped him.[17]

But what's this got to do with National Art? Well, a friend of mine went to Salamanca specially to interview Unamuno, the great Spanish Nationalist.[18] He had read Unamuno, but he wanted to find out first hand, or as they say in Scotland, by word of mouth, what he meant by National. So my friend said, 'Could you give an example, say a book that you could say really expressed a national point of view?' Unamuno went direct to the shelf and produced a copy of Burns' works. One can hardly think of any intelligent person dismissing Unamuno's opinion as negligible, and it's about Scotland, so we may be coming to something, and here I reprint a notice from *Apollo*, February, 1939.[19] The writer '*gives it up*.'

THREE SCOTTISH PAINTERS: S.J. PEPLOE, LESLIE HUNTER, F.C.B. CADELL AT MESSRS. ALEX REID & LEFÈVRE'S GALLERIES

These three artists, all recently deceased, as well as J.D. Fergusson, happily still going strong and holding an exhibition this month in the same galleries, really belong together in time and in metaphysical space. Mr D.P. Bliss, who has written a foreword to the catalogue of the triple show, would persuade us that 'for all the Frenchness and Modernity of their style' these artists take their place in the pictorial tradition of Scotland. Mr Bliss is also a Scotsman, so he can probably see more than a benighted visitor from south of the border, who must profess himself puzzled, the more so as it is even asserted that these three painters 'carried out and brought up-to-date the tradition of the Glasgow School'. Scotland, it seems to me, has no 'pictorial tradition', and the likeness between our triplets or quadruplets and the Glasgow School is about as striking as the likeness between, say, Princes Street, Edinburgh, and Sauchiehall Street, Glasgow, on an autumn day – sparkle and colour in one, gloom and greyness in the other. To step from Sir James Guthrie's room in Burlington House into Peploe's room there illustrates what I mean. It has the effect of stepping from fog and murk into sunshine and air. And as fog and murk more or less characterise all the other rooms in the Academy at present – there are, of course, exceptions, such as McTaggart – the Peploe-Hunter-Cadell-Fergusson School seems to represent a break into tradition, rather than a continuance. The real point of interest is whether these light and colour-rich four are more essentially Scottish. But then, what is the essentially Scottish element in a Scot? Knox or Burns? Or both? I give it up!

I'm not surprised, after seeing the Scottish Art Show at Burlington House which *most faithfully* represented the Royal Scottish Academy, and which does not, or to be more careful, certainly did not represent Scottish Art. *I'm not surprised the writer gave it up.* Any person trying to understand instead of merely accepting the recognised authorities *did* give it up. The Peploe, Hunter section *was* Burns. But Knox was a great strong man and did great things for Scotland, and Bliss's statement was correct and well understood. But no one could be expected to see what he meant if they took the Scottish Show at Burlington House to really represent *Modern*

Scottish Art. To try to find a painting tradition among that stuff was impossible, for *it wasn't there.*

Was it a sense of justness that made them place an effigy of John Knox at the entrance to receive us?

I don't know any of the organisers. They were faced with an impossible task. They had to have the work of every dead Scotch Academician, and I suppose every Associate, so what could anyone do. No one *not* in the Scots Academy had a right to be there. Everyone of the Academy had a definite right. Had this Show happened at the time when the Glasgow School was at its best, no Glasgow School man would have been in it because they weren't in the Scots Academy.

This brings us back to the Glasgow School.[20] Why should they have been in such a show? If it is to be regarded as an official academic show there is no reason at all why they should even be expected to be there. But the point is that most people, even intelligent people wanting to know, accept this show and such shows everywhere as representing the art of the country, and that is unfair both to the artists, the country, and the people who go to the Exhibition.

The French had at the time of the 1936 Exhibition an exhibition of what they called Independent Art and that was fair and honest. If you didn't like Independent Art you didn't need to go. No one claimed that it was *all French Art,* and it in no way prevented the official Salon from having *all* the visitors, if no one wanted to see the Independent Show. But people *did* want to see the Independent Show, went and thought it wonderful, which it was. My opinion. Yes, of course, but not only mine, and certainly not the opinion of the old Salon.

We are talking of modern painting. I am submitting that official art does not represent the art production of a country with any independent art spirit. I don't say that all countries have an independent art spirit. Some are artistically or in the art sense, dead, as some are politically or socially dead. Whether these 'deads' are separable is too long to discuss in this book.

But about National Art! Why should we say that one art is more representative of a country or of a race than another? I know Scotland and Scotsmen pretty well, and I've never met anyone that put Holy Wullie as more representative of Scotland than William Wallace, Bruce or Robert Burns. I've certainly come across people who were ashamed of Robert

Burns. In fact the generation I had the misfortune to be born into *were* for the most part ignorant or ashamed of Burns and only associated him with drink. But supposing that the worthy Scot admires Wallace and Bruce and the spirit of the Arbroath Manifesto then he should admire painting of the same spirit. Does any sane person suggest that the average painting expresses the courage and independence of Wallace, Bruce, Knox or Burns? Has *any* painting? Certainly. The Glasgow School from the *Galloway Landscape*, Hornel and Henry at their best, Melville till the last, Guthrie's *Garden Party* and his portrait of Ned Martin, Lavery's *Miss Burrel* in Kelvingrove Gallery, Crawhall; in fact the whole school at their best had the Scots characteristic of independence, and vigor, colour and particularly quality of paint, which means paint that is living and not merely a coat of any sort of paint placed between containing lines like a map. Theirs was paint that expressed the envelopment of things in light, low tone or bright, and their own people backed them.[21]

At the same time, McTaggart, *not* the Glasgow School, was producing without official recognition work that is thoroughly Scottish. I find it very difficult to believe that anyone has painted the sea better than McTaggart. I've seen a lot of painting. I've never seen any as good. It's always been a mystery to me how he survived and brought up a family on his painting. Then there was the charm of Walton and Roche. This is just to mention those that come to my mind. They are what I call representative Scottish painters.

In those days among the great supporters of Melville and McTaggart was McOmish Dott, a most sympathetic dealer, with great taste and judgment.[22] His little gallery called the Scottish Gallery always had McTaggarts and Melvilles well presented, a charming oasis in the dried up desert and a great help to me. His enthusiasm for the things he believed in was really heartening. It is a great pity that his lead has not been followed up. I also owe a great deal to the sympathetic talks with that very charming dealer Van Vissenleigh.

CHAPTER III

The Glasgow School

An unorthodox blast has been blown in the west.
Burns[23]

BUT THERE IS still the word modern. I don't mean merely paintings of today, contemporary or up-to-date. I mean by *modern* Scottish painting, painting that attaches itself or can be considered to be related to the modern movement of Europe of the last 40 years. Progressive painting would be a better title, for progressive should mean liberating, liberating by a persistent attempt to find the fundamentals, the essentials or truths, instead of adding clever gadgets, or by using fashionable stunts. Up-to-date generally means with all the latest gadgets.

The modern movement in art was an attempt to get down to truths, to fundamentals, and start afresh to create a free art, or an art freed from the academic imbecilities which at that time dominated the world.

The Glasgow School was an attempt to do the same thing in Scotland, but it started about 1880, nearly 20 years earlier. By started I mean took definite form. If there was any considerable progressive art in Scotland before the Glasgow School, I didn't see it or hear of it. I was there devoting myself to trying to see or hear of any free art, and as I have continued to do so that is not an unreasonable claim. The Scottish Academy at that time was *hopeless*, had nothing to do with progressive art. It was just the RA of Scotland, which is all right for people who like that sort of thing.[24] For those who think that that is not a fair statement, I ask them if they noted the room that represented that period in the recent Scottish Exhibition at Burlington House, 1939, which was representative, I suppose, of the best of the RSA for that period. Compare it with what was happening in France at the same time and tell me if there was anything to give a lead to the art student or young painter of that time. I was one of the art students and I decidedly saw no lead, nothing helpful or even liberating, to allow me to go on and help myself. I said so then and I say so now.

84

But at that time (meaning the nineties) the Glasgow School was not merely starting but *established*, and was a most inspiring lead to any young Scots painter. There were probably 25 painters in the Glasgow School Group. The 14 I mention in this book were outstanding and still can stand among the modern men of today. When I go to dinner with some friends I see a Moorish market by Melville looking at me just as it looked 35 years ago. I saw an E.A. Walton the other day, May 1939, in the French Gallery in London – 'Harvesters' – which gave me the same feeling as it did 35 years ago. It was between two recent strong Peploes. And I had just come from the de Segonzac Show and the Monets in Bond Street.[25] This from my point of view justifies the use of the word 'modern' in relation to the Glasgow School, for it would apply equally to another dozen of the group.

But the Glasgow School! It won't do to assume everyone knows about them. I should think most people of this generation, even in Scotland, haven't even heard of them. I don't intend to give their history. David Martin in his book, *The Glasgow School* (Bell & Sons), has done that very well, and Francis Newbery, the head of the Glasgow School of Art, has written the introduction.[26] The word 'school' in Glasgow School, he explains, has nothing to do with any educational establishment. It simply means a group of painters, grouped by sympathy of purpose.

Although my book does not pretend to be historical, for what it sets out to say it is necessary to give some history, or to give what seem to be the things that go to make up the character of the group. Jean Jacques Rousseau has said that 'history is the art of selecting from a mass of falsehood something that *seems* to be true'. I intend to proceed as I do in my painting; that is, *to select from a mass of information what seems to me to express what I want to say.*

What then do I think is the difference between the Glasgow School and the rest of the Scottish painters of their period, with a few exceptions, which I will deal with later? I would say first of all that they were Scottish, and not because they were not influenced, but for the best reason possible, that they couldn't help it.

And what do I mean by Scottish? I refer you to page 79, the Arbroath Manifesto (see chapter on 'Art and Nationality'). They were Scottish because they wanted liberty; to express themselves freely, which in art means honestly. Then they were directly emotional. That is to say they were moved by beauty in nature instead of being moved by literature or moral sentiment, or a desire to illustrate it. But the chief characteristic was that they were painters; people with a feeling for the fulness, quality, solidity and expressiveness of paint. I mean the difference between a painting by Rembrandt and a coloured drawing, called a painting! by Ingres.[27]

To try to state it in another way, they were concerned with the quality and substance of things, and not content with a coloured diagram or map of things. This substance is reality, it is the fullness and richness of things made apparent to the painter by light. The difference is like the difference between two suits cut from the same pattern, the one in the best Harris tweed (and there is no material more beautiful), and the other made of 'sleezy', trashy, thin material. The good tweed suit will be something, even if *very badly* cut. The Glasgow School men, from my point of view, were best in the homespun period, and Guthrie was like that to start with. Later, as seen in the Scottish Show at Burlington House, he got among silks and satins and frills. Bad luck for Scotland! Then, although I have no intention of going into the *detective critic* business which people seem to like, some detective business seems necessary. Where did these Glasgow men get the encouragement or support for this feeling for substance and quality in paint, for without *some* sympathy and support one can't go on, and they did go on for quite a long time, till apparently some of them saw that the thick homespun stuff was not sufficiently *refined* for the portrait painting business.

Well, where did they get the support for this feeling of the fullness of things, like rich earth, foliage, clouds, etc? In his book David Martin keeps telling us of the *great advantages* many of them had in having studied under the Parisian professors at Julian's or elsewhere, under Bastien-Lepage and Dagnan Bouveret.[28] He talks of a *thorough artistic training* under the tuition of Bougereau, Collin and Courtois, Jean Paul Laurens, Gérôme.[29] Well, has anyone ever seen anything that could be called painting by any of these people, meaning by painting what the Glasgow men themselves put forward as painting, and what all the modern movement would accept as such? Or again meaning that Giorgione, Rembrandt, Velasquez, Monticelli, Corot were painters, and obviously great influences on the Glasgow Group.[30] No. Very evidently, to put forward *these* Parisian '*pompier*' professors as any aid to progressive art is the height of

                                          MODERN SCOTTISH PAINTING

absurdity.[31] A *'thorough artistic training'* under them could have done *nothing but harm*, and perhaps that's what sowed the seeds of the disease that made the Glasgow School fade out as a force for a Scottish tradition in painting. While they were Scots, they could not be academic. When they aimed at the Royal Academy and the Royal Scottish Academy, then the Bougereau, Gérôme, Jean Paul Laurens influence was a help, of course. It *was just what was wanted*, and the homespun was shed for the 'Braidclaith' which 'gie's folks an unco heese', makes for 'respectability' and conformity.[32]

I feel really depressed as I think of it. Here were 25, all *painters*, probably 14 whose good work will stand anywhere to-day. Twenty-five men, independents, who established themselves without any official recognition; who even trained a public to accept their work in spite of it having been at first received with ridicule; who were recognised and bought all over the Continent. Twenty-five men who were *not* conscious of the tremendous contribution they had made in founding a first-class tradition of Scottish painting. Twenty-five men who mostly preferred academic honours and success to the Wallace and Bruce example of patriotism, of fighting to the last for Scottish Independence. A birthright, and for what a mess. Well! The Group must have had the right instinct at the start when they elected William Kennedy as first president, who was steadfastly opposed to all academies till the last.[33]

'But tae oor tale' or our history.[34] It certainly was *not* Monsieur Bougereau and Co. who helped to give a feeling for independence or quality of paint to the Glasgow School. Who then? Well, as Scots they had the feeling of or desire for independence and liberty as their birthright, and as Westerners not poisoned by the modern Athenianism of the East, they still had the natural instinct for the beauty of nature (which the Greeks had not), for light, and colour, and quality of light and colour, but some sympathy and support is necessary even to keep to these things in spite of ridicule and lack of recognition. The sentimental idea that one can stand alone may satisfy people who haven't tried to stand alone. Some of us haven't that idea, and know that it is not even desirable. Sympathy, apart from the idea of just handing over some money, is quite necessary, and the use of a Group is not, as most people think, to be constantly meeting and agreeing, but to create what the French call an 'ambiance', what Burns calls a 'clime' meaning climate. 'To mak a happy firesides *clime* for weans and wife' – to create a climate or ambiance which gives a feeling of freedom for expression.[35] This applies in the case of climate to flowers, trees, crops, animals. The ambiance is something more human and in the best sense social, not independent of climate of course, but not feeling, rightly or wrongly, entirely at the mercy of it.

Well, where did this come from to help the Glasgow School men? I can't say exactly, but one day on the rocks at George Davison's bathing place on the Cap d'Antibes, a girl introduced me as an artist to her mother.[36] The mother said she was interested in art and artists; had I heard of a Scottish artist called Arthur Melville?

Strange question! I *had* heard of Melville; he was my first influence. Although I never met him or even saw him, his painting gave me my first start; his work opened up to me the way to free painting – not merely freedom in the use of paint, but freedom of outlook.

Then we talked, and this charming, sympathetic woman is Mrs Harrower, daughter of the late John Forbes White (*John Forbes White* by I.W. Harrower, Published Foulis) of Aberdeen, a most remarkable man. He brought the first Corot to Scotland, and made, by introducing the work of Israëls and the Dutchmen (who were based on the Barbizon School) *another link between French and Scottish painting*.[37]

White bought pictures by Israëls, Corot, Diaz, Bosboom, Mauve and James Maris, and so launched the modern Dutch influence in Scotland. Good dealers sold the Dutchmen all round the West, and that was the start of the Dutch influence on Scotland.

Writing in 1897 in his introduction to David Martin's book on the Glasgow School, Francis Newbery says:

> Glasgow has been extremely fortunate *for the last twenty years*. The finest examples of the work of the Barbizon School, and of the modern Dutch Masters, of Millet, Corot, Diaz, Monticelli, the Maris brothers, Israëls and many others have been bought by Glasgow buyers, and were brought before the eyes of the Glasgow artists *long before London had recognised even the existence* of these continental influences.[38]

The Maris brothers started about 1880.

So the Dutch, who, from my point of view, had earlier put Scotland on

                MODERN SCOTTISH PAINTING

the *wrong* tack (but probably the Lowland Scots and East Coast people) with the photographically accurate materialistic interiors, *copies* of silks, tiles, furniture, etc (very well done) came this time to show the West of Scotland men the possibilities of the beautiful atmospheric greys they lived among. It was easy for people not yet full of Bougereau, Gérôme and Co. to accept this. And, of course, Corot was easy – I mean the grey ones.

The International Exhibition in Edinburgh in the year 1886 brought together a collection of Dutch and French pictures such as it would be almost impossible to surpass; and these examples were eagerly studied by the Glasgow men. Private collections, where these same pictures were hung, were always open to inspection, and it was undoubtedly such influences as these, slight though they may appear, that were the first motors in the movement.

Francis Newbery, in his introduction to Martin's book, *The Glasgow School*, says, 'The enterprise of a Fine Art dealer in Glasgow in bringing these pictures to the city was of paramount use and importance'.

Great credit is certainly due to these Glasgow Fine Art dealers, [William] Craibe Angus and Alex Reid, and great credit is due to John Forbes White of Aberdeen.[39]

We couldn't call Forbes White a businessman. He started as a medical student, but at the death of his brother had to go into his father's business. He was a real, what the French call 'amateur', by which they mean an 'art lover'. He was a just critic, and went by his *feelings*, and bought with confidence on his judgment.

Partly perhaps because he was a first-class amateur photographer, he did not expect a painting to look like a photograph. Writing about his Corot *Souvenir d'Italie* (the first Corot brought to Scotland, now in the Glasgow Corporation Gallery) he says, 'The human eye is here rather than the lens of the camera. *The heart of the painter rejoices in his works!*'

Then, writing about Rembrandt – 'He is the creator of the man, or at least his interpreter, perhaps his judge. The subject is no longer merely what he seems to all the world. He is like a ray of light *split up by passing through a lens* – the lens of an analytical mind.' This appeared in *The Quarterly Review* in 1899. This 'split up by passing through the lens of an analytical mind' makes me think at once of a Picasso portrait.

White was instrumental in the acquisition of the Rembrandt *Hendrijke*

Stoffels for the National Gallery in Edinburgh. He was a rich man, an erudite, and knew everybody, but said, 'I have found more real taste and discrimination and feeling for art among artisans than among any of the upper classes'.

Arthur Melville said of White's house that it had 'Flowers in the garden, meat in the hall, a butt of wine, and a spice of wit' (Robert Louis Stevenson), which helps to give a portrait of John Forbes White.[40] With a few men like him, Scottish Art could again take its place in the world.

It was strange that I should meet Mrs Harrower, John Forbes White's daughter, in the property of George Davison, a man of the same sympathetic character, and also a famous amateur photographer, and a great friend of artists and musicians.

All these French and Dutch painters introduced by John Forbes White were painters who used paint as painters and had nothing in common with Bougereau, & Co., but why were they accepted and bought in the West of Scotland? *Evidently* because the West of Scotland was not yet controlled by the Royal Academy or the Royal Scottish Academy. I remember the horrible shock at the varnishing day of the Glasgow Institute, when I found the chief places occupied by Royal Academicians for the first time. It was said, because the Glasgow men had gone to London, the lay members had taken charge of the Institute.

But it is easy to say that the men who put up such a wonderful fight didn't do enough, although for Scotland's sake one can't help regretting that they didn't 'keep to it' more. *Let's raise a cheer for their great achievement*, especially when many, perhaps most of them, started with no advantages. What they achieved was wonderful. It's not easy to keep on. But, as I have said, they must have started with the right idea, for they elected William Kennedy for their first President, and he was *solidly and to the last, against academies*.

The unfortunate thing is that these men made a track which is followed by the young Scottish artist, that track is from Scotland to Burlington House. It was, and is, natural for the Edinburgh young men to fix their eyes on the RA Art on the east coast and in Edinburgh being represented by a Scottish RA, which is a branch of the London RA, most natural, Edinburgh being an academic town.

But for the west coast and Glasgow where they are great engineers,

MODERN SCOTTISH PAINTING

build great ships, beautiful yachts and all that sort of thing, to be academic is *not natural*. Glasgow creates things and not imitations of old things, but ships like the *Queen Elizabeth*, yachts like the *Britannia* (G.L. Watson's perfect masterpiece). They made the Clyde navigable up to Glasgow. They make their International Exhibitions a success.[41] In doing all this they do make a mess of their town with smoke, which is most regrettable. It could be charming, and the mess is for the most part unnecessary and wasteful. I hope they will tackle that, too, and make their town worthy of the most beautiful country it is surrounded by. But they do make, create things, and on that account I say that it's not natural for them to be academic. What we'd like to see is west coast Glasgow art in the same class as the *Queen Elizabeth*. Art that would take its place as the *Queen Elizabeth* takes her place. In the days of the Glasgow School it was not so easy to see that art had anything to do with engineering. Tennyson being the Poet Laureate, poet to the Queen, was taken very seriously by most people with any claim to being cultured, and as he said, 'He was only a landscape painter'. Perhaps the Glasgow men felt they should pay attention to Bougereau, & Co. as they were 'real' artists, figure painters; that's to say, doing classical subjects. This perhaps is the truth about the psychology of the Glasgow School. Their weakness was their feeling of inferiority in face of the alleged culture of their time. This alleged and accepted culture was represented by Lord Leighton who was a Lord, the President of the Royal Academy, and a painter of classical figure subjects, so what more could anyone ask?

This is still the awe-inspiring combination for the bourgeois artist, and this brings us to something that for a long time I couldn't understand. It is, that these men, even Melville who had complete freedom in landscape, seemed generally to become paralysed when dealing with a portrait or figure subject, apparently quite terrified that he might 'go over the edges' of accuracy, meaning by accuracy not emotional accuracy, but photographic or anatomically exact measurements. Paint was used freely and fully in dealing with anything but flesh. Liberties could be taken with landscape, but to paint figures you had to have a discipline that could only come of what's called a *sound academic training*, such as that of Leighton, Bougereau, & Co., the super *'pompiers'*, expert extinguishers of the youthful fire of inspiration and free expression.

So now we come to realise that the Glasgow School's achievement was wonderful, and if they weakened they did so on account of an atmosphere in which it was impossible or nearly impossible to carry on.

But it was possible. Whistler did not give in, and Sickert did not become academic, and is, I am glad to say, *salut!* still going strong. And Ethel Walker, that wonderful woman, at the age of 73, is painting with a freedom and vigor that makes the painting by most of the young men seem like doddering imbecility.[42]

And there is James Pryde, who has never had anything to do with academies, and is undoubtedly one of our greatest Scottish artists.[43] And this brings us to Whistler, a great point in the history of Scottish Art, for as he said, 'Am I not a McNeill of Barra?', and if he hadn't said so we'd have thought so, and there was nothing strange or unnatural or affected in the Glasgow men accepting the lead to freedom in figure painting offered to them by Whistler. Nothing could have been more natural. Here was a man, a fighter, a man of feeling, of sensibility, not muddleheaded enough to be impressed by the academic imbecilities. A man with a real sense of design, a real sense of colour and quality of paint (see *The Little White Girl*) but above all with *confidence in himself*. It was easy for the Glasgow men to accept his beautiful greys, and they saw that his sense of design was something that was a great help to them. His art was obviously not very full-blooded, but it had spirit and wit, if not humour. It was definitely art just as much as the academic stuff wasn't, but it was the twilight, the Celtic twilight, brought to Chelsea. It was too like the Fiona MacLeod, white wind blowing through everything. It was *not* gloom or dirt. It was the white mist, and compared to the art of the time in Britain, amazing and charming.[44]

Again the Glasgow men might have joined Whistler, formed a solid group and kept out of the Academies as he did. For a time they did, and at the Grafton Gallery the International with Rodin as President was a great show in its time.

But let's get back to Scotland at that time. The Glasgow men were trying to get into the RSA where they were hated, and as often as possible rejected, coming from Glasgow, an industrial town not considered a seat of learning. The youthful vigour and bright colour of the Glasgow School was considered by the Scotch Academy as the vulgarity to be expected from an industrial

　　　　　　　　　　　　MODERN SCOTTISH PAINTING

region. They were detested and rejected, till purely by accident, Guthrie became President.

There was and still is in Scotland a Society of Scottish Artists, the SSA. This society was founded by the younger and less academic painters, I think in the '90s. Compared with the complete impotent senility of the RSA it became very strong, and so strong that it was evident to anyone of intelligence that this was the representative Scottish Show. When this point arrived the usual thing happened. The RSA *asked the leaders in,* and with one or two exceptions they came in like lambs, and the SSA not being the Royal Academy of Scotland has become merely a stepping stone for the RSA – in other words, the first step to the RA.

The greatly respected man in the SSA was McTaggart, at that time not welcome in the RSA. I often meet people who have the idea that McTaggart always was a great accepted success in Scotland. Certainly not so, and in the old days he had nothing in common with the Scottish Academy.

About that time two young men were evidently outstanding in the east – S.J. Peploe and Robert Brough. They were students together, and shared a studio together in Paris. They were very different. Peploe came back very much impressed by Manet, I *think* after reading Zola's *His Masterpiece*[45] Brough apparently resolved to be a successful portrait painter. They both sent to the RSA. Brough shot ahead at his job, portrait painting. *Peploe was nearly always rejected.*

One man that did stick to his point of view till the end was Charles Rennie Mackintosh. Though this book is about painting, I'll take the opportunity to say that Scotland, and particularly Glasgow, ought to be ashamed of their neglect of Charles Rennie Mackintosh, undoubtedly one of the best architects of the world in modern times.

Apparently they could not stand his honesty and independence, and bamboozled by buildings and pretentious imbecility couldn't see that his simplicity had the dignity of the traditional architecture of Scotland.

He thoroughly established a style of architecture and interior design which did not copy existing buildings or bits of buildings, Scottish or foreign, but created something new and Scottish. Had it been carried on it would have made Scotland one of the leading schools of architecture of the world.

Mackintosh's work was recognised and taken up on the continent and made use of everywhere except in Scotland.

I think the Glasgow Art School designed by Mackintosh to the smallest detail of wood and ironwork, inside and out, is a masterpiece of constructional integrity.

Most Glasgow people haven't noticed it, haven't even heard of Mackintosh, and I don't think a book on his work has been done in Scotland, although he may be considered the father of modern architecture.

He told me that as people didn't want architecture as he wanted to do it, he preferred to give it up, and he took to painting and did very good water colours which have the same constructional integrity as his architecture.

Both Mackintosh and his wife Margaret MacDonald always insisted on their great indebtedness to the director of the Glasgow Art School, Francis Newbery and his wife for their wonderful sympathy, understanding and encouragement, without which they said they did not think they could have got a start, so all respect and good wishes to the Newberys.[46]

CHAPTER IV

Art and Engineering

Predestination in the stride o' yon connectin'-rod.
John Calvin might ha' forged the same – enorrmous, certain, slow –
Kipling's 'McAndrew's Hymn'[47]

PERHAPS ONE OF the most important contributions Calvinism has made to Scotland is that it has made the Scot a first-class engineer. In the whole range of that field, without worrying ourselves too much about history, we can accept, I think, the idea that Scotland before Calvinism was distinctly lacking generally in the feeling of responsibility necessary to the accuracy required in engineering.

I say *generally*, and I am talking about accuracy in the sense of instruments of precision, machines that work, and men that work like man-made machines. To the artistic person (in the Victorian sense), this is just a thoroughly bad, poisonous affair. It isn't, it's too much of it, like too much whisky that is bad and poisonous.

Some of this sort of accuracy is necessary, and particularly to emotional people. Otherwise you get what existed in Scotland before Calvinism – a state of affairs that was 'just a mess' – some or lots of good things in that mess, but generally 'a mess'. Scotland at that time needed a purge and it got it from Knox and artistic people (not artists) have since blamed Knox just as the teetotaller blames drink. Might as reasonably blame the sun because people get sunstroke. We constantly hear that sort of complaint in the South of France from people who refuse to behave differently there from in Scotland.

Well, Scotland got its *purge*. It needed it and it did it good. Had I lived in Knox's time I'd have been on his side. I don't blame him for the state of Scotland now, which I think is heartbreaking to anyone that loves it and its traditions. I blame and blame thoroughly and curse the people who have *misused* the purgative (see modern medical opinions on purgatives). The people who, having benefited by the purge, have tried to live on purgatives ever since and naturally have become weak and unable to live a decent human life – I mean to function fully as human beings. The feeble (I don't mean physically) have of course accepted the condition. Some strong ones have stayed and given weak ones the satisfaction of seeing them worn out and defeated, and what a joy it gives the weak ones to see the independent or courageous one reduced to a state they consider defeat, hating his heroic attempt to preserve what all Scots are always talking about: freedom.

The wiser ones left in order to preserve their national character – independence. There always are exceptions – some hero who comes through – and we are always having the idea put forward that if you are good enough you can do it. Did William Wallace? No! Then he wasn't good enough, neither was Christ, nor Bruno. Galileo was good enough to survive. He was a 'Yes man' at the critical moment, proving that he realised that the dead weight of stupidity and prejudice was too much for men even of his power. Then clearly we have to be better than Christ, Bruno, William Wallace and Galileo to survive.

What has this got to do with art? Well, what is art and what makes it? Independent art is created by an independent people. Is that saying too much? Well, gaze around in this year of grace.

Can it be proved that art should be independent? Can it be independent? Don't let us try to prove things. Let's try to examine things and let's each act according to our decision after examination.

I don't pretend to say exactly what art is, I don't know. But I believe that no people lacking in independent spirit can be creative in the first class sense whether it concerns procreation or art creation. But! About engineering and art? Is it not that the creative power of the Scots has been diverted from literature, painting and the recognised art mediums, to the wonderful engineering feats like the Forth Bridge or the *Queen Elizabeth*? That's not so easy. Is the Forth Bridge, which I've *always* admired, a work of art? Is the *Queen Elizabeth* a work of art? If not, why not? We can cut the trouble by saying that *art is what you think it is, for you*. That for a Scotsman is too easy. Let's examine it a bit, this question of a diverted or changed creative power, and let's examine it, not for the sake of proving what art is, but for the pleasure of trying to clear our heads – in other words *to be free* and not slaves. Let's be Scots.

This subject was never as interesting as it is at present, when lots of

MODERN SCOTTISH PAINTING

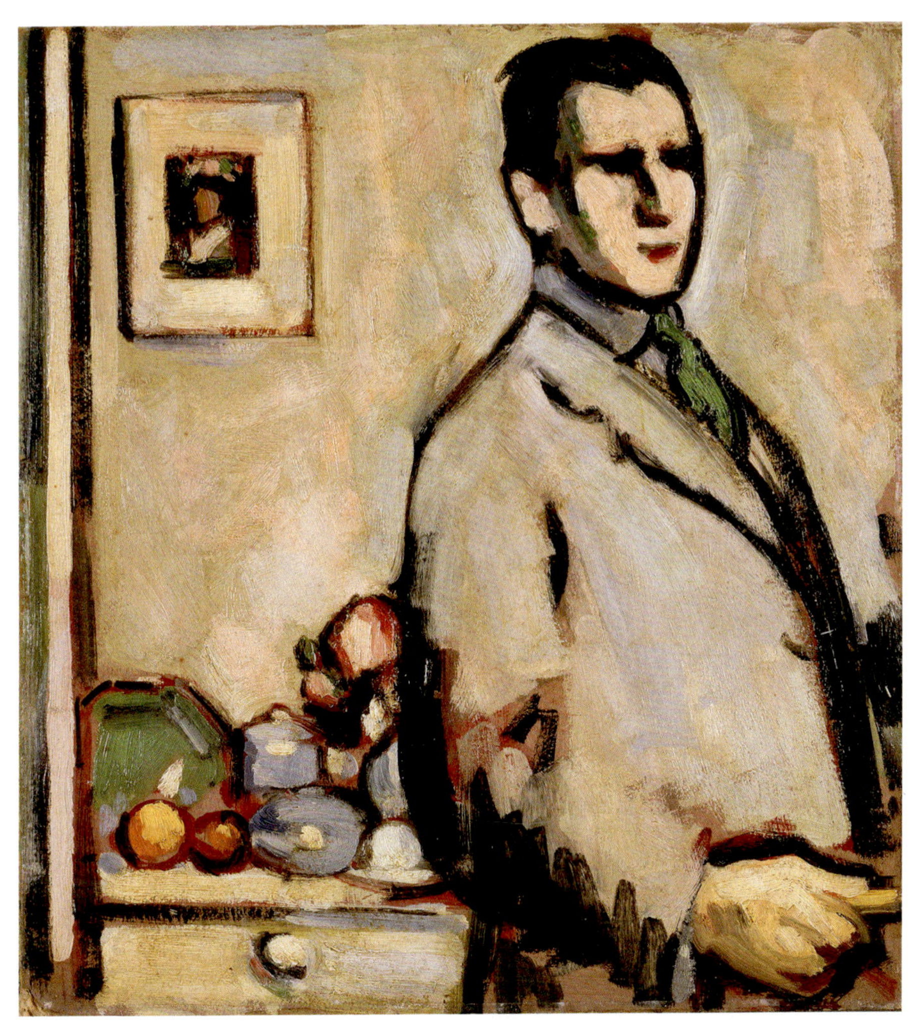

Self Portrait · 1907

Oil on canvas · 54 × 51 cm

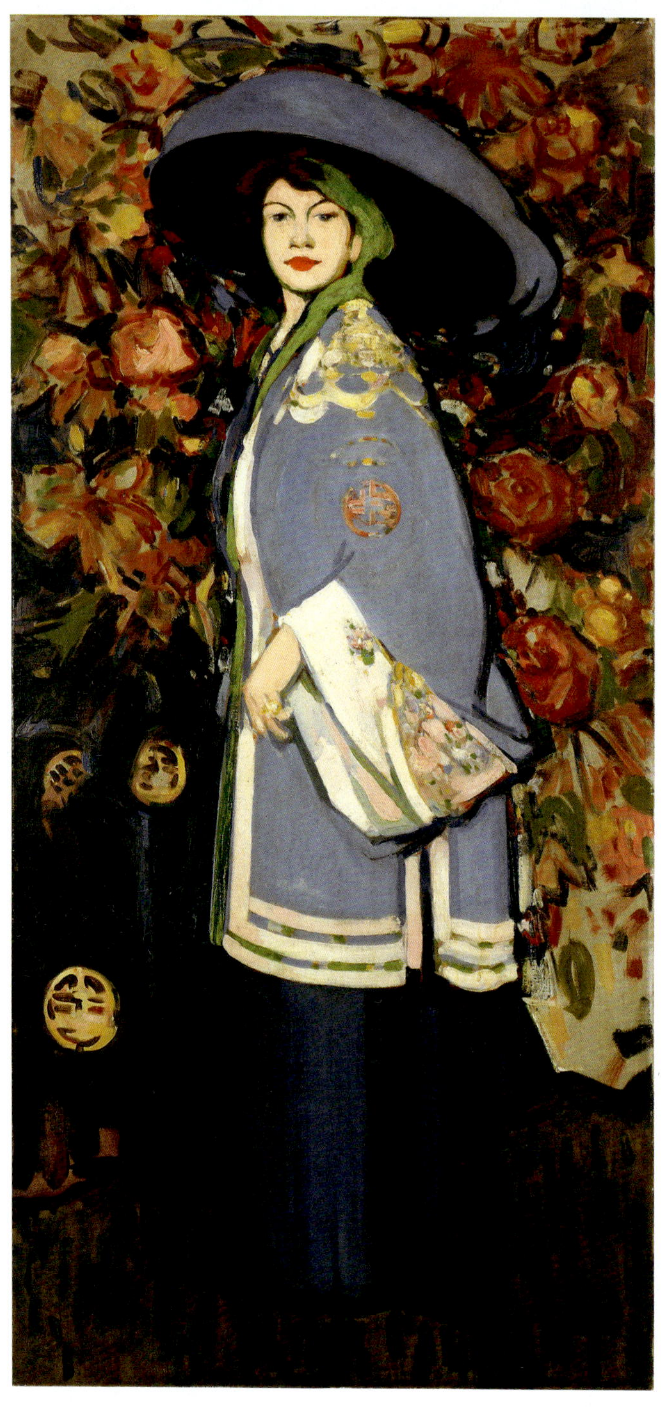

Le Manteau Chinois · 1909
Oil on canvas · 199.5 × 97 cm

Bathing Boxes and Tents at
St Palais · 1910

Oil on board · 25.6 × 35.5 cm

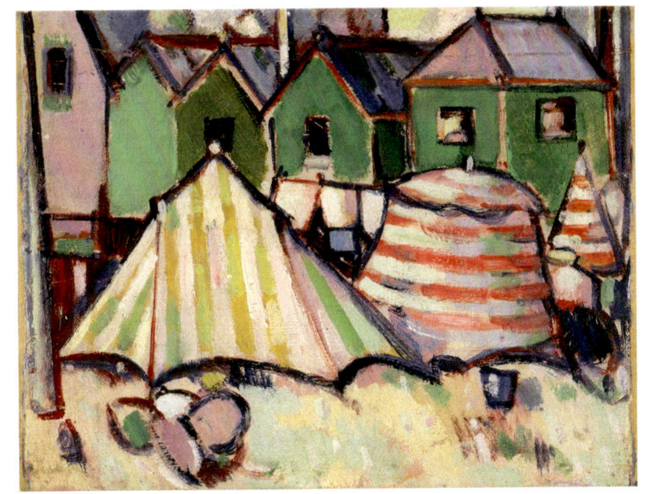

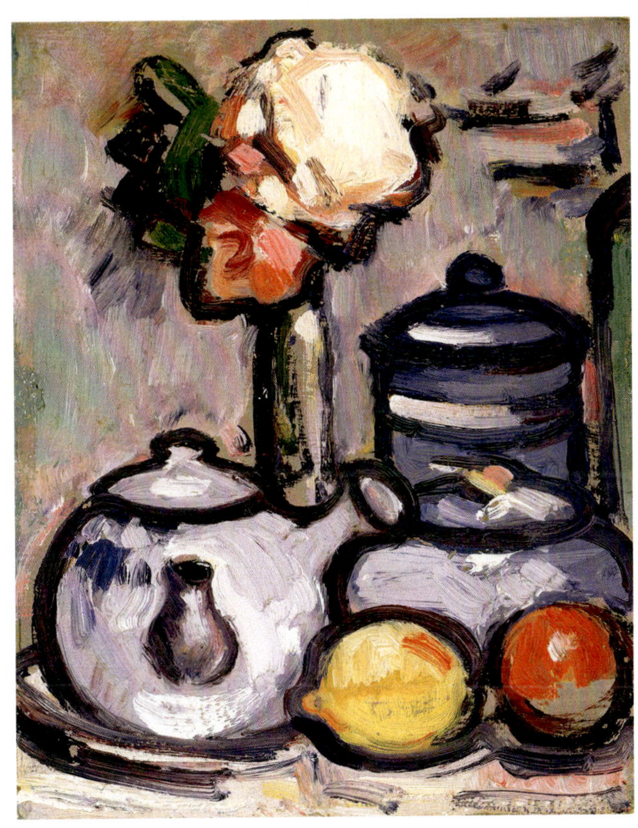

Still Life, Teapot with Fruit
and Flowers · 1912

Oil on board · 24.1 × 19.7 cm

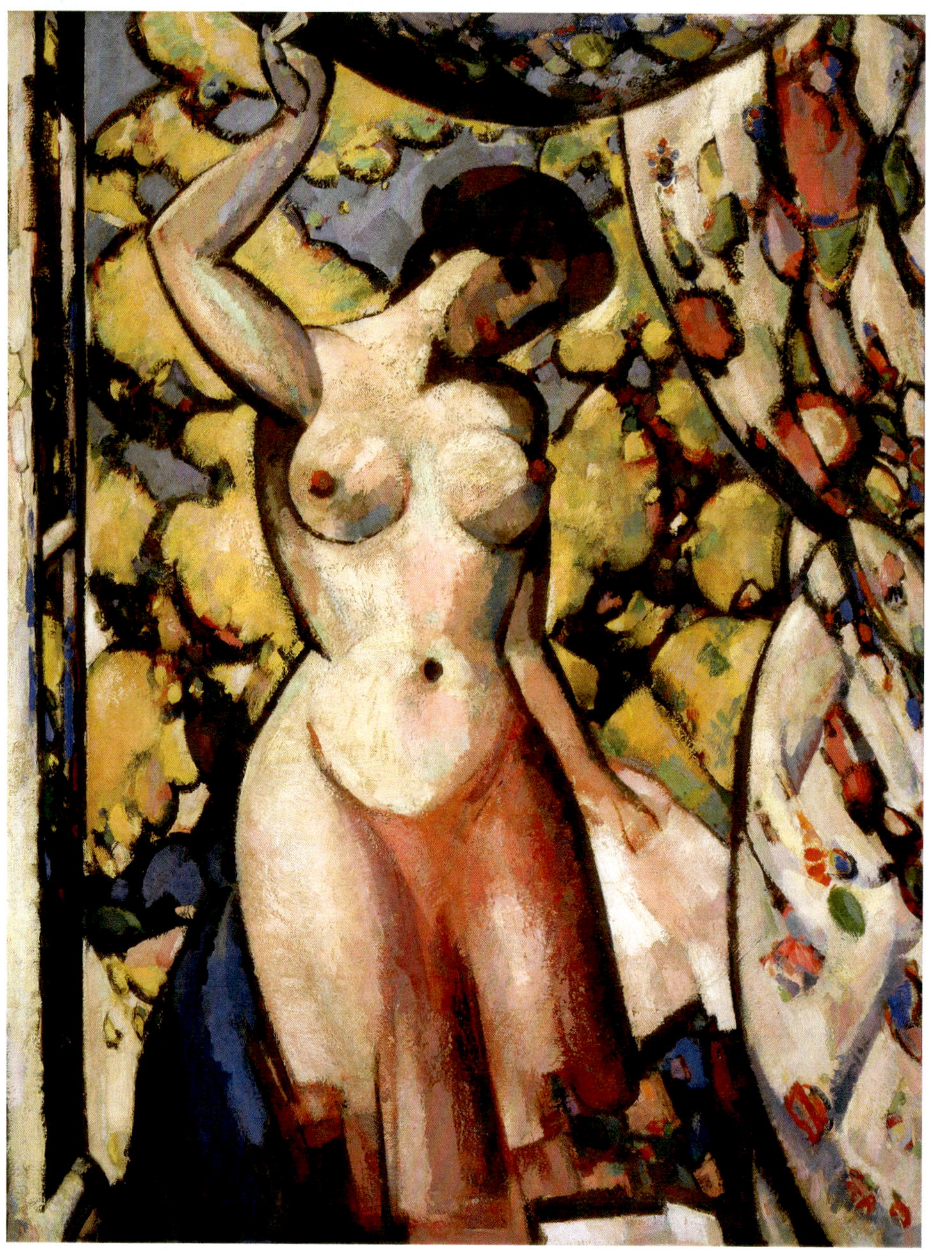

At My Studio Window · 1910

Oil on canvas · 157.5 × 123 cm

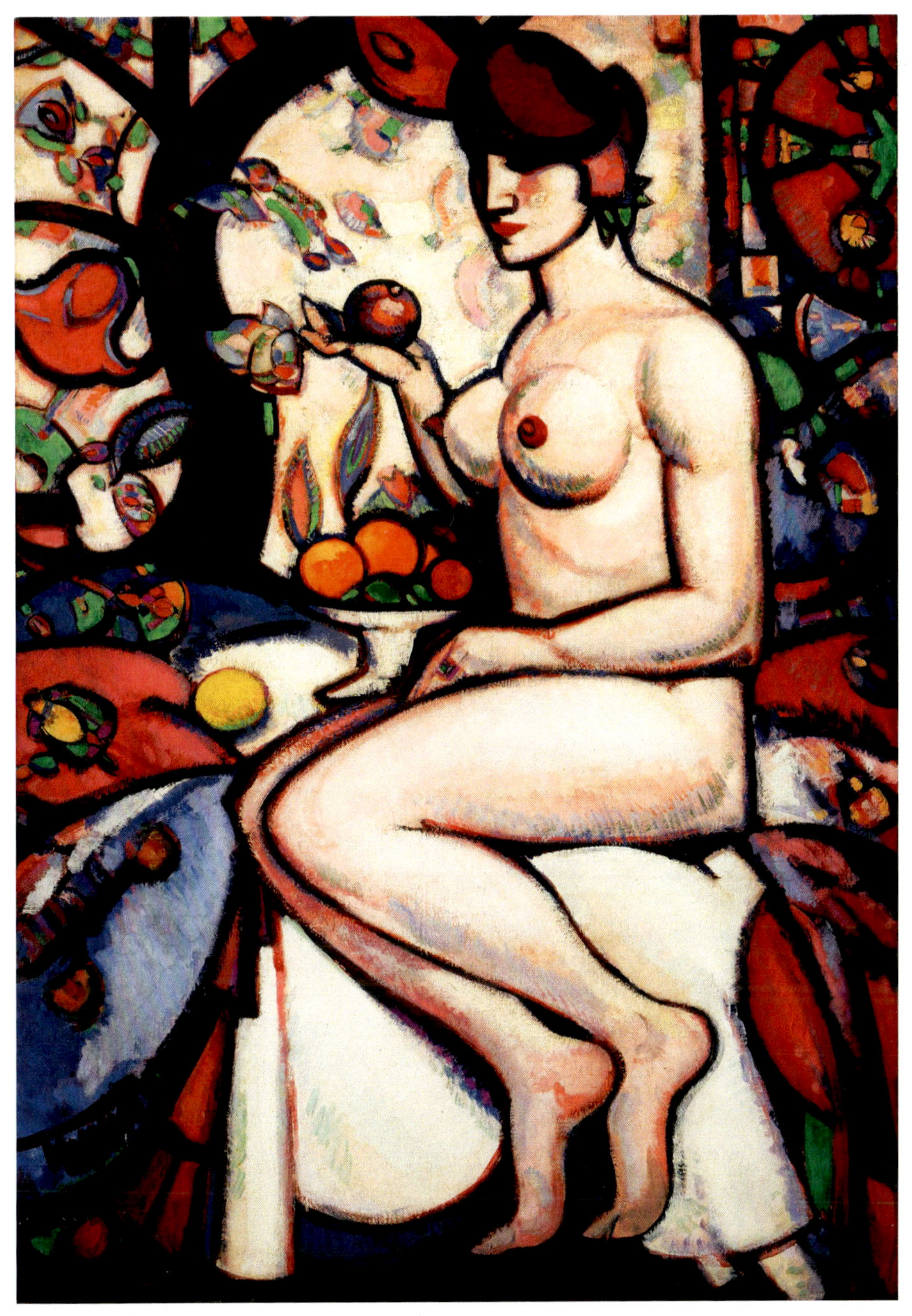

Rhythm · 1911
Oil on canvas · 163.5 × 114.3 cm

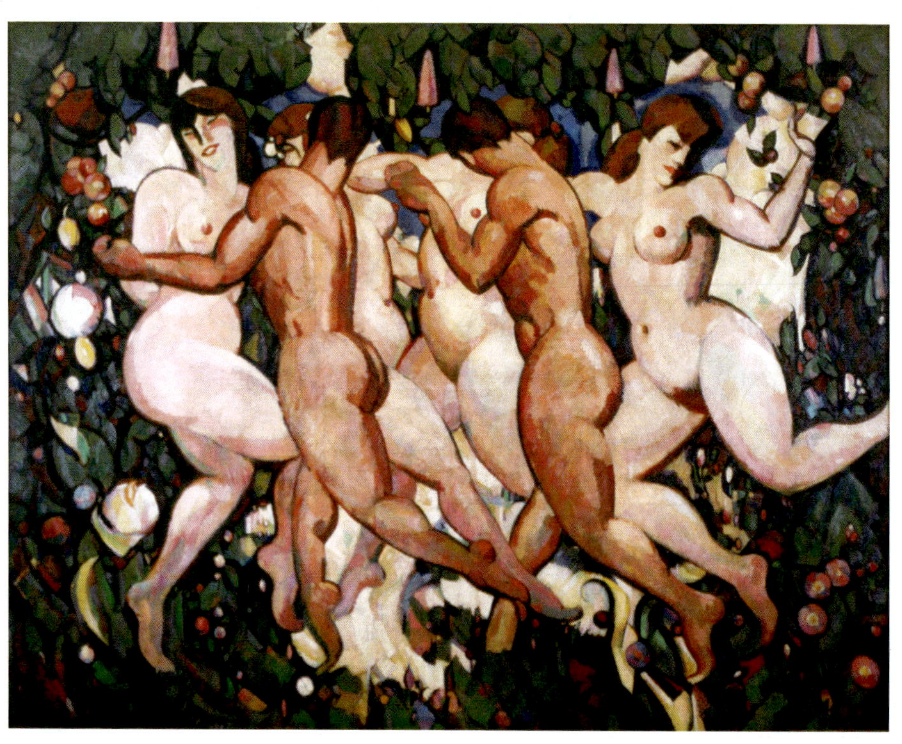

Les Eus · 1913
Oil on canvas · 157.5 × 123 cm

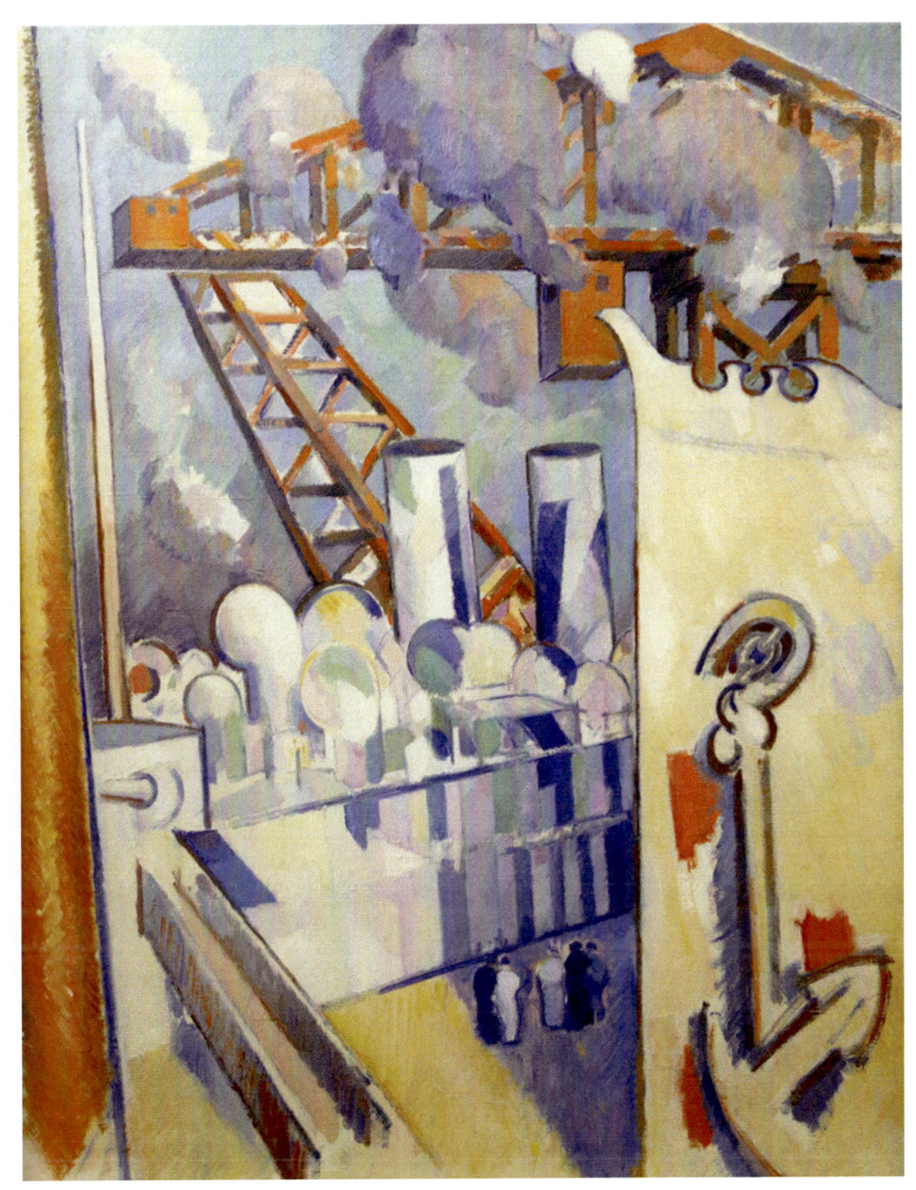

Portsmouth Docks · 1918
Oil on canvas · 72.6 × 68.6 cm

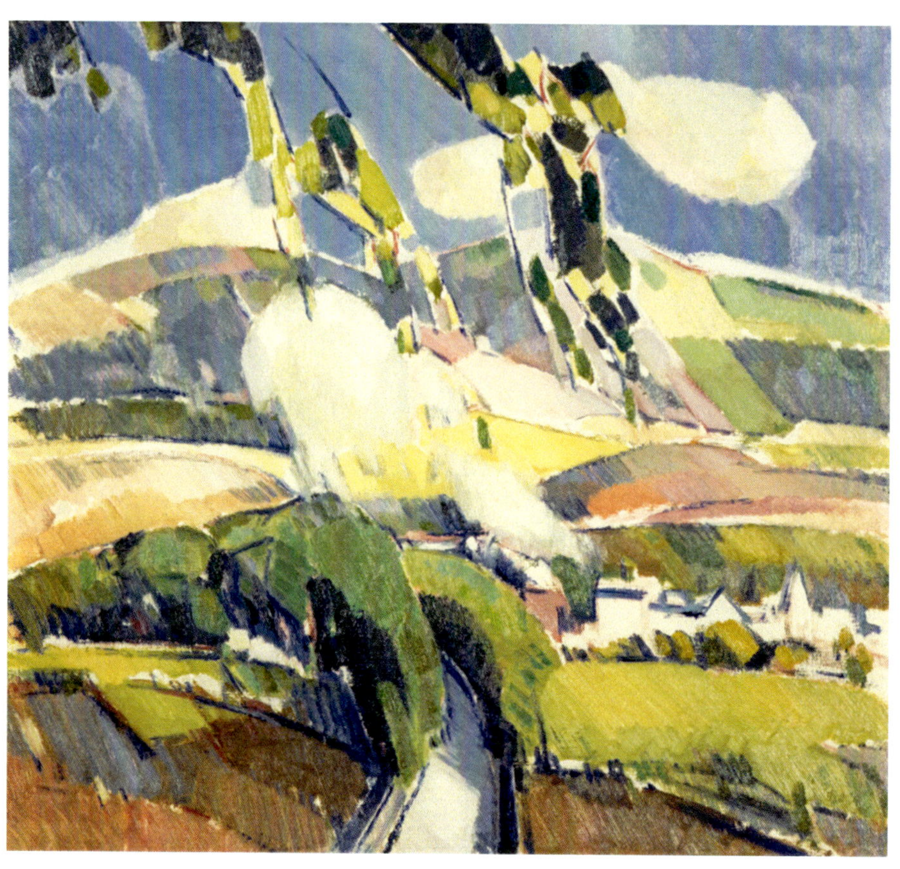

A Puff of Smoke near Milngavie · 1922
Oil on canvas · 56 × 61 cm

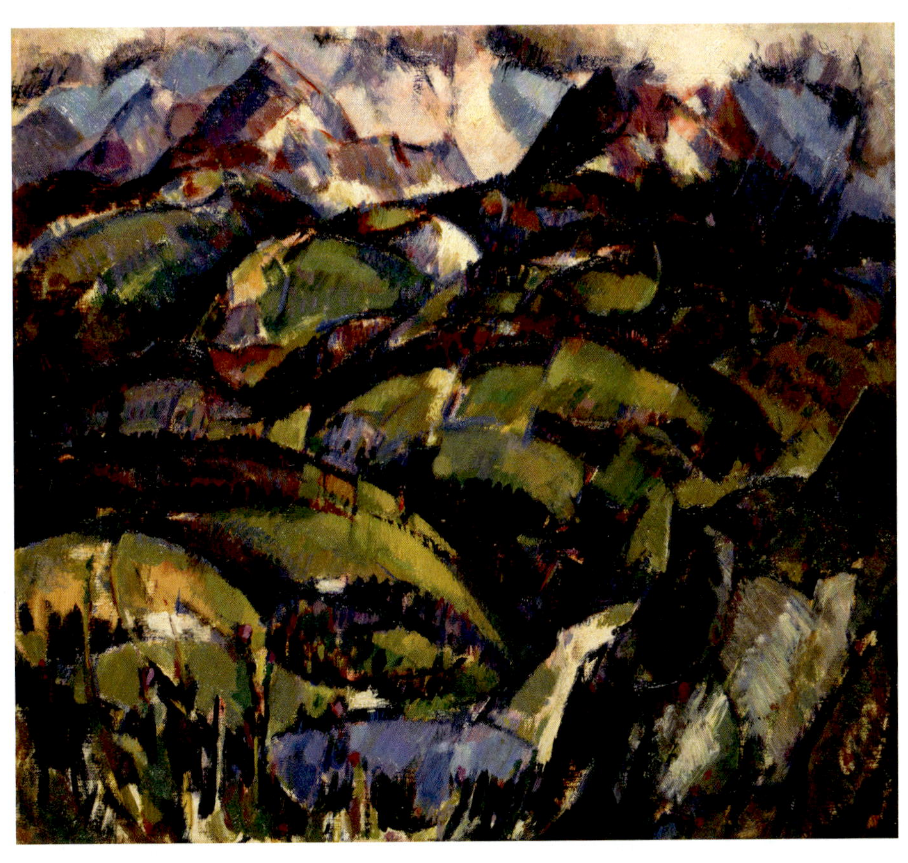

Storm Around Ben Ledi · 1922
Oil on canvas · 54.5 × 55.8 cm

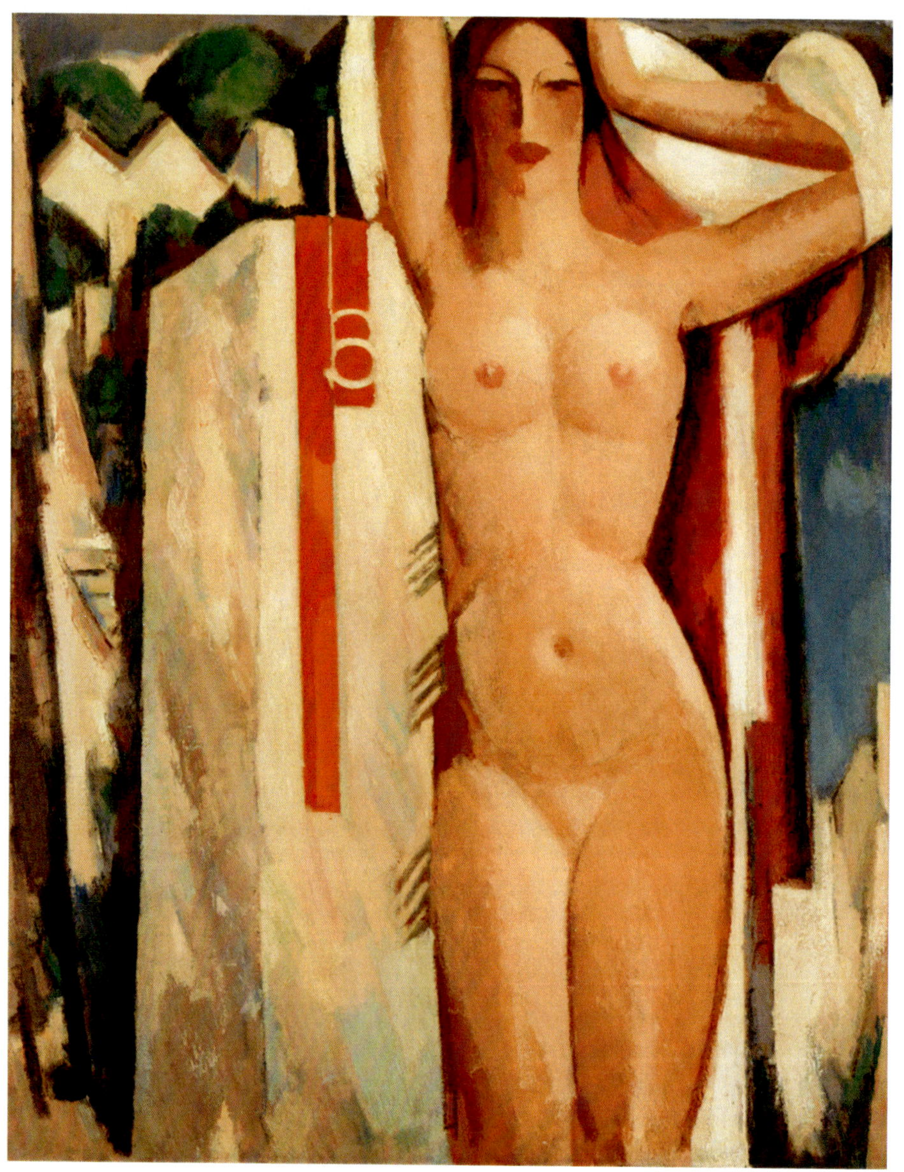

Megalithic · 1931

Oil on canvas · 92 × 73 cm

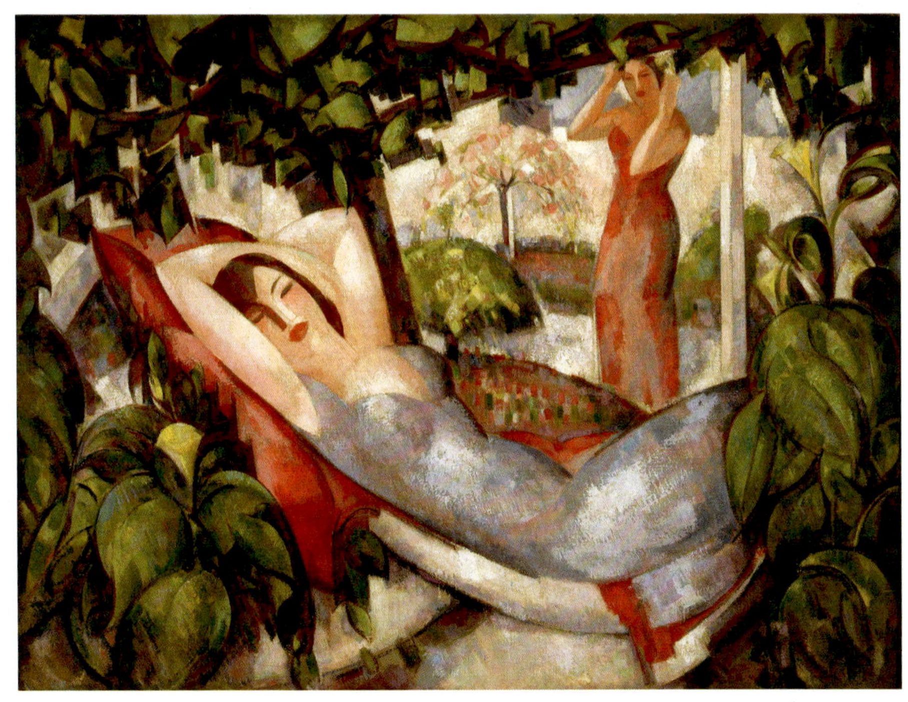

Summer, 1914 · 1934
Oil on canvas · 88 × 113.5 cm

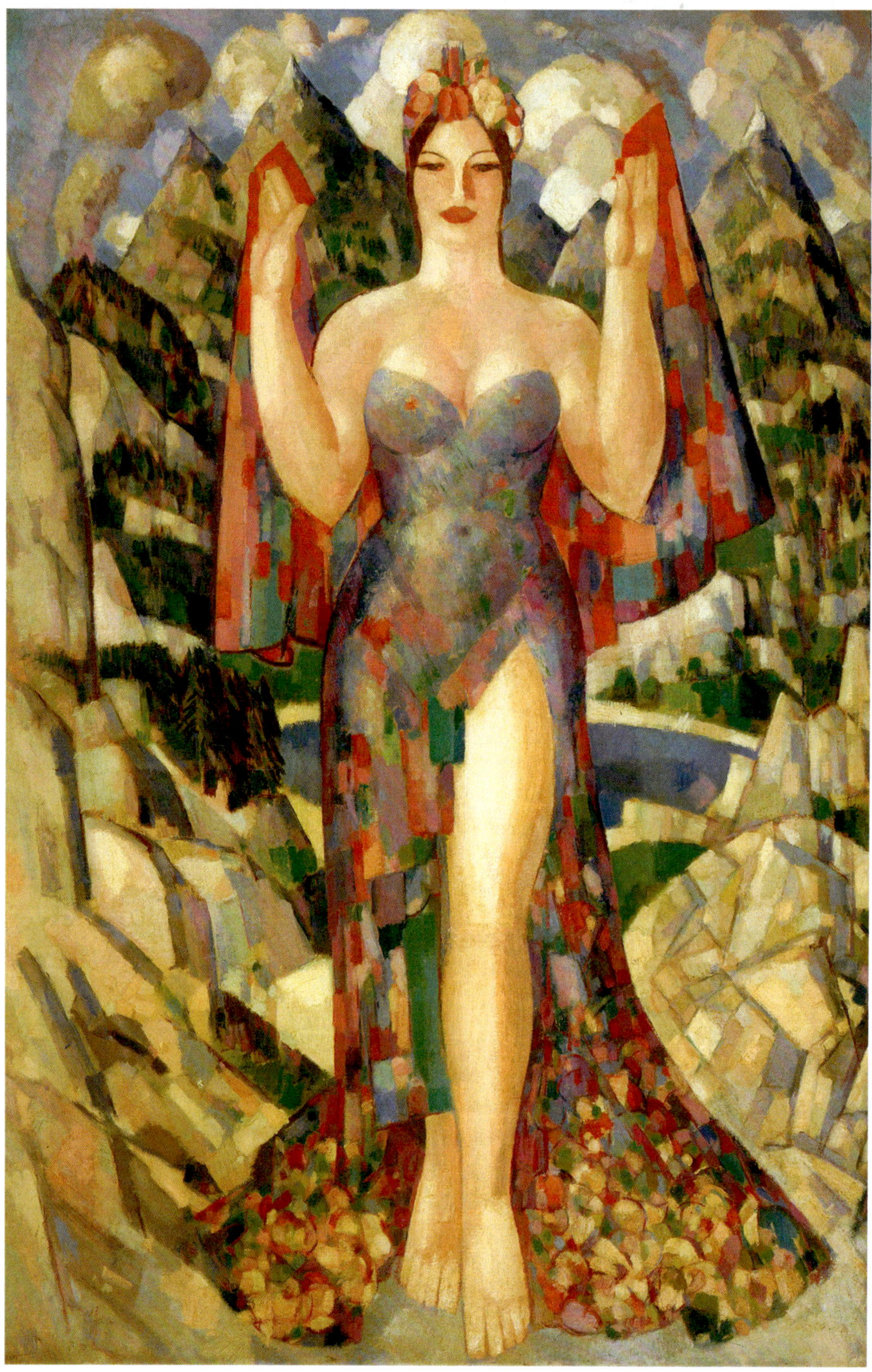

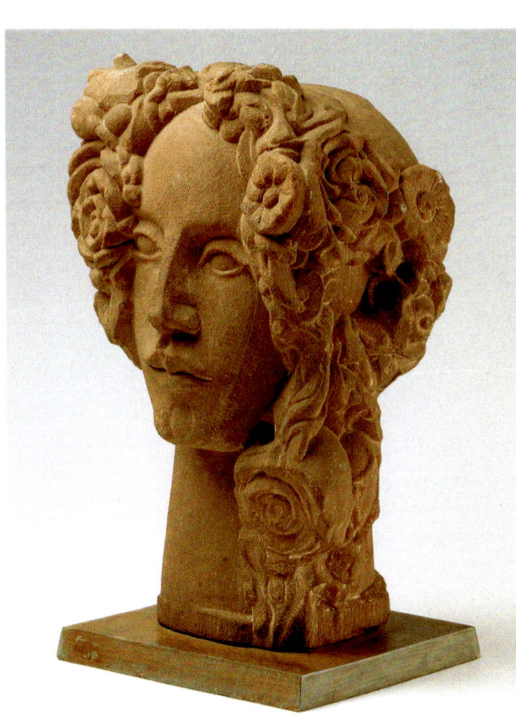

Summer: Head of a Woman · 1916
Red Sandstone

Female Dancer · c.1920
Plaster

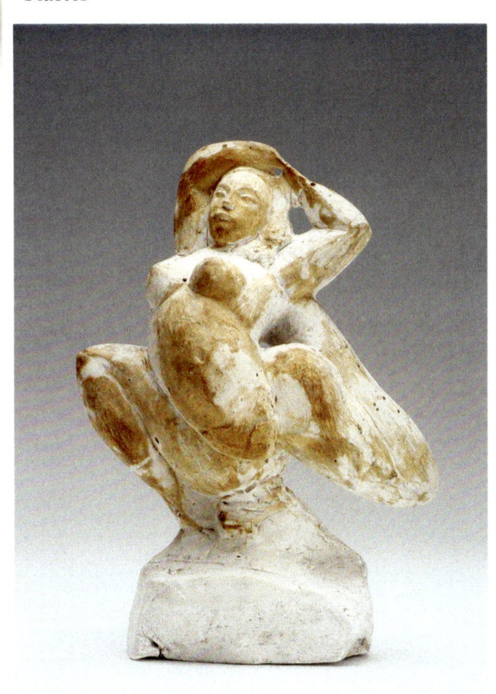

<   *Danu, Mother of the Gods*
1952–53
Oil on canvas · 184 × 123 cm

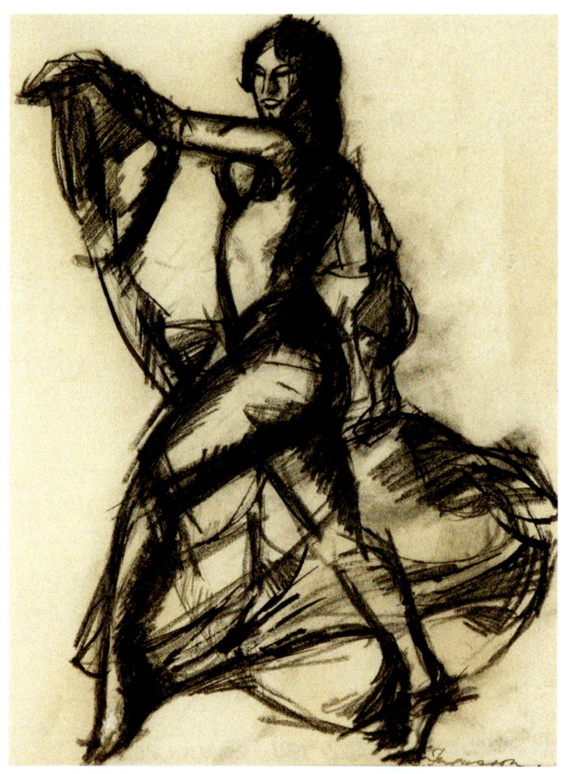

Margaret Morris Dancing · 1913
Charcoal on paper · 34.3 × 26.7 cm

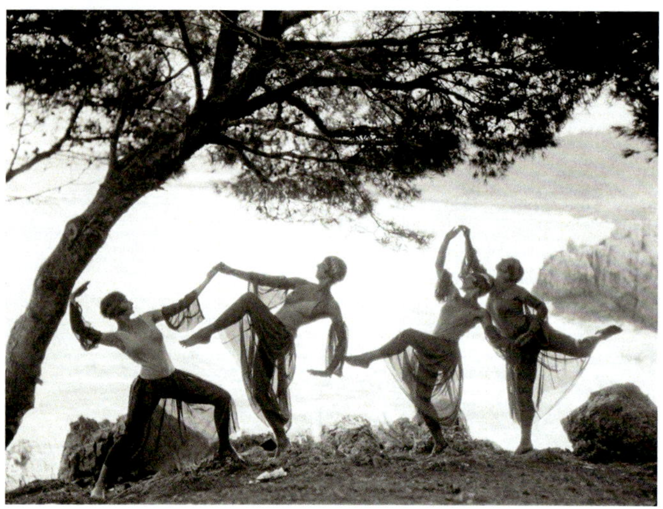

Margaret Morris and her
dancers in Antibes · c. 1925

Letter to Picasso
1911

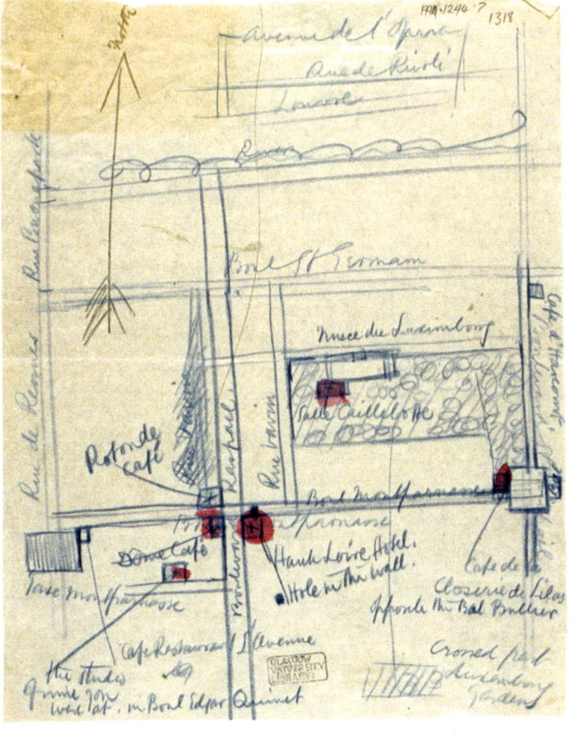

Hand-drawn map
of Montparnasse by
Fergusson, showing his
first studio in Paris at
Boulevard Edgar Quintet

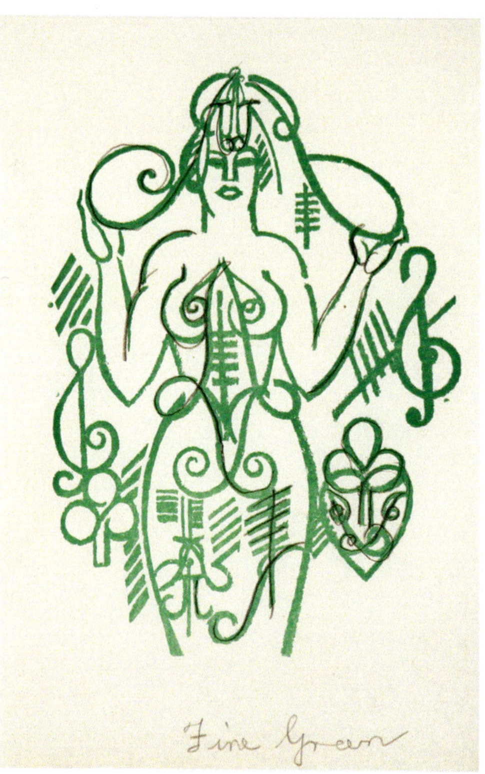

Frontispiece for *In Memoriam
James Joyce* · 1955

Original book cover of the first edition
of *Modern Scottish Painting* · 1943

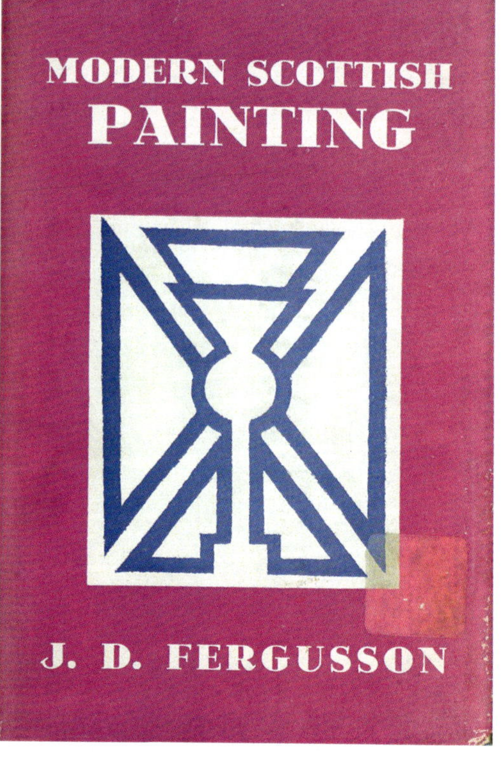

most intelligent, interesting and courageous young men are producing works resembling pieces of machinery, just as at other times artists were producing works that resembled human beings.

I admire these young people. These machinery-like works are not *imitations* of machinery any more than any work of art in the old days was an *imitation* of human beings. Only the uncreative (not artists) are imitative.

These young people are impressed by the dignity, the wonder of machinery and engineering achievement. In the windows of the motor shops we see engines wonderfully lit, compared with which *most* sculpture, specially the not modern, is merely stupid and boring.

We don't need to be motor engineers to be fascinated by the beauty of these things, any more than we need to be physiologists or anatomists to admire a beautiful nude woman. In the case of the woman, if we have a healthy natural reaction and not that of the aesthete, we admire the woman that looks as if she was capable of procreation, in other words healthy and capable of functioning, therefore lack of breasts would be to the natural healthy man, even if an artist (not an artistic person) a deficiency. I'll leave you or the motor engineer to work out the analogy. To the Calvinist, of course, any sign of breasts or other necessary functional parts is indecent and immoral. That's what is really distressing about Scotland, that disgustingly unhealthy idea. Then what about it?

Well, all that is not a problem. The point is, where does the art come in? Evidently the real woman can create the man who creates the machines. Then things begin to criss cross. The machines can all contribute to creation. We *can* imagine ourselves without machines, but not without woman. Is she then a more worthy subject, a more permanent symbol? Less merely *à la mode*, belonging to all periods rather than only to-day. Is she more expressive of reality than of actuality? I leave it to you.

It seems that what you like is your affair, but it doesn't prove that a work of art based on a woman is better than one based on an engine. Then where are we? *We each are where our experience of life has brought us.* We can't go round the world either of imagination or reality without moving. There are people who behave as if they thought that no one outside their own house, street, parish, town or country, could tell them anything; who seem to think that icebergs or the Gulf Stream cannot affect Scotland, because they have not been produced in Scotland; that the Scots have never travelled till Cook and Sons showed them the way, and so on. They may have this point of view and live almost entirely on imported food, and still think that anything they are not accustomed to 'can't happen here'.

But about Art and Engineering, I submit that as a result of research in form (which cannot really be separated from colour) the artist can only make his research for form by *seeing*. By his research the artist sees *in advance* the functional form necessary for the best results in *Queen Elizabeth*s, submarines, aeroplanes, etc. The real artist is always *a research man*, and not as people seem to think, *an imitator of recognised forms*. This brings us to accuracy in form, and then we have to ask, accuracy for what, and we immediately realise that it has not even occurred to most people that there is *emotional* accuracy, and that all real precision is *emotional*, in other words human. Mass production produces an amazing standard of mechanical accuracy, but when work has to be first class it has to be done by a really sensitive emotional human being. Even in the machine accuracy the adjustment must be human. It takes sensibility to sharpen a razor or to adjust a machine to sharpen razor blades.

One would think that it was evident that a musical ear, a sense of time, of beat and rhythm; a sense of visual balance and order, a sense of just relationship of things in movement, were necessary in the make-up of a good engineer.

A good engineer can probably tell by the look of an engine if it is any good, and he can certainly tell by the sound of it, which is a composition of lots of sounds.

Well, who are the people who devote themselves *specially* to research in these fields? In everything concerned with the visual side the painter and sculptor, on the side of sound the musicians, on the just relation of things in movement the composer of dances, and the Association football player. It may be useful to remember that inventions and improvements in the mechanical world are not always made by people thoroughly involved in that side of things, but often by complete outsiders. But these people, although outsiders, are evidently not possessed of less imagination or sensibility. They are in the position of the artist, lookers on, and consequently objected to and opposed by the orthodox people. They have not practical *experience*, but they have *imagination*.

At the time when Kipling wrote 'Mr McAndrew, don't you think steam spoils romance at sea', hardly anyone would have even started to consider that there was any relation between art and engineering. Steam was just a bad thing that had arrived and was destroying the soul of art, which meant something that belonged to the Middle Ages or the Italian Renaissance, and certainly required the conditions of those times to exist at all. People were painting Tennysonian types and subjects. A workman had to look like a Greek god or something Italian. The thing that was hailed as a masterpiece was Stephen Phillips' *Paola and Francesca*.[48] Every cultured person collected Japanese prints, and Whistler was the ruler of advanced painting in the Anglo-Saxon world – *not in France* – and the Anglo-Saxon world was certainly fortunate to have Whistler to attack and defeat the stupidity of the academic art of that time, which oddly enough, though they didn't think so, was mechanical, but in the most feeble way. To Whistler the Anglo-Saxons are indebted for re-establishing feeling and sensibility as a basis for painting as opposed to the domination of Bougereau, Lord Leighton, Alma Tadema, Marcus Stone, MacWhirter, Leader and Company.[49]

Young people must find it hard to believe that these people were considered to be anything at all, but they were all-powerful, and it is a thing that has to be stated in order to explain what follows. Someone will certainly say that there were plenty of people who were not stupid enough to be impressed by Bougereau, the old Salon and the Royal Academy. I was there. I know about it. *There were not plenty* of people, and I don't think there are *plenty* even today. The average young Scottish artist of today, if he is at all intelligent, wouldn't claim that being a Royal Academician is the same thing as being an artist, but he wants to be an RA, and the *average* artist always will, and why not? I don't see why he shouldn't. I think he should. We should have a place for everything, and the *average* artist is often heavily disguised as a fierce revolutionary till he is 'asked in', which always reminds me of the Salvation Army who used to sing, 'If we can't get in by the Golden Gates we'll climb the garden wall'. 'But tae oor tale', art and the engineer.[50] As far as I know, and I watched very carefully, Kipling was the first to put forward the engineering side as an inspiration for a work of art. Whether you think his effort was a work of art or not is 'another story', and although I was watching I didn't notice any recognition at that time of his discovery, which I think it was. And that brings us to John Calvin and Romance.

> *Predestination in the stride o' yon connectin' rod*
> *John Calvin might ha' forged the same – enorrmous, certain, slow –*

Have most of us any useful working idea of what we mean by romance! I certainly don't mean an *absolute definition*. Only a fool thinks he has an absolute definition of anything that matters, but a working idea that allows us to talk without being stupidly muddleheaded. Being muddle-headed isn't always stupid. It can be intentional and can be amusing.

Is the word romance perhaps like the word art, sincerity, and so many words that were entirely satisfying; *absolute labels* to the Victorian. When the Modern Movement began to be heard of in England people came to Paris to ask me as the most representative Briton, what it was all about. It was impossible to say anything to such questions as: But is it art? Is he sincere? But is it painting? It's merely decorative, perhaps it's all right, but it's not sculpture. It doesn't seem to have occurred to people that the Scots' habit of asking another question instead of replying is because the question as put is not answerable, or to be more exact, the asker has not put forward anything that could be called a question. He has merely made some sounds which are useless. So, 'Mr MacAndrew, don't you think steam spoils romance at sea?' only means 'Mr MacAndrew, don't you think steam has produced at sea something that I can't see anything interesting in, because there has not been centuries of art, storytelling, writing, painting and music to get me to accept it?'

So perhaps romance to most of us means the sum, or synthesis, of what the contribution of all the arts, storytelling, song, literature, painting, music, have made for us about life. But there are people who are not prevented by the accumulation of the past, from seeing romance in the present. And what is the present? That's too long. But clearly concerning art, time cannot be settled by the clock, the calendar or any other conventional measure-ments, and there it becomes difficult, too long for this book.

There is emotional accuracy and emotional time. I know very well that this to the average person is sheer nonsense. He may not believe in God or himself, but he believes absolutely in the clock, weights and measures, and instruments of precision.

                                        MODERN SCOTTISH PAINTING

This is a pathetic manifestation of inferiority. The *average* artist is always proclaiming his inferiority by attempting to justify his work by comparison with the photograph, anatomical diagram, instead of being surprised when the camera does something that looks human, which is the operator's human feeling coming through. As to the absurdity of justifying art by anatomical measurements which one cannot see emotionally or humanly, but find to be there by cold examination, I have a right to an opinion as I started life as a medical student.

This attempt to justify art by accepted measurements is really consciously or unconsciously commercial and cowardly, founded on the fear that the buyers will be in a position to prove, by means that they have had to accept in order to make the money they buy with – to prove that the artist is wrong. So, being afraid, he accepts their standard, but is always telling you that they are damn fools and know nothing about it.

We can, of course, make the necessity to earn a living an excuse for anything, air raids, poison gas, pogroms, religious persecution, and so on, so no discussion is possible. William Blake ran great risks of losing his living and losing his life, and must have known it. I suppose he was what is commonly called just a mug.[51]

I know very well that courage is generally thought to be something that belongs only to the battlefield, or dying for religious convictions, and it is evident that without the courage on the battlefield, Scottish independence that we Scots are all so proud of would never have existed. The point that is missed is that it is unlikely that a people lacking in courage in the ordinary conduct of life will suddenly show it in time of war, and many of us hope that the spaces between wars may be increased. Therefore courage must be sustained in other fields, as has been done by Pasteur, the Curies and television Baird, and I think it takes courage to keep to an unaccepted point of view in any art, which means persisting in being independent.[52]

But about Art and the Engineer – well, I think all this *is* about it. The point is that it is necessary for Scots really to have a working understanding of what they are talking about, and to try to find out not merely what is necessary for living from one day to another, which we certainly have to find out, I'm not an amateur. But to know or try to know at least, what is necessary fundamentally for living a happy human life (and by human

I mean not only being a human being, turned into a Robot, but a human being capable of enjoying life even if machines stopped, or diminished in their power to control our conduct). We need not go back to cruses, rush lights and tallow candles. Let's have the benefit if you like of electricity, but let's be able to do without it. We may have to.[53]

The idea that without machinery the world is hopeless is not so convincing to most people as it was. At the moment it looks to most people, and they hardly talk about anything but the idea, that on account of amazing developments of machinery civilisation may come to an end. If it does and some people are left, the storyteller, the singer, the dancer and artist will soon again be under way, and civilisation's tragedy will become a romance. Already people are asking how we are going to make use of our leisure, and we see that the more industrial we are, the less we can entertain ourselves. There are nations which, without money to pay *to be entertained*, just don't know what to do with themselves. There are nations capable of spending evenings just talking about things, making music and singing to amuse themselves. In my own lifetime my friends and I have found that it is becoming increasingly difficult to discuss things, gossip and scandal having replaced the exchange of ideas.[54]

But about Art and Engineering! Why this refusal or inability on the part of the Victorian artist to see any inspiration for art in engines. Who or what started the change of attitude? Now this is where we can leave Scotland, leave Spain, leave any country that has a fixed idea of what art is and what is suitable material for art. We must go to Paris. I hear a moan or groan or growl from the 'narrow Nationalist' – the people who don't want Frenchness in Scotland. Well, art and nationalism is another chapter, but I'd like to point out that Frenchmen do not consider Paris French. They say it is difficult to find a Frenchman in Paris. No-one in France has ever said that I or my painting was French or Frenchified. They all find me very *Scotch*; influenced by France certainly: is that new for a Scotsman? Look up the history of Scotland. Even Scotsmen (or should we say *only*) don't seem to know that there was an *auld alliance* between France and Scotland, and when Scotland was at war with England it was obviously not convenient to go to Oxford or Cambridge. In these days the Scot went direct by sea to France and to Paris, to the Sorbonne. Dunbar walked to the channel preaching, and walked preaching to Paris. He says:

     MODERN SCOTTISH PAINTING

In Derntoun Kirk, and eik in Canterberry,
in it I passed, at Dover oure the Ferry,
Throw Piccardy, and thair the peple teichet.[55]

The works of Dunbar are full of French words and the Latin he used was French, not English Latin. In those days nobles and poor looking for education went to France. The Scots noble was naturally received at the French Court, and as there were not Hotels de Luxe, passed on to the chateaux of the French Court (hence Scots Baronial architecture); then on to Italy, and that was the *Grand Tour* that every young nobleman was expected to make as he is now expected to go to Oxford. The poorer young man, we are told, had two barrels, one filled with his clothes, the other with oatmeal, securely closed. These were put in the hold of the ship at Dundee and he sailed to Dunkerque [Dunkirk] and then went on to Paris. By the time the oatmeal was finished he was expected to be able to earn his living by tutoring, and there was, and perhaps still is, a Collège des Ecossais in the Boulevard St Michel, and there still is a Rue des Ecossais.[56] To go to Paris was the natural thing for the Scot. It is not as the modern Scot or the Teutonic Scot seems to think, a new fantastic idea. Besides that, it doesn't seem to have occurred to the modern Scot that the Scottish Celt, when in France, was among his own people, the French Celts. French culture was founded by the Celts, and invasions have not changed the fundamental character of the French people. Every Celt feels at home in France. The '*ésprit Gaulois*' (the Celtic spirit) still exists and has not been submerged by Calvinism as it has been in Scotland. If Scotland or Celtic Scotland would make a 'new alliance' with France, *not political* like the 'auld Alliance' but *cultural*, it would perhaps put Scotland back on to the main track of her culture, and let the Scots do something Scottish instead of imitation English, or rather second-rate British, such as following the R.A. for example. So let's not forget our ancient friends and allies, and let's stop using the word French as if it is meant something that has nothing to do with Scotland.

The academic Spaniard will no doubt say that Picasso is not Spanish. The same thing would be said by the same kind of Dutchman about Van Gogh or Van Dongen, and of Modigliani by the Italian. Paris is simply a place of freedom. Geographically central, it has *always* been a centre of light and learning and research. It is a place that has always been difficult to dominate by mere deadweight of stupidity. It will be very difficult for anyone to show that it is not still the home of freedom for ideas; a place where people like to hear ideas presented and discussed; where an artist of any sort is just a human being like a doctor or a plumber, and not a freak or madman, and where he doesn't need to look fantastic. After going there over 30 years ago I have some right to speak – *Salut!* to Paris. It allowed me to be Scots as I understand it, and has *made* me so Scots that I am leaving it and coming home. I wish it was to the Highlands, but I'm not strong enough to cut myself off completely.[57]

> *A hunter's fare is all I would be craving*
> *A shepherd's plaiding and a beggar's pay*
> *If I could earn them where the heather waving*
> *Gave fragrance to the day.*
> Neil Munro[58]

Charming, gentle, hielan' Neil Munro's own story in a few lines. Well, I live by my painting, and couldn't even show anyone in the Highlands my pictures, and I certainly couldn't expect them to buy them (though the Scots do buy them) and there are no galleries in the Highlands.

But Art and Engineering. Yes! Well! ''twould be ower lang to tell the tale' *in full*, but about 1909 or 1910 Picasso and Bracque simultaneously they say, realised the possibilities, or became intrigued in, the idea of compositions of forms; forms that were quite representational, and resembling objects or things as definite as roofs of houses, boats or trees, but not necessarily in the juxtaposition as they were in nature, but in the juxtaposition that seemed to them good in the composition of forms they were presenting. *At a stroke* these two liberated the world of art from the slavery of trying to make things fit the ordinary accuracy of position according to recognised conventional measurements, topographical, anatomical, or otherwise.[59]

Form had then taken its place on its merits, not merely as something to imitate a composition of forms that was considered necessary in painting such as an anatomical nude, an architecturally correct building, or as I remember Mr Ruskin demanded a geological landscape.[60] This was indeed a liberation, and a great responsibility which these two men have upheld so splendidly till to-day. To the average artist (I know, I was there)

                    MODERN SCOTTISH PAINTING

all this was pure lies and fake, and showed entire lack of responsibility in these artists. Well then, the point had arrived when an engine, or a piece of machinery being a composition of form, was a perfectly good source of inspiration for a composition of form in painting or sculpture, even if the artist was not an engineer and didn't know the 'anatomy' of engines. The average artist of course pointed out that, as no Beaux Arts kind of academic training was necessary, no knowledge of anatomy or architecture, 'anybody could do that sort of stuff'. With his usual muddleheadedness, what he was saying was that you couldn't be an artist without academic training, the trust being that if you succeed in being an artist in spite of academic training you are wonderful. So that's at least something of what I have to say about Art and Engineering. Everybody knew all this. 'Oh yes! I'm meeting artists, and these everybody's, and not all stupid, every day of my life.'

> *God gie's a man like Rabbie Burns to sing the sang o' steam.*
> Kipling[61]

CHAPTER V

Art and Philosophy

Philosophy
Not harsh and crabbed as dull fools suppose
MILTON[62]

AFTER TALKING TO people for an average lifetime I have found that most people and most artists are convinced that philosophy has nothing to do with art, that it is another thing altogether; that a philosopher is a 'dry as dust', is unaffected by anything, and that any sign of being emotional is a sign of lack of philosophy; that the artist is a sort of inspired idiot, incapable of examining or understanding what he does, and that any attempt to examine, reason, or understand, puts him outside the artist category.

They believe that the philosopher *does* understand, and that the artist just *doesn't*.

The artist, if he is an artist, should know that he doesn't understand why he does things, he can't know. The craftsman can, and *ought* to know and understand his '*métier*' or trade. We are constantly having the idea put forward that the artist is, or ought to be, just a super craftsman. Then why use the word 'artist'?

I can see no excuse or reason for accepting supercraftsman as a meaning for the word artist. I don't think even the person who hasn't thought about it means that doing a job exceptionally well makes an artist. To earn the name artist it seems clear that one must *create* something, must make something, be a '*makar*'.[63] The modern movement has stood for that, and that's the difference between the modern movement and the academic craftsmanship, which enables people to pass examinations on accepted academic lines, what is called a *thorough artistic training*. How many great artists have been Prix de Rome winners? Obviously every Prix de Rome winner must be a proficient craftsman, must have passed the tests.[64]

We immediately hear the person who talks in absolutes say, 'Then it's *not* necessary to be able to draw or paint' – exactly the expected and invariable remark. According to the 'absolute' type there is either academic training and qualifications, or *none*. Drawing is academic; that is to say, anatomically, or photographically correct, or it's all wrong. The human response to form and colour ought to be corrected by academic conventions. Anything that departs from the exact measurements of the foot rule, the photographic exactness, and the test by the calipers, however human, is wrong, is a caricature, and the artist is a faker and not sincere.

Now this is where a little thinking might help the *artist*. I don't mean the supercraftsman. Then what do I mean by Philosophy? Well, I think the etymological meaning of the word is clear and good. The Americans have launched the expression 'getting wise' to a thing, which I think is quite useful and sound. The only useful meaning of the word philosophy is, I think, a persistent attempt to give things their just values, and that involves dealing with things in their groups or categories.

Again it has to be repeated that we cannot talk in absolutes, and we use categories or groups because we want to make a statement, not because we have absolute belief in them; just as we put a line or an *'arrêt'* or accent in drawing or painting not because we see it or believe it exists *absolutely*, but because we see that it is necessary *relatively*, in order to make a statement.[65] The fellow that always puts the same line, accent, or *'arrêt'*, is a bore and an ass, and that's what the academic fellow does. He knows exactly what to do and does it *invariably*. The fellow that refuses to allow himself to use the accent in the same way more than once is another kind of ass. The accent, movement or rhythm is or ought to be the natural gesture of the artist, and there's no reason why it should be constantly entirely different or constantly the same. Now if philosophy means, and it does, trying to 'get wise' to things it is part of the artist's job to find out what his reaction to form and colour is, *as a human being*. The contribution that the modern movement made to art was that it attempted to get back to *human* values.

It put forward the idea that 'to step aside is human', that the human being is not, and need not try to be, an instrument of precision, and that he need not try to justify his statements by anything but his own 'honest to God' feelings.

To Caesar what is Caesar's. It is just this justifying by one's own 'honest to God' feelings that brings in, or is, philosophy, and this is the real and the most serious and severe discipline. It is very difficult. For as man changes constantly so do his ideas of value, and what is good for to-day may not be good for to-morrow, *if he is honest.*

The academic discipline is much easier. It is a thing *arreté*, fixed and defined absolutely.[66] Once learned or acquired, further thinking or examining or awareness is quite unnecessary and undesirable. All that is necessary is to apply it and keep on applying it till it can be done automatically, and the *métier*, the trade is mastered.[67] But someone has said that 'the price of liberty is constant vigilance' so now we come back to the Scots, and the Arbroath Manifesto (see page 79), liberty, free or liberated art, free artists.[68]

At this point we are not surprised to hear the kind of person that asks what philosophy has to do with art, ask what the liberty referred to in the Arbroath Manifesto has to do with art, for, having no sense of liberty, the categories that we have been proposing to *make use of* are to him absolutely watertight compartments.

Now there are evidently nations, races and people who reason and want to reason, and others who don't and do not want to; who want to be told, and like to accept what they are told, and are quite happy about it. I have never heard a Scotsman say that he was quite pleased just to do as he was told, and the desire to examine, reason and discuss is a Scot's characteristic. In the old days there were 'sermon tasters'. At political meetings they pride themselves on being *great* 'hecklers'. They are proud to have produced first-class philosophers. Then there's no excuse for them being muddleheaded.

So to come back to the categories, there's no excuse for them being muddled about the categories. On the contrary they should be able to juggle with them, to let them criss cross and then put them back in their compartments. If they do so in anything they do not do so in art, and why? Well, here we need to digress and come back to Calvinism. Looking at it by and large it seems that before John Knox the Scots were undisciplined, lacking in control, emotional, or whatever you like to call it, compared with their *since* John Knox temperament, or rather *conduct*.

We're told that Knox had all their songs changed from their honest, *natural expressiveness* to sanctimoniousness. Even Burns had to adapt the old songs to make them presentable. Restraint wasn't the feature of Scots conduct before Knox. I don't think at that time they had the control that

   MODERN SCOTTISH PAINTING

Calvinism gave them, which has made them the most reliable marine engineers in the world, the successful bank managers, heads of departments and all that.

I don't think there's anything to suggest that their songs were produced with the controlled accuracy of an actuary, or the unfailing reliability of a marine engineer.

In the days of the clans, accuracy with the claymore was necessary, and that sort of accuracy is *very like* the accuracy of emotional painting, dancing and music.

Well, perhaps Calvinism accounts for the Scot of today applying the test suitable for one category to all others, spiritual or material. The Scot has come to be considered a person who can only admit what he considers provable or justifiable, what is called hardheaded, and that state of mind lands him in a very limited field of thought and action.

Since the union with England perhaps, and the industrial boom, his conduct has been that of a person content most of the time with the results that came from material things that he could prove to his own satisfaction to be workable. His *conduct* has been that, but there is something deeper than conduct, and he has at times shown, as at the Glasgow School period, that there was deeper down a feeling for art, for most of the time submerged, and the belief that this still exists makes it worthwhile to try to get the Scot to apply his reasoning powers to the examination of art and its place, value and contribution to the social condition of a free nation.

I say to a *free* nation, for to a *slave* nation freedom of thought, invention and creative ideas in any form are not necessary. A slave nation can always steal, and exploit by cheap slave labour, the ideas and inventions of a free nation.

Now the Scot has always had the idea that 'Freedom is a nobil thing'[69] I have never met a Scot who admitted that he didn't think so – 'these Scots wha hae'.[70] Then why does he not apply this to art? Does he really think that academies stand for, or encourage freedom? As we give him credit for being able to think, the only answer is that he hasn't thought about it; that it hasn't occurred to him that art has anything to do with freedom.

Freedom is to him something won by battle, by warfare and in support of that freedom no one can say he has ever hedged. So now on behalf of art, we submit to the Scot that freedom is necessary in art, and that free art contributes to the freedom of a nation. Any art ought to be the expression of a point of view, and not as is generally thought, merely supercraftsmanship.

Art must be philosophical in its expression. By that we do not mean the illustration of an accepted philosophical idea, *but wise in itself* – in other words free.

The only use of philosophy is to liberate, and until the Scot can think clearly enough to see that everything cannot be decided by the same test, that there are different tests for different categories, and that using the tests and measurements of the material category to place a value on a thing in the spiritual category is absurd.

Until he can think clearly enough his field of thought and action is inevitably very restricted, and he has no right to think he has freedom, or to believe that he is building up a free nation or a desire to be a free nation. He has the power of reasoning and thought necessary to achieve great things in engineering, to test and accept inventions in that line. Why not in art? Artists have always been aware of the streamline that the engineer has come to accept for his great ships, and that form when most efficient is most simple, like the present day engines.

The artist has always been aware that a human figure was healthiest and most efficient when it was what is now called streamlined. Only in the last few years has the engineer accepted this. He accepts the streamline, which only means the *free* line, because he can't deny the tests in that category. If a ship goes across the Atlantic better streamlined then it is good; if a streamlined athlete wins then he is accepted; but these things are in the category that can be '*proved by walking*', and there are more and more people every day beginning to realise that there is a power in love, in good will, in thought, in ideas, in short in things spiritual, the importance of which cannot be decided by the tests and measurements applied to material things.[71]

We admit that the categories are not watertight compartments. We know that they criss cross. We are using them to try to explain something, not because we believe that they are absolute.

But then what are the tests for spiritual values, for art values? Well, evidently that is what worries the Scot, for he is always ashamed if he cannot justify his statements or his likes and dislikes. So as he knows no tests for art he applies to it the material tests and measurements, the footrule and the calipers and the photograph. The artist, in order not to appear a fool to his buyers, accepts these tests for his work; says the buyers, the public, are damn fools and understand nothing, but is afraid to oppose them as he has no material proof that his opinions are of any value.

In many places it is accepted that the artist is good if he makes plenty of money. 'To Caesar what is Caesar's' doesn't come in. Evidently then what is wanted is a sort of *litmus paper* test; some means of deciding *absolutely* if a thing *is* or *is not art*. Can philosophy do this? No, it certainly can not, but it can free people from the idea that there can be a sort of litmus paper absolute test, material or spiritual, for art, and that is a start.

Having reached that freedom the person is then in a position to accept the idea that 'art is what he thinks it is, *for him*', that his ideas, appreciation and comprehension may change for what he thinks a greater range or better understanding, and that he need not feel apologetic when he says he 'knows what he likes'. Nothing, if he is honest, could be more true. Certainly no one else knows what he likes, and he will be saved from reading masses of books telling him exactly what art is. He will also be relieved of his feeling of inferiority.

By this time I can imagine I have given the impression that if there is an escape from reading masses of books on art it is by reading masses of books of philosophy. I certainly don't mean that. I mean use your brains to get to a state where you can be free to go by your feelings, and not be afraid to like something, because it's not like some acknowledged master-piece, academic or otherwise.

But this just seems to leave you with nothing. It does. It doesn't give you the litmus paper. 'Freedom is a nobil thing', but it can't be given. The Scots ought to know by now that it has to be fought for.

CHAPTER VI

Scotland and Colour

Honour the Gods, do nothing low and be courageous.
DRUIDS

IF SCOTLAND IS TO be accepted as only gloom and greyness then all the tartans must be false, out of place and exotic. I haven't seen any tartan that isn't a colour composition. The old tartans were brighter than the present ones. They were, I believe, made in Scotland and dyed with natural dye. I haven't seen a grey tartan. I think tartans are today admitted as being characteristically Scottish. I haven't heard any one put forward that they didn't go with the Scots temperament, or the Scotch landscape.

The hunting tartans clearly anticipated the camouflage of the Great War. In other words were made to go with the region they were worn in. (There's a great deal of heather in Scotland, there's a great deal of gorse.) I am glad to hear that the earlier and brighter colourings are regaining favour greatly, and are more worn.

It seems reasonable to suppose that in Scotland's great times of black suit (the now accepted 'stan' o' black') was not the idea of a gala dress. Then where does this black and gloom and grey come from? Who or what caused it? Is it really in the soul of the Scot? We are told that Scotland, including the West Lowlands, was Gaelic and Gaelic-speaking till the end of the 11th century. There is no record that the Gaels ever had any love or respect for black. On the contrary, everything, all the information goes to show that everything black was hated and abhorrent.

As an idea, let us start with the Druids – an early enough start. They said that three things were created or appeared simultaneously –

'Man, Light and Liberty.'

In my father's Gaelic dictionary under the word 'Breacan' we are told that the Arch Druid wore a garment of the six colours: –

BREACAN – breechg -an, *or* bruchg -an N.M. Tartan, tartan plaid, a Highland plaid; a parti-coloured dress used by the Celts *from the earliest times.*

The *breacan* of the Highland King had *seven different colours*; the Druidical tunic had *six*; and that of the nobles, *four*.

'Breacan an fheilidh' – *the belted plaid*, consisting of twelve yards of tartan worn round the waist, obliquely across the breast, and over the left shoulder, and partly depending backwards.

(From old Gaelic dictionary)

The heaven of the Gael is a place where the sun always shines. It's in the west where the sun goes, full of colour again. In Scotland they work with the sun, stir food in cooking *with the sun*, away from the north which is dark and black. In Celtic legend you have the Formors, the gods of darkness and the depths of the sea, the black people, the enemies of light and life.[72]

Lugh was the sun god, the god of light. Corrigu was the hoodie craw, the symbol of evil, and I was told so when a child. In Dunbar's poem, 'The Golden Targe' describing his idea of a brilliant court, he says, 'this court usit no sable', and the opinions of Fergusson and Burns about 'braid claith', the garb of respectability, we need not mention.

Then it was cheering to see that the Ramsays at the Scottish Show at Burlington House had the effect of being devoid of black. From what I have said, I think any intelligent person will be able to decide that black is certainly not fundamentally characteristic of the Scottish temperament. It is characteristic of Calvinism, night, degeneration, despair, disease and death.

Since this blight of black struck Scotland she has steadily gone down hill, till according to lots of people, her state is nearly hopeless. If black is still dominant don't let us accept it as *permanent*. Everyone in Scotland should refuse to have anything to do with *black or dirty and dingy colours*, and insist on clean colour in everything.

I remember when I was young *any colour* was considered a sign of vulgarity. Greys and black were the only colours for people of taste and refinement. Good pictures had to be black, grey, brown or drab. As someone will immediately start to deny this, I will refer him to the Exhibition of Scottish Art at Burlington House, 1939, which represented, and faithfully, the accepted artistic taste of the period I refer to.

Well! let's forget it, and insist on things in Scotland being of colour that makes for and associates itself with light, hopefulness, health and happiness. For those who seem to believe that there is something fine, something grand about this black grey grimness, I'd point out that most thinking Scots today are utterly failing to see this alleged grandness, and are on the contrary dismayed by its destructiveness.

If the winters in Scotland are certainly long and dark, the summers are certainly long and light, and we have plenty of waterpower, or plenty of water for power to make electric light for the dark winters, and the young artists can apply colour by electric light to make a Scots town as cheerful and beautiful as any town in the winter. No excuse! Fortunately, the cinema, which for a long time influenced many artists to put forward monochrome as a preferable thing to colour, has now gone in for colour. Most people are beginning to enjoy the colour, and soon will not be able to accept monochrome films. Glasgow free from dirt would be a beautiful city.[73] So all Scots should refuse to have anything to do with black, dirty, drab colours. *It is the duty of* artists, architects, decorators and designers to give a lead to make a brighter Scotland. Stores and shopkeepers should stop wrapping *everything* in brown paper, the accumulation of which all over a town has a most deadening effect. You see brown paper everywhere. The general public should refuse, as far as possible, to contribute to gloom by wearing anything black, drab or dirty in colour. For both men and women there are to-day clothes that are beautiful in colour and design, and well cut, at prices that even poor people can pay. So when the working people are through with their jobs, let them put on cheerful clothes and not crawl about in the traditional holy Willie 'stan o' black'. Of course I know there are people who enjoy being in black, and going to funerals, but I don't believe that all Scots are like that. I hope not, and I repeat to those who still believe that there's something wonderful in gloom and grimness, that to a great many of us who are seriously interested in Scotland there is no sign that it has done anything for Scotland except chase out her best men, or most of them, to the benefit of other countries.

CHAPTER VII

Independent Art

But for the glorious privilege of being independent.
BURNS[74]

Scotland should have an independent art.

SCOTLAND SHOULD HAVE an independent art. No one has a right to decide for others what *is* art and what isn't. The public has a right to decide for itself, and to like what is considered to be bad art if they choose. Any intelligent person ought to be able to see that in any properly composed community art is an important social asset.

I can hardly imagine that any intelligent person thinks that art is not part of education, or that art can develop without research. Research demands free thinking. Therefore there ought to be encouragement for free thinking or free *feeling* in art.

Here we can hear a moan from the Calvinist (religious or otherwise) the idea being that free thinking or free feeling is damnation, and that is just where the average academic minded person, artist, art teacher or bourgeois is.

Why should the restraint and discipline of the academies and academic art schools be accused of keeping back the artists or thinkers? They are not keeping them back in the *academic* sense. The student is perfectly free to do what the academies think he should do. They encourage him, give him prizes and scholarships, but it is very evident that the academic successes have hardly ever, I should say never, been the *research men* and the *explorers*, inventors and discoverers.[75] Here again the voice of the absolutist. And here it is evidently necessary to explain that I *do not*, and definitely *do not*, object to such institutions as the Old Salon (generally called in Britain *the* Salon), the RA and the RSA. It is as idiotic to object to them as to object to the Derby, Ascot or a Cup Tie final (though I must apologise for dragging these in, for the performers in all these events are first class). Why object to these official and political art exhibitions? The public has a perfect right to have them if it wants them, and the British public is famous for its want of taste in food and art.

What I *do* object to is that these exhibitions should be taken as *entirely* representing the art of a nation, and succeed in preventing from being seen any art other than what they, the RA, without any right at all (chiefly in order to protect themselves) decide the public should see.

These official, or supposed to be official, (the RA is I believe private) academies naturally hold their exhibitions at the best time of the year, and even if their galleries are used for other exhibitions it is at a time of the year bad for light, or when people are not in town.

In Paris the Autumn Salon is in autumn, when the official building is not wanted by the official Salon, which is the only Salon that most people in Britain, and certainly in Scotland, ever go to see, or have even heard of.

This is of course greatly because people naturally would rather go to Paris in May. Very few people in Scotland have heard of the Autumn Salon, the Salon des Indépendants, or the Salon des Tuileries, and consequently don't know that *all the leaders in modern painting* (this is quite exact) have started and *gone on in these Salons*, have never shown in the official Salon, and haven't been using these salons as stepping stones to the official Salon, as almost all British Artists do with the non-official exhibitions.

The old Salon was the salon of Bougereau, Gérôme & Co., and sculptors of the same kind, and these were the people who did so much harm to the Glasgow School when they tackled figure painting. These men are called in France 'pompiers' – firefighters – and there's no doubt that they were experts at extinguishing fire, the fire of youthful inspiration.[76] They have the power and the habit of distributing medals and mentions, and these medals impress greatly people outside France who know nothing about painting and French art, and believe them to be a *proof of the approval of the best French artists*.

I am writing this because it is someone's job to tell the young artists and art students and people of Scotland that this is *decidedly not so*. Obviously every student, young artist or person interested in art is not able to go to Paris (which *is* the centre of art for the world) and stay there long enough to find out for himself. He goes if he can in May of course, and then sees at the official old Salon the worst French art. The international

　　　　　　　　　　　　　MODERN SCOTTISH PAINTING

Exhibition of 1937 gave him a chance if he was able to take it, to see the Exhibition of Independent Art which in spite of fierce official opposition was held and was a revelation to most people who had not been in the modern movement of the last 40 years.

Scotland should have an independent art

But here we hear the voice of the 'defeatist' saying Scotland isn't France – it's not an art centre! Perhaps not, but in the time of the Glasgow School, Glasgow *was* an art centre. But the question is, why did it not continue to be? Who was to blame for the Glasgow School fading out? Was it Scotland's feeling of inferiority? Was it the lack of sympathy or financial support from the Glasgow people? Was it the desire on the part of most of the Glasgow men to have academic success or recognition (inferiority feeling), lack of patriotism in the artists, in the public or what? These are questions that every Scotsman interested in art and the worth of his country should consider. He either ought to consider these questions or admit that his independence, which he has so much to say about, is gone; that instead of being a free man he has become a servant even if a good well-paid and successful one, which may be enough for some or most, but I hope not for all. But if

Scotland should have an Independent Art

how is it going to happen or how is it going to be done? Well, it must be *wanted*. Someone must want it, and first of all someone must find out if it *is* wanted. This means an effort by a group of people representing the different interests that go to make up a social organism, not only artists, politicians or business men, but all sorts of people who want to know if there is any reason for art trying to exist in Scotland when there is a bigger market in England.

The first thing that should be understood is that it is not desirable to attempt to create by force an art movement or an improved market for art. Certainly the hope is that both these things will result, but because the people want art and want to take an interest in it, and because it is living art, and not copies of ancient art, or an attempt to be 'arty' or artistic, but something that will give people a starting point for creating a stimulating and not merely a pleasant or agreeable atmosphere.

The Scots of my time detested the sugary, affable stuff. Then supposing it is found that the people of Scotland think that

Scotland should have an Independent Art

what are we going to do about it?

Well, I once put forward a complete plan for a London Salon of Indépendants, and here is the circular.

THE LONDON SALON

OF THE

INDEPENDANTS

(Allied Artists' Association, Ltd.)

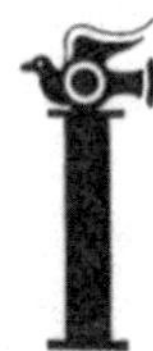

MANAGEMENT COMMITTEE

Malcolm Arbuthnot	Alexander Jamieson
Frank Dobson	Frank Rutter
J.D. Fergusson	Randolph Schwabe
Charles Ginner	Charles Rennie Mackintosh
E. McKnight Kauffer	

THE BRITISH INDÉPENDANTS was first organised in 1908 under the title of the 'Allied Artists' Association, Ltd.', for the purpose of holding 'open' exhibitions of Painting, Sculpture, and Craftwork of every kind. There was no selecting jury, and any artist was eligible to show three works with one on the line. Successful exhibitions were held at the Royal Albert Hall until the outbreak of war, an average of 4,000 exhibits being displayed.[77]

The Society has now been reorganised, and it is hoped greatly to enlarge its activities on an international basis. It is the first necessity for every artist to be able to submit his work to the judgment of the public, freely and without restrictions. The Association enables him to do this without the intervention of any middleman, whether artist or dealer. It has a membership of over 200 British artists, and the support of considerably more than this number is assured, together with many continental workers and societies such as the Salon des Indépendants in Paris.

This Society, having similar aims to the British Indépendants, has always had assistance and facilities granted to it by the Government, and its exhibitions are the most important art functions of the year. In view of these facts, representations are being made to the British Government for the national need of similar facilities being given to the British Indépendants.

Exhibitions will be organised on much the same lines as those of the Allied Artists' Association, but on a larger scale. Wall space will be balloted for, but in the future it will be possible for two or any number of exhibitors to agree to apply for consecutive numbers in the ballot.

For the furtherance of these aims the Society is no longer restricted to exhibitors only, but appeals for support from all interested in the freedom of art.

Annual subscription for exhibitor, two guineas. This subscription entitles the associate to show three works; but any person may join the Society upon payment of not less than five shillings per annum and subsequently qualify as an exhibitor by paying the balance up to two guineas.

All communications and subscriptions to be addressed to the Secretary, 1 Robert Street, Adelphi, WC2.

And how did this London Salon of the Indépendents get on? *It didn't get on at all,* because it was impossible to find a place to hold it in. After a year of hunting everywhere, the only place we could find was the parade at Brighton. In London it was not possible. The official people told us that there was *the* Royal Academy, and anyone was free to send there. The other galleries of any size were too expensive.

My idea was to have it in Army huts with glass roofs on one of the walks in Hyde Park. (On the walk because there would be no turf to replace.) Charles Rennie Mackintosh had that part in hand. We were to have as many huts as the space subscribed for demanded. Groups could take one or more huts, and they could do what they liked with their huts. This was the cheapest way to do it, and to avoid expense for *light and heating*, most important, it was to be held in May. But we were told that the parks belonged to the King and that was impossible.

My idea was that it should go on to any town where it was wanted, and that any town could organise its group for the London Show. After a year, having failed to find a place, the Society had to be wound up, and the subscriptions returned. *It wasn't wanted*, and that's what I mean when I say that it has to be found out whether Scotland wants such a thing.[78]

The whole plan is ready. It's the least expensive form of exhibition possible. There's no risk, for the huts are ordered according to the space subscribed for, but we want *the ground free, central, and in May*. The subscriptions would be reduced as far as possible according to the expenses. The 200 members we had, had no fault to find with the scheme at the general meeting, but they thought the Committee were going to do all the work. The Committee were all men who *did not need the Society at all*, who could have private shows of their own. They were merely offering a scheme whereby the artists who *did need a place to show in*, could help themselves. That's the story of 'The London Salon of the Indépendents' – *not wanted*.

I think *Scotland should have an Independent Art*. Does anyone else think so?

CHAPTER VIII

The Journeyman Artist

THE IDEA THAT THE artist is a supercraftsman and that there is a technique of painting that can be *completely* acquired by study, application or *a thorough artistic training* (I suppose in anatomy, etc.) simply means that there is an apprenticeship and that by examinations or tests it can be decided that the apprentice at a certain point becomes a journeyman, what the French call a 'patented plumber', or gets a degree like a doctor. What could be more confusing? Further, that if he proves exceptional ability he can become a professor. Then his work and opinions on art are not to be questioned by the ordinary man or the student or unrecognised artist.

This actually is the idea of the average man, and the average artist about art. Anyone not accepting this point of view is immediately classed as revolutionary.

It must be evident that the journeyman mechanic, say in wireless, has not invented wireless; that the air mechanic has not made the research necessary to allow an aeroplane to fly; that the doctor gets his degree not for discovering medical treatments, but for applying them. The doctor's degree proves his ability to pass the necessary examinations. It does not prove that he is able to invent anything.

The research man needs no degree, the only excuse for using the name artist is to mean a *creator or inventor*, and certainly not to mean the person who uses or exploits the creations of others however well.

At this point we can hear the 'absolutist' say, 'but we must use the creations of others'. Well, we can't start every paragraph by saying that we are not even *attempting* to talk in absolutes. If we use an absolute it is used relatively. We say, for example, that X is an absolute ass, meaning in relation to the subject we were discussing, say art. He may be an absolute genius at darts and we didn't even know he played darts, but the 'absolutist' wants us to mean that however, wherever, and under any circumstances whatever, X is an absolute ass. Well!

The belief or whatever we call it, in the apprenticeship, journeyman, master, and all that, brings us to the word '*content*'. When I came to England and heard people talk of 'the content', I was rather surprised and perplexed. In all the years in Paris involved in the modern movement, in all the discussions about art, and meeting all different nationalities, I never heard this word used. I wondered what was meant by the word 'content'. For example, what did '*but the content apart*' mean? It suggested that there was a container and what it held was the content apparently meaning that we can accept the idea of a mould or receptacle, and what is put into it is what makes it art, whether a stationary engine, flying machine, wine bottle, railway train, steamer, submarine, elephant or snake; or that a building could be equally suitable for a blast furnace or a habitation *if you got the right pattern.*

I can see that it could be applied to the Victorian painting where the content was generally some historical incident or philosophical idea (in the ordinary sense) and painting was merely used to illustrate it. But leaving that, what does it mean? All I can think it could mean is that there is some means of arriving at a form, a mould or container that is suitable for any subject or feeling, for anything that has to be represented. That anything expressible has to be thought of as a fluid, and should fit into this fixed form. All this again suggests the belief that there is something that can be arrived at that is adequate for expressing all the human feelings and emotions if the artist has mastered his medium or produced his container. Now it seems to be evident that there is a difference between being an artist and having been an artist, and that the word artist strictly applies to the person who *persists in being* an artist. The awareness that form is constantly changing, never fixed, is the quality that makes the artist; that is the inventor or discoverer as distinct from the exploiter. If we admit this then we cannot accept the container idea, for going on means *incessantly* seeing new aspects and combinations of form and colour (separating these things for the sake of examination for they are not really separable). That the same mould, container, will do for all the new combinations is obviously absurd, and the absurdity is evident to any intelligent person when they see academically drawn map-like figures, *filled in* with the colour inventions and discoveries of the impressionist. And the map-like division of the figure from the background persists with all the academically trained painters, and I suppose always must. It is what is called good drawing. Again the container idea; the *containing line*; the idea being that having mastered the art of putting the containing line anatomically in the right place, the artist can express anything. To be seen, the figure must be in some sort of light, and therefore must be part of the light and not *apart* from the light.

Here we hear a voice say – but there's the light of imagination, the light that never was, except in the mind of the artist. This is merely another manifestation of the belief in the *container idea*. And here we touch on difference of *ideas*, not merely about art, but about life and death, quantum mechanics! light, Einstein and all that; that light should bend no doubt seems to the Calvinistic Scot a terrible weakness on its part, and he is probably incapable of admitting it. Here again the voice asking what all this has to do with art. Well! The container, the watertight compartment, the absolute category, all that.

So if content is something that is contained, then it seems to me that the *work of art is not a container*; that it does not contain, but *is something that allows something to pass through to someone in sympathy*. Its value may depend on the sympathy of millions, or the intense sympathy of one, and someone may understand greatly, without being sympathetic, others may be entirely sympathetic without understanding.

But the voice again saying that *I* don't understand what is meant by 'content'. There must be lots of other people who have spent much less time on such matters who are also at a loss. It is for these people I am writing in the hope that they will find for themselves whether *content as used in* relation to works of art means anything that matters or means anything at all.[79]

Then we come inevitably to the other word so *freely* used, technique, and not merely *freely*, but as if it was quite unnecessary even to think what it meant or to give it even a useful working meaning.

I don't admit that it's my ignorance of painting or lack of thinking about it that makes me wonder what people mean when they say that *technically* a work of art is wonderful, meaning, I suppose, that there is something called 'technique' that can be separated from the work of art. I can see that the 'technique' of french polishing may be applied to the very finest grand piano played on by the greatest master, or to the 'table de nuit', and I suppose following the same line of thought or lack of thinking, the really great french polisher is an artist. If that's what is meant by technique, all right, I see. That puts painting into the same category as french polishing, and what the house painters call 'graining', that is, imitating in paint the grain of different woods. Both allow great technical skill, and differ from painting (except abstract painting) only in that they are more admittedly abstract; or don't even pretend to be art, and are not usually put into frames and hung in picture exhibitions. Why not?

And here we come to something I won't tackle in this book. What do I mean by abstract? Now what do other people mean by abstract? I was in Paris when Picasso and Braque started what has come to be called abstract painting. I watched its development very closely and carefully, and made a tremendous lot of research in order to see the possibilities and uses of it; but it's long, and there are hundreds of books on it. Young men tell me about it. It started over 30 years ago.[80]

But to come back to the *containing line* it reminds me of Walt Whitman's 'Open Road':

From this hour I ordain myself loosed of limits and imaginary lines.

WALT WHITMAN, 'Song of the Open Road'[81]

We know that there are artists who do not want to travel or explore, spiritually or otherwise, but for the artist who wants to take to the open road, in other words wants freedom, and I think anyone worthy of the name must, the artist who wants to be free should say with Walt Whitman, 'From this hour I ordain myself loosed of limits and imaginary lines'. He will be forced to use *limits and imaginary lines*, but he should ordain that he is free to use them as he *feels*, and not according to academic rules or mechanical measurements. He should decide that the limit and lines are concerned with quality of light, as he *feels* it, through having *seen* it, and be proud of his human reaction, instead of trying to dehumanise himself and attempt to compete with the machine or instrument of precision, which is the worst possible manifestation of inferiority, – although it undoubtedly is the aim of the average artist who is apparently convinced that it is the highest achievement, and a thing to try for.

The idea or belief that map-like, two dimensional division of space is drawing, design or composition is something that should be examined, for it is generally accepted that that is drawing, design (for which I find no

                    MODERN SCOTTISH PAINTING

word in French) and composition. This amounts to admitting that *quality* does not affect design. In other words that in painting, paint is something filled into the design. This of course means that any freedom or feeling in the use of paint is impossible. The drawing or design or composition is fixed in advance, and to lose it is to be lost. And with *what's called* good design, drawing or composition, any paint will do, and to express light, *quality* of paint is unnecessary. And it is pretty clear that most people have not even thought of *quality* of paint, and that many think that quantity of paint is quality. Quality of paint like quality of line or quality of tone is not a thing that can be fixed. It is the artist's statement in paint of his reaction to form created by the play of light, and is poor or full according to the painter's sensibility and experience of life.

CHAPTER IX

The Master

ONE OF THE GREAT mistakes of the artist is to desire to become a master, that is 'to be called Rabbi' – master of one's destiny, 'master of one's medium', '*cher maître*' and all that. The word master and artist seem contradictory. Can any real artist be a master? A great craftsman should be a master of his medium, or his trade, which only seems to mean that he can put the final polish on his productions.

The artist, I think, is not concerned with final polish but with ultimate truth, and no one worthy of the name artist can really believe he can reach the ultimate truth.

To the real artist life is continuous defeats, some less discouraging than others, some that for a *moment* almost *look like* successes, but never even for *a moment*, success. The artist to live, must go on.

The expression 'renewing himself' doesn't seem to apply, although it is happy. He merely recovers from one defeat to go on to another, and he goes on hoping that next time he will have more strength and understanding to allow him to make some progress on the journey he has undertaken, the wonderful adventure in the world of beauty, full of obstacles, enemies and temptations, and if he is a real Scot of the old belief he hopes that he will go on stronger and freer in the 'land o' the leal', the 'Tir nan Og' (the land of the ever young). No, I don't think the artist has any right to expect the 'salutation in the market place'.[82] The craftsman has a right to expect it. 'To Caesar what is Caesar's.'

This brings us to the question of courage. The Scottish artist ought to have the courage to be submissive. I mean to take the risk of submitting to his emotions or feelings, instead of trying to justify them or correct them by Calvinism or calipers. Why this fear of acting as a free human being? What is it based on?

It is of course based on the knowledge that to act as a free human being makes it quite impossible to compete with the Calvinist or rather the Holy

Wullie, who is quite prepared, even willing, to sacrifice all liberty in order to be considered respectable, and having succeeded in making the Scot accept that money-making and church going are the only moral things, uses the power money and respectability have given him, to restrict by a form of blackmail everyone behaving like a free natural human being.

By this means the Dutch Calvinists ruined and starved Rembrandt to death, and are now making money by the fame he has brought to Holland. These Holy Wullies (for they are *not really Calvinists*, merely hypocrites), having gained power of exactly the kind that the reformation was meant to destroy, have succeeded in producing in Scotland a state that exists all over the world today, a condition in which fear and mistrust and blackmail has replaced love; a condition where there is no love or friendship for your neighbour or *anything*. Scotsmen of independent spirit have if possible left the country, or have stayed only on account of a stimulation from the feeling of being persecuted.[83] This is true about the crofter, the artist, painter, poet or writer. They find the English, if rather indifferent, at least kind, live and let live people, and London hasn't the small town or village power of interference with the private affairs of life and liberty. To quote *The Times*, 7 July 1939:

> The Scots, for instance, make no fuss about *Lebensraum*, they have all too much of it in their own country; their one idea is to get away from it as rapidly as possible, and settle down in over-populated cities like London, for they know quite well they will have more fun, and more scope for their talents in a crowd.

The Scot has for a long time, thousands of years, been a fighter. I believe he still is. I hope he is still. He has been a fighter, but for liberty, and that liberty meant to a great extent the liberty to live his own way and think in his own way. He has been concerned with primitive ideas of liberty. That is to say the first things concerned in liberty – his land, his religion, his government, his laws.

It seems that he has hardly ever associated any form of art with liberty or freedom. Thinking of it broadly he has never encouraged or been much moved by any attempt at establishing free art in any form. Fergusson and Burns might be considered attempts to establish a free art. The Glasgow School certainly was; but they had not *general support*.

The Scot is perhaps justified in thinking that a free art should naturally be produced in a free nation. That seems quite right, but it's the survival after its birth that the nation should be concerned about. It certainly is the artists' affair to start a free art, that is to say, to express himself freely and honestly, but if the nation is against or negligent of free and honest art expression, the artist cannot exist in that atmosphere, climate or surroundings, and must stay and die, or move to a more hospitable surrounding. And that brings us back again to courage. Were the victims of the clearances cowards, gutsless or worthless people? The colonies are the answer.

Has Scotland been able to do as well without them? Well, has it?

Now there's an idea that if you're good enough you'll come through and that if you move away from discomfort or persecution you are a coward; that a Scots artist should stay in Scotland whether he is wanted or not, and that if he is really an artist, lack of freedom, persecution and neglect will only help him to become a greater artist.

Some Englishman said, 'The fox is a good athlete but his trainers are sometimes too hard on him.' Dunbar, Fergusson and Burns stayed in Scotland. Perhaps the Scots trainers think their treatment of them was all in order. I don't think so.

A curse upon your whunstane hearts ye Edinburgh gentry,
Half what ye spend a year on cairts would filled his pantry.

BURNS ON FERGUSSON[84]

MODERN SCOTTISH PAINTING

CHAPTER X

The Artist and The World or The Public

AN AMERICAN ARTIST I know, a very good painter, was commissioned to do paintings of the Klondike.[85] He wanted to, and was very pleased to get the chance. When he was getting near the Klondike he thought the other passenger in the railway carriage looked very like the kind of fellow one would expect to belong to the region, and found he was. He decided to question him about it. Having talked about things in general up there, he then came to the point and said, 'Have you any painters up there?' 'Aw no,' said the Klondiker, 'we do our own painting.' 'Oh no!' said my friend, 'I don't mean house painters, I mean artists, picture painters.' The Klondiker fixed my friend with a Klondike eye and said, 'Why Hell! We'd shoot a guy like that.'

Now that strikes me as first class, quite honest and free from hypocrisy. If people don't want artists and don't feel the need of them or object to them, *then let them say so*, so that the artist may know where *not* to go, just as the gold-rush man doesn't go where there is no gold to rush for.

But does the average man say that he doesn't want art? Oh no! Even if he's not interested he doesn't say so, and feels it would be showing a hopeless lack of culture or refinement to admit it. When then! If he feels that, what does he do about it? Generally nothing. He has been trained to believe that art just happens and you can't stop it happening. That the real artist carries on and succeeds because of a *gift he has got* and *hasn't earned*, and the gift does not require to be sustained or developed. *It does itself.*

For other achievements one has to work and therefore should be paid. In fact the only way to become an artist is to starve, and if the nation or the world neglects the artist it is doing the best thing for his development.

The world or the nation will take the artist's works and praise them, boast of them, exploit them, use them for every money-making purpose with the feeling that it has a perfect right to do so, although it has not paid for them. It never even occurs to them that they should have paid for them. The artist is a 'mug' who produces whether he is paid or not. Why bother. They do it. (I am, of course, talking of the research artist, the inventor artist, not the commercial artist.)

Now this attitude if extended sufficiently in the world produces the condition where everyone wants to sell something, and not waste any time making anything, and the end of that state of affairs can be seen without any great vision.

The excuse is that one has to make a living, and that non-commercial art can only be followed by artists with private means. That's true, but it should not be so. It's an unhealthy state for society. A nation of shopkeepers is not a very good kind of nation, a nation all of salesmen, any more than a nation all of artists would be. It's cock-eyed. What then? Well then, society should understand that they have to pay for all sorts of contributions, and that invention and research are among the most important contributions.

The salesman ought to realise that the inventor in art or anything else is supplying him with something to exploit, and he ought to have enough sense of decency to feel that he should contribute to the creator type, even at the risk of making the mistake of sometimes backing the wrong man, that is to say, taking a sporting chance.

There are always plenty of people willing to help the man who is, or appears to be, a proved success. Academies are always ready to honour the accepted artist, and we know the immortal reply of Sam Bough to the RSA when they offered to make him an ARSA.

The point of view that the artist will produce whether paid or not, and that he should not even expect sympathy if he insists on trying to create, exonerates the public entirely from every feeling of responsibility for the welfare or existence of the artist, that is to say, the inventor or creator.

The commercial artist disguised or otherwise can always look after himself, and he should be able to. He is not contributing. He is exploiting. Really creative people are rarely interested in making money, but they cannot live without some, and what they make they generally use to help them to go on with their work.

It is merely a business proposition to give the creative person enough to allow him to produce his best, which goes finally to the country directly or indirectly; and every artist or creative person who leaves a country or dies of starvation or neglect is so much loss to that country, and his work generally has to be paid for very highly after his death.

Again the voice of the 'absolutist' – 'The commercial artist can be a creative artist.' Of course he can, and many are, and often more creative than artists who despise commercial art, but the commercial artist is always telling us how limited his chance for original work is, and how his best work is always being spoiled by the interference of people who know nothing about art. What I mean by a commercial artist is not a bad artist or an artist without creative instinct or power, but one who willingly or from necessity, and often with great suffering, produces what's wanted and not what he wants to produce.

I greatly admire many of these people who, with great courage and against the kind of opposition I could not face, persist in doing as good work as they are allowed to do, and it's often very good. An artist may have to keep his mother, or his wife and children, and it is not his fault if he finds it impossible to do this by producing his best work. Well, whose fault is it?

And here we come to the wonderful idea, which I know does exist, that everyone but the artist knows about art, and that it is only by severe criticism and the control of the necessity of making a living that he produces anything worth anything – meaning, when you examine it, worth anything commercially or at least in money.

> Pure art praises the Lord.
> Commercial art praises a product.

I have said most definitely that I do *not object* at all to institutions like the RA, and I *do not* object to commercial art even when bad, but I do *definitely* object to commercial art or art that is made to sell being considered the *only art that should be encouraged.*

And when I say commercial art I don't mean only the kind of thing produced in Commercial Art Schools. The Commercial Art Schools are quite frankly and honestly commercial, so nothing can be said against them. On the contrary, a great deal can be said for them, for they can and *often do* manage to persuade their clients to accept better stuff than they would if left to themselves. And that's helping art, without pretending to be non-commercial.

One man I know has persistently tried and succeeded in improving tremendously the standard of what he would frankly say was commercial art. Good luck to him. It must have been a tough job, but of course, without an intelligent and sympathetic patron it would have been impossible. Then good luck to them both.

This brings us to the question of who is responsible for art, good or bad, or for the lack of it. *Obviously everybody. Everybody is responsible*, aware of it or not. The artist cannot go on producing work without some sympathy and enough to live on. The buyer cannot be expected to be studying art and making money, so he consequently must rely on being helped by critics, writers, dealers and, of course, last of all by the artist himself.

He always mistrusts the artist. Naturally, because he sees that according to the business standard (which is the standard he knows) the artist is unreliable. Quite right, the artist is according to that standard unreliable. Then naturally the businessman goes to the dealer who is in his own category, and can be dealt with in a business way. What could be more reasonable and desirable? This ought to relieve the artist of the most disagreeable side of his life, that is, being a contact man and salesman.

Francis Newbery, in his introduction to Martin's book, *The Glasgow School*, says, 'The enterprise of a Fine Art Dealer in Glasgow in bringing these pictures to the city was of paramount use and importance'. This brings us to the dealers.

No one can be of more use in making art known than a courageous dealer with enough taste and self-respect not to be willing to sell just anything that will sell.

And commercial art and selling brings us to the Royal Academy and the reasons for sending there.

If intelligent young painters don't believe in the Old Salon, the RA and the RSA why do they send to them? The reasons and excuses are that although they are bad exhibitions, and do not represent the art of the country, there is no charge for having pictures hung, and no subscription. That the fees for showing at other exhibitions are too high for people who have not a private income, I agree. That it is a good discipline to prove to yourself that you can do work that will be accepted. That one has to make a living. That successful people in the RA sell well at high prices. That everyone goes. That the buildings and galleries are excellent and central, and the Shows are held at the height of the season and are social functions patronised by Royalty. That a condition made by people having their portraits painted is that they should be hung in the Academy, and work is often refused by the patron if not hung. That it is not all bad (like the curate's egg, good in places!). That there is a rich benevolent fund and pensions for the artists' widows. But I think the best excuse of all is that it is the duty of the artist to send, to try to raise the level, or at least to keep it from getting too low. Dear me! This sounds to me like saying that if the stew is admittedly bad, stale, unpalatable, or in the opinion of some, even worse than that, the thing to do is to put in some really good fresh meat, or other really good, fresh ingredients, to save the stew. That if the new ingredients are really good they will transform the rancid stew. Well! Anyway, there will be some good stuff in it. There will be, but we have seen that the good stuff never lasts long in the bad stew. It's what business people call throwing good money after bad. Though I am a Scotsman I won't quote the Bible, or the many Victorian proverbs; I'll quote Barnum and say 'enough said'. *No one* claims that, although a very rich and very well-run institution, the RA really represents the art of the nation. These opinions are not merely mine, or the opinions of the *extreme* modern painters. What intelligent people with a sense of humour thought of the Royal Academy in the 'nineties' was very well expressed by Walter Emanuel in *The Butterfly* – 'Is the Royal Academy worse than usual, Pa?' – 'The Royal Academy, my son, is a very rich and very influential body, but even it cannot achieve the impossible.'[86]

Humour or a sense of humour is perhaps merely natural philosophy, that is to say, the spontaneous reaction to human values, regardless of values according to artificial (man-made) standards, man-made laws or conventions. Real people and real things can always stand being laughed at, and the real people generally laugh at themselves and see their limitations and weaknesses. A really good work of art always makes me laugh, and once when I said so to Peploe he replied 'at a certain point you have to laugh or cry'. There is no more sure proof of the feeling of inferiority than the fear of being laughed at. The snob being an inferior person is always terrified he'll be laughed at. That's the cause in art of his fear of taking sides without the support of recognised power and authority such as the Old Salon, RA, RSA. He is also always afraid to approve of or see any wisdom in anything comic, or amusing. He is prepared to admit that any work of art which is approved by the authorities, and which he does not understand and is bored by, is great and serious.

CHAPTER XI

Responsibility of Art Schools and Directors

IF THE ART DEALERS are very important in selling art, the Art Schools have a great influence on Art Students, and a good Head (that is to say a Head with ideas beyond the mere winning of scholarships and producing success-ful teachers) can do great things for the young artists.

But the Head is employed and paid only if he continues to satisfy his directors, and the directors feel that as they are entrusted with the money that is to be spent they cannot take chances; that it is their duty not to gamble with the money. Safety first is the only honest thing to keep in mind, and naturally, not necessarily having any ideas of art, safety to them means following the academic (in the sense of recognised) lead.

This is quite to be expected. So the Head, whatever his ideas may be, if he wants to keep his job must find out what the directors want and do it; teach his pupils to make their work look nearly enough like the old masters, which the directors have not the courage to question because they know that they are accepted and safe.

What else can they do? I don't see what else they can do, and I don't object to their doing so, but I object to that being the only art education, or rather I object to people (and specially art students) being under the impression that is the only education possible if you want to become an artist.

If you want to become an art teacher on purely accepted lines I see nothing wrong with it.

Then what would you do? If the young artist can't afford models, if he can't afford a studio, if he needs a scholarship to travel and see the art of the world, if he must convince his parents (a most important point; most parents seem to mistrust their children), that he really is studying, what's he going to do? If he feels that he must have a model, that is, that he must make anatomical studies of the nude; if he feels it must be done in a real studio light; if he feels he must have a scholarship to travel and see the art of the world, and that he must go to a recognised Art School *to convince* his parents that he's not just loafing, then the Art School is his affair, *and we'll say no more about it.*

But if he wants freedom to express himself in his own way, regardless of academic or popular recognition, if he wants to study form, and realises a hired model in a studio light is the most artificial condition he could deal with, if he is intelligent and honest with himself, he will realise that he has more chance of becoming an artist by working in human conditions from still life, his people or friends as models (they need not be nude), or street scenes, landscape and the endless subjects of human interest instead of the set model in the set light.

If he realises this and wants what is to be got by it he will then not go near an Art School, and if he has got there he will be glad to leave it. If he wants to work in a group he can form a group and share expenses of a room to work in where each can work in his own way.

His group can have an exhibition of the work they want to send, and hang the works in their own way. In short, have freedom. It has been done. But he won't have everything provided for him as he has in a school. No, of course not. You can't get something for nothing. He'll have to pay for this freedom, do without things, make sacrifices. Certainly it's not easy. It merely depends on what is wanted.

All I'm putting forward is that the Art School is not the only way to train to be an artist. It is a way. I'm not putting forward a scheme for 'How to become an artist without trouble', or 'Art made easy'; rather 'art made difficult'.

As I have been saying this for an ordinary lifetime, and know most of the replies, I can hear the usual reply that all this sounds all right in theory, but how are you going to put it into practice unless you have a good private income? My reply is that I have put it into practice and without a private income, but I have contented myself with the least possible money. I mean I have been very happy because I have been, and still am, delighted with my job except when I have to attend to the business side of it, like having exhibitions, and attending to paying rent, etc. It is difficult, I can tell you, but not impossible, and if artists would keep to it, it would be much easier, and France, the nation that has kept to this point of view most, is the strongest nation in art in the world.

There is always an *independent art* in France *as well as* an academic art, and that's the *best that any intelligent person can expect in any nation.*

There is also independent scientific research in France. The workers (the Curies for example, if you don't know what I mean), and Branly, to mention only one other, make hardly any money.[87] They are great scientists not *because* they are very badly paid and work under difficulties, which seems to be the point of view of the person who believes that he can't be an artist unless you starve, and that you do good work if you have to work in order not to starve to death. *What a point of view to have.* Even the mass production factories have to reconsider it a bit to get the most out of the workers, and some people are beginning to feel that they don't like things produced in sweat shops!

But how are we going to know who is the artist deserving of support if we have not the guide of academic success of approval? Well! You can't know. *You must take a chance on it!* Use your judgment. How do you know your children are going to be a success? How do you know what's going to win the Derby? Or the Calcutta Sweep? How do you know what is the future of Europe? Must you know before you do anything, or even before you pass an opinion of your own? How does the artist or the scientist know that he is going to manage to exist and go on with his work? 'Gazing around the fair assembly', there's not so much to encourage him but 'he takes a chance on it', and a lot of them have done things that the type that is never willing to take a chance has successfully exploited. Why shouldn't he exploit their discoveries? He should. He is an exploiter, and necessary, but it is necessary that he has something to exploit, and he ought to realise that that's what the inventor provides. 'The goose that lays the golden eggs.' Well, even the good earth can be exhausted by stupid treatment.

All this is a long way of explaining what I mean by saying that it is everybody's business to attend to, and see the importance of the creative or inventive member of society, and the reason for the explanation being long is that after a lifetime of discussion I haven't noticed that the short and snappy, or epigrammatic statement explains things enough to most people. I knew the 'nineties', the delightfully bright flashes of Whistler and Wilde.[88] They were most valuable, and for the people who were willing to use them as a starting point for thinking about things, were quite

	MODERN SCOTTISH PAINTING

sufficient, but it seems to me that generally to explain things more lengthily is necessary.

I repeat, this is my impression after an ordinary lifetime of discussion, and not with stupid people or one nationality. And I repeat, I am not writing this for people who know it all already, but for the young student or artist, or man who is interested in art but has had less time or chance of thinking about it or discussing it with a great variety of people in different countries. In short, for the person in the position I was in when I began, without anyone to discuss things with, and a great desire to.

Although I am aware that at the moment art doesn't seem to be the thing of the first importance, that ARP is the thing to think about, I am hoping that the use of the preparations for war will be that they will bring about conditions of peace, and that art will be taken more seriously as part of the life of the person who will have time and a desire to think of other things than defence. And I think 'we've got to be prepared' for peace as well as for war. Starting to think about art only when we are quite certain that war can't happen, seems to me to be a hopeless state, for *everyone* to be in.

Anyone who has devoted his life to the arts of peace should not be expected to throw everything aside until he is sure that peace has come for good. At the moment the problem is 'how to make a living' when only war is in everybody's mind, and all the money is being spent on war preparations.

The pressure on the artist to become commercial is daily increasing, and research in art or science must be immediately applicable to the needs of the moment rather than attempting to develop people capable of making better conditions for the future.

I have heard that it has been frankly said that in an Art School the main thing is to turn out people fit to make a living. *That should not be the main thing.* That should be a *by-product.* The making of a living should be the result of having created or produced something.[89]

I think that the public or most people believe that Universities are seats of learning and scholarship, and that they have been established and endowed by men who believed in the necessity or importance of study and research in the different branches of thought, and that people still expect something different to what they expect from places where one merely learns to make a living. And I think the public put the National or Municipal Art Schools in the same category, only dealing with a different subject, and I feel that once the public feels that these institutions are merely places for learning to make a living, that their respect for them will quite justly cease.

There are commercial colleges and commercial art schools without number, and unless the national municipal endowed universities and art schools are at least trying to do something higher what is the excuse for them? That's what I think the public can be expected to ask. Speaking broadly, the public have lost faith in the churches. I don't see why they should not lose faith in the universities and art schools if they are just used to train people to make a living. For there is a great difference between being trained to be a doctor or a scientist and making a living, and being trained to be a doctor *in order to make a living*. This will sound to some people like nonsense. I don't think it is.

Again the voice of the absolutist. 'What you want then is a lot of arty people quite incapable of making a living.' No! I haven't said so, and I don't want arty people. What I want is people who want to do something, to create something, or try to find something that will be a help to make life more agreeable than it is at present, and to create a state of mind in the world where that seems a good and reasonable way to spend one's energy, instead of the idea that it's good and reasonable to steal or *take for nothing* the inventions or discoveries of others in art or science, and be proud of having cleverly exploited them, and made lots of money by them.

I want the people who are *not* inventors or creators to realise, or admit at least, that research and invention is an important part of any first class state of society (the slave state doesn't need them), and that they should even from the purely practical point of view be willing to contribute to allow the research people to work without having to think *first* of making a living. *They* should be free to think first of their job, and the public should have enough pluck to risk sometimes backing a loser – in short, to take a sporting chance.

Art is, or ought to be, the purest form of free self-expression and free self-expression is the life of any free country.

One of the first moves in the creation of a slave state from the outside is the suppression of free self-expression. One of the first symptoms of the slave state *creating itself* from the inside is the fear of self-expression, and if real art is the purest form of free expression it is evidently something that must be supported, or at least given freedom, by the people who claim that they want a free country. The suppression of self-expression and the development of fear to express oneself freely is most dangerous when it is least evident.

Interference with the freedom of the press is soon evident, and soon resented, but the effects of Calvinism on free expression in Scotland are much more penetrating. When the average person speaks of freedom he means freedom to criticise, to express his opinions of the Government. He apparently doesn't think that anything else needs freedom. In the case of art, I think he rather feels, if he is concerned at all, that art should not be allowed freedom, except, of course, to do what is approved by the orthodox schools, and that everyone departing from the orthodox is a crank or a faker.

Here I think it is necessary to say that I *do not object to the real Calvinists,* I mean the people who really want Calvinism and believe in it; but I do object to a nation which does not want Calvinism and does not believe in it, being so gutsless as to be afraid of it, and so lacking in independence as to allow it to restrict their freedom, definitely hinder their development, and reduce them to a state culturally and consequently commercially, admittedly worse than it has ever been.

I say consequently commercially because I do not mean by culturally something only to do with art and letters, but what should go with art and letters if they are concerned with living culture – a state of mental awareness and alertness that leads to invention and creation in everything including, of course, commercial enterprise.

The Scotsman who opposes this may as well remember that I am a Scotsman, not partly, but 100 per cent; that I've met lots of Scotsmen and that I've never met one who was in favour of Calvinism, and never met one that wasn't afraid of it. I can hear the reply at once that they never think of it; that they don't bother about it. Quite true, they don't, and it's high time that they did think of it and bother about it, and stop behaving as if it was a perfectly natural thing for all Scots to accept. It will probably be indignantly denied that it leads to hypocrisy. Well, it's useless to tell *me* that. I know better.

But what has this to do with Modern Scottish Painting? It has to do with freedom of thought, and consequently with modern painting every-where, for one of the chief characteristics of modern painting is free thinking and free expression, and Calvinism has produced a state of mind in Scotland that makes the Scots artist afraid to paint a nude, and the Scots buyer afraid to hang one on his walls – unless perhaps by an old master. Even then, generally not. A Frenchwoman writing about the Scots has said, 'Calvinism has not left them frightened of hell although it has made them ashamed of being caught looking at a naked body.'[90]

I *haven't* said anywhere that it is necessary to paint nudes to be an artist. I *have* said that it *isn't* necessary. But I do say that the artist must have enough courage and freedom of mind to paint nudes if he wants to, and I don't mean nudes that try *not* to look like nude human beings and made to look like sugary angels, by way of being apologetic, but wholesome, healthy statements of wholesome healthy people. Not nudes painted to show how daring the artist can be, or to show his knowledge of anatomy, but because he wants to express some beauty seen in the best subject for many artists, the beauty of light on healthy skin.

And here we seem to come to the point – who invented or launched the idea that a good-looking man or woman without clothes was an indecency? Who started this poisonous unnatural idea, and how has it come about that a nation claiming to be an independent and thinking nation has allowed such a perverted and unwholesome point of view to come to be considered by other nations *one of its outstanding characteristics* and not just pathetic hypocrisy.

Do they really believe that it was ordained by God? Is it the result of some bad translation or stupid misinterpretation of the Bible? Did Christ say so? Or what? Who started it? and as such people go by authorities, has the modern Scotsman asked himself on what authority he submits to such imbecility? The modern Scot thinks himself in touch with modern scientific ideas. Does he find any support for this anti-nude idea anywhere in science, medical or otherwise. No! It's a fear and a *well-founded* fear that any sign of real interest in nudes will be used against him as blackmail, to starve him out of business, and prevent him making a living as the Dutch Calvinists did with Rembrandt. He may do nudes at school, in fact he *must*, but that is in order to study anatomy – just like anatomical dissecting in the medical schools – but he must not show any sign of being

　　　　　　　　　　　　　　　　MODERN SCOTTISH PAINTING

humanly interested in the nude woman as a thing of beauty. And, anyway, no one in Scotland would buy nudes, and the galleries wouldn't hang them. Is it because the Scots are not interested in nudes? Let's hope not. Let's hope it's pure hypocrisy. I repeat that it is quite unnecessary that in order to be an artist one should paint nudes, but I repeat that to be an artist it is quite necessary to be free and have the courage to paint what may, at a certain moment or period, appear to be the best subject.

> *Hail May, hail Flora, hail aurora sheen!*
> *Hail! princess Nature, hail Venus Love's Queen!*
>
> WILLIAM DUNBAR, 'The Thistle and the Rose'[91]

It's as natural for an artist to be interested in a woman as a subject as in a suit of clothes, which is the main thing in a male portrait and apparently is considered natural and paintable.

But perhaps I'm missing the point. The whole thing may only be a 'racket' launched by the tailors and dressmakers. They've put trousers on the Highlander and crinolines on the women, and I suppose the Scots Calvinist feels that makes them really moral people. *There ought to be some independent thought in Scotland.*

> *O wad some power the giftie gie us*
> *To see oorsels as ithers see us!*
> *It would frae mony a blunder free us,*
>   *An' foolish notion;*
> *What airs in dress an' gait wad lea'e us,*
>   *An' e'n devotion!*
>
> BURNS[92]

CHAPTER XII

Calvinism and Art

An honest man may like a glass,
An honest man may like a lass,
But mean revenge and malice fause
  He'll still disdain,
And then cry zeal for gospel laws
  Like some we ken.

Burns[93]

BY CALVINISM I MEAN *what is called Calvinism* and that may have no more to do with Calvinism than what is called Christianity has to do with Christianity.

But why worry about Calvinism? Why bother about it? It's quite negligible. Well! Is it?

The destructiveness of Calvinism is much more subtle than merely interfering with political liberty. Under the directors of the Reformation and the Puritans, the works of Dunbar and his contemporaries were carefully set aside.[94] Sanctimonious words were put to popular tunes so that nothing of the folk songs should remain. They succeeded in suppressing natural Scottish poetry till the time of Allan Ramsay. Meanwhile the educated were doing imitation classical poetry.

Fergusson and Burns followed Ramsay, and again gave Scottish national poetry a start. Burns apparently had not the opportunity of reading Dunbar, for *The Ever Green* was rare and not within reach of people without money, but the real reason was that the Calvinists had suppressed the works of Dunbar and the poets of his period. That was the effect of Calvinism up till Burns' time.[95]

But to show how persistent and far reaching it had been, poetry being a thing I'm too much interested in to read in a public library, I decided as a result of a discussion 25 years ago that I ought to own a copy of Dunbar and *really* read *all his* works.

I took it for granted that for about five shillings or perhaps seven and six I could get a second-hand copy of the works of the admittedly greatest of the old time Scottish poets. I went to every likely bookshop in Paris, London, Glasgow and Edinburgh and got the only one existing at a reasonable price in Edinburgh, and of course *not at all complete*. This means that the Calvinists have kept the work of Dunbar from the *poor* student of Scottish poetry, from the time of the Reformation till the time I asked for it – from say 1565 till 1914.

Is this negligible? Not worth bothering about? I asked these booksellers to let me know when they had a complete Dunbar. I got from one a letter saying that I could find three volumes of Dunbar in volumes 1–10 of the Scottish Text Society at £25, and that the best Dunbar had been done in Germany. In other words, Dunbar was for the rich antiquary.

This has the effect of making me feel a great admiration for David Laing of the Signet Library, who in 1834 published a complete Dunbar, without apologies or whitewash. So, if 'Time still spares the Thistle and the Rose' no thanks to the Calvinists.

No decent-living person needs Calvinism. The Calvinist is self-condemned by admitting the necessity of it to force him to conduct himself decently. Why doesn't he try Christianity? No decent drinker needs prohibition and no healthy decent eater needs restricted diet. The effects of Calvinism on Scotland have been as destructive as the effects of prohibition in America. Aware of and allowing for subtle side reasons, they were both intended to be correctives. In the case of America, a young and vigorous nation, a stupid law inevitably produced lawlessness. In the case of Scotland the submissive submitted, and the others just left for some place where life was reasonably human.

Every other reason but Calvinism has been given to explain the de-populating of Scotland. According to the Times Atlas most of it was less populated than Siberia about 25 years ago. Trade is diminishing. Do the people who are supporting the present out-of-date state of affairs really expect the country to produce workmen, business men, statesmen, writers, musicians, artists, etc., with imagination or creative force?

I should think they would say they can do without the artist, writer, musician type. Well then, suppose all the imagination and creative force is going into the business men, on the kind of life offered, can they raise them?

Perhaps what is at the back of their minds is, 'Let others take the risk of inventing things, we'll sell them'.'

I had an interesting experience in London recently. I was asked to dinner with some successful businessmen, *very nice people*. After dinner naturally they discussed business. As I am well aware that business people think artists are merely inspired idiots unless they can show they have made lots of money, I kept quiet and listened. Perhaps on account of an extra glass of port I stupidly said, 'But where do you put the inventor in all this?' One of them turned and looked at me amazed and said, 'Oh! Those mugs are being born every minute.' The man that wastes his time inventing, which means creating, is a mug. The only person they respect, or at least feel they have to watch, is the clever salesman, the person who takes inventions and makes money by them.

The salesman type of artist takes ready-made accepted forms of art and sells them. Why not? No reason why he shouldn't. I am not trying to show that he is inferior; I am trying to explain that there's a difference, and I am submitting that a country can't thrive or develop on only one of these.

It is necessary to have people to sell things; it is necessary also to have people to create things to sell. The Americans talk of selling an *idea*. Quite right, but can ideas, even saleable ones, be produced where life is restricted, and among people who have come to accept restriction as a *normal state*? For a time as a recreation, yes! possibly, but I don't believe it can go on.

Bernard Shaw said, 'Beer is the anaesthetic that enables the British working man to undergo the operation of living.'[96] I think that the greatly accepted idea that art is only produced by artificial stimulants is all wrong, and has led to a great deal of opposition between the creative type and what's called the normal person.

The position has been that the independent creative type has had so little support or so much opposition that to survive even long enough to do something he has had to take to artificial stimulants instead of doing the work on good food, fresh air and sunshine, in short in healthy conditions.

Someone has said that 'Art flourishes where food is most plentiful'. They probably meant that the artist could have *some* when there is an overflow. But if the value of the artist was understood people would see that he got *enough*, and if he *was* an artist that wouldn't need to be much.

In India it has always been understood that the teacher had to be supported, and if the artist is not a teacher, who is? That is again if he *is* an artist. This will, of course, be immediately understood to be asking charity for the artist. *Not at all*. It's paying for a contribution to the *spiritual side* of life which anyone worthy of being called a human being will admit necessary, but it can be done without! It's not absolutely necessary! Yes! It can be done without. It is not *immediately* necessary.

This is where we come back to Calvinism, which tries to reduce life to necessities, and thank God few people have arrived at the point where they accept a life consisting in mere necessities.

But a little more examination of the Calvinist quickly shows that he does not live on mere necessities, he revels in the enjoyment of seeing people stopped, frustrated, deprived. He can do with little food, without alcohol, without theatres, dance halls, cinemas and other abodes of the devil; with plenty of strong tea, bread and jam, the exultation of seeing someone fail in the attempt to get some joy out of life, and the conviction that Calvinism is Christianity. He is, no, not happy, for that would be immoral. No, certainly not even pretending to be happy. He is, he considers, qualifying for the next world by his misery.

I haven't read the life of John Knox, but I like to believe that he wasn't like that. Anyway, if that is to be accepted as the character of Scotland the sooner the Scot leaves it the better for everybody, for the non-Calvinist Scot is quite a useful cheerful fellow, at least when in a country or surroundings where cheerfulness is not out of place and suspected of being only the result of too much drink. He even produces works of literature, music, painting and other signs of interest in worldly enjoyment, of beauty in its varying manifestations.

In other words, from the point of view of the Calvinist, he is lost; and that's where his tragedy begins and his malady which is nostalgia. I say it's true that the real Scot, and certainly the Highland Scot, never forgets a good turn or a bad one.

He forgives a bad turn, yes! But after he has been away from Scotland for a little time he begins to forget that he left it gladly, in the hope that there was a place where life was a fuller, more generous affair, where his ideas would be accepted – an idea for a railway from Canada to the Pacific, an idea of making it possible to see by wireless – to write something that would honour Scotland, 'that I for puir auld Scotia's sake some useful plan or book might make, or sing a song at least'.[97] He forgets what happened to William Wallace. His name may be MacGregor or his grandmother may have been a McDonald of Glencoe. He forgets that Fergusson asked his mother when he was dying, to sit on his feet to keep them warm, that Burns, when dying, wrote to borrow £5 to see his wife through childbirth. It all gradually fades out and is replaced by a 'nostalgie de la boue'.[98] Yes, it's a nostalgia for the land, for the mountains, lochs and sea and islands of his country, not for the people. It's the nostalgia of Deirdre, or expressed by her for some, and by the Canadian boat song for others, which, as Neil Munro said, has sung itself into the hearts of the highlanders:

> *From the lone sheiling on the misty island*
> *Mountains divide us, and a host of seas,*
> *But still the blood is strong, our hearts are highland*
> *And we in our dreams behold the Hebrides.*[99]

And today for thousands of Scots everywhere, by Kenneth MacLeod's 'Road to the Isles'. The memories of the meanness and misery of the Calvinists fade out and there begins to appear to the mind's eye of the exile a wonderful country of beautiful mountains, sea lochs, forests and moorlands in sunlight and rain, rivers that sound like their names – the Bruar, the Tummel, the Garry and the Tay, and the islands in the western sea towards the setting sun, that take his mind to the 'Tir nan Og'. It is because all this is in his mind's eye that I *still* believe that he can produce art if he gets any decent chance, for the mind's eye is the only eye the creative artist sees by – the eye of imagination,

> *for I'd rather be a craven, with no name or fame or scars,*
> *than turn a wanderer's heel on Moidart Bay.*
>
> NEIL MUNRO[100]

I don't blame him. No one can say that the Highlander is likely to accept the name of craven readily, but I believe that his love of the beauty of nature is to him more important than being considered courageous. So he comes back from all the ends of the earth to find that this wonderful land is much more wonderful than he dreamt; wonderful, almost uninhabited,

MODERN SCOTTISH PAINTING

and perhaps not habitable if he has ideas about freedom. Who does it belong to, this wonderful land? Anyway, when he comes back, God bless him,

> *may all evil sleep*
> *and all good awake in his way.*

KENNETH MACLEOD, 'The Blessing of the Road'[101]

Notes

[1] The Dedication: Johnnie and Lily and Harry and Jean: John Ressich and Harry McColl were two of Fergusson's close friends, Lily and Jenn, respectively, their wives. Margaret Morris, in *The Art of J.D. Fergusson* (1974), tells us that McColl was a businessman working in Paris and one of Fergusson's best friends; John Ressich she describes as Fergusson's oldest friend, a writer (his books include *Voices in the Wilderness*, 1924, *Dago Red*, 1932, and *Thir Braw Days*, 1933, collections of short stories) who in articles and in various ways helped promote Fergusson's work, and drove him on the tour of the Highlands and Islands of Scotland in 1922.

[2] The Foreword: The penultimate paragraph of the Foreword is strikingly similar to the note the great American poet Ezra Pound (1885–1972) placed at the opening of his *Guide to Kulchur* (1938). It is not likely that Fergusson was emulating Pound but their intentions evidently arose from the same impulse and commitment, and it is salutary to read Fergusson in the constellation of the great modernist artists, poets and manifesto-writers who were his contemporaries. This is Pound's note: 'This book is not written for the over-fed. It is written for men who have not been able to afford a university education or for young men, whether or not threatened with universities, who want to know more at the age of 50 than I know today, and whom I might conceivably aid to that object. I am fully aware of the dangers inherent in attempting such utility to them.'

[3] *À nous la liberté* ('Freedom for Us' or 'We want Freedom') was a 1931 French comedy-satire film directed by René Clair with music by Georges Auric, in which an escaped prisoner becomes a rich industrialist. Its satiric edge was the model for Chaplin's *Modern Times* (1936).

[4] The crisis of September 1938 was the Munich agreement, when Germany, the UK, France and Italy permitted Germany to 'annex' Sudetenland in what was then Czechoslovakia. This was effectively the prelude to Hitler's further Nazi 'occupations' in Europe. Fergusson

and Davidson must have felt that if Britain, France and Italy had not approved this Nazi move, things might have been different. Jo Davidson (1883–1952) was an American sculptor of Russian-Jewish descent, specialising in realistic portrait busts. Commissions included J.M. Barrie, Charlie Chaplin, Joseph Conrad, Arthur Conan Doyle, James Joyce, Rudyard Kipling, D.H. Lawrence, George Bernard Shaw and H.G. Wells. Stylistically his work is close to that of Auguste Rodin (1840–1917) and the Scottish Pittendrigh MacGillivray (1856–1938).

[5] *Painting and Sculpture* by J.D. Fergusson at London, Reid & Lefèvre (February 1939).

[6] The Manoir of Bécheron: Originally built in the 15th century, the main building was added in the first half of the 18th century. Davidson bought and converted it in 1925, the huge barn becoming his workshop. He lived there until his death in 1952. In April 2011, a plaque commemorating him was placed on the portal entrance.

[7] *tilleuls*: linden trees; *The Lily of the Valley* (1835): novel about love and society by Honoré de Balzac (1799–1850).

[8] Kenneth MacLeod (1871–1955), best known as the Gaelic collaborator with songwriter Marjory Kennedy-Fraser, working on a series of four volumes of Hebridean songs. His book *The Road to the Isles: Poetry, Lore, and Tradition of the Hebrides*, with an introduction by Marjory Kennedy-Fraser (Edinburgh: Robert Grant & Son, 1927), ends with 'The Road to the Isles' (p.244). This song begins:

> It's a far croonin' that is pullin' me away,
> As take I wi' my cromak to the road.
> It's the far Coolins that are puttin' love on me,
> As step I wi' the sunlight for my load.
>
> Sure, by Tummel an' Loch Rannoch an' Lochaber I will go,
> By heather tracks wi' heaven in their wiles,
> If you're thinkin' in your inner heart braggart's in my step,
> You've never smelt the tangle o' the Isles.
> It's the far Coolins that are puttin' love on me,
> As step I wi' my cromak to the Isles.

The poem that begins the book is 'Blessing of the Road', from which Fergusson quotes at the very end of *Modern Scottish Painting*. Evidently, Fergusson held this sourcebook of Celtic songs, lore and poems, in high regard, taking references to open and close his own manifesto, to emphasise the distinctively Celtic identity he wanted to endorse.

[9] James MacNeil Whistler (1834–1903), *The Gentle Art Of Making Enemies* (1890), partly a transcript of Whistler's famous libel suit against critic John Ruskin (1819–1900), who in a published review had referred to Whistler's painting *Nocturne in Black and Gold: The Falling Rocket* as 'flinging a pot of paint in the public's face'.

[10] Leo Frobenius (1873–1938), ethnologist and archaeologist whose writings with Douglas Fox introduced African traditional storytelling and epic to Europe. Ezra Pound corresponded with him from the 1920s.

[11] Moustiers-Sainte-Marie is a tourist resort village in Provence, southern France; the 'Moustiers' man is shorthand for a superficial observer.

[12] Robert Burns, 'A Song – ' ('To Mary in Heaven', 1789). In Burns, *Poems and Songs*, edited by James Kinsley (Oxford University Press, 1969), number 274. The last stanza is:

> Still o'er these scenes my mem'ry wakes,
> And fondly broods with miser-care;
> Time but th' impression stronger makes,
> As streams their channels deeper wear:
> My Mary! dear departed Shade!
> Where is thy blissful place of rest!
> Seest thou thy Lover lowly laid!
> Hearest thou the groans that rend his breast!

[13] John Barbour (*c.*1320–95), *The Bruce* (*c.*1376). These words are from Book 1, lines 225–28:

> A! Fredome is a noble thing!
> Fredome mays man to haiff liking;
> Fredome all solace to man giffis,
> He levys at ese that frely levys!

[14] The Declaration of Arbroath is a letter written in 1320, attributed to Bernard, Abbot of Arbroath and Chancellor of Scotland, signed by 51 senior noblemen, addressed to Pope John XXII in Rome, though possibly drafted by Robert the Bruce himself, in confirmation of the independent sovereign state of Scotland, and the authority of Robert the Bruce, King of Scots. It is the foundational document of Scotland, making two fundamental points. One is that the people of Scotland

constitute the sovereignty of the nation, not the King, and that if the
King betrays the people, he will be replaced. In other words, the head
of state is a King by selection. The second point is that the people
have the right to freedom and the responsibility to defend that
freedom. Although what we understand by democracy in the 21st
century was not a political option in 14th-century Scotland, it is
nevertheless possible to read the Declaration of Arbroath as a
foundational document in the development of the western idea of
what democracy would become.

[15] Burns, 'A Man's a Man for a' That' (1795), Kinsley 482. The third
verse runs:

> Ye see yon birkie, ca'd, a lord,
> Wha struts, an' stares, an' a' that;
> Though hundreds worship at his word,
> He's but a coof for a' that:
> For a' that, an' a' that,
> His ribband, star and a' that:
> The man of independant mind,
> He looks an' laughs at a' that. –

When this was sung by Sheena Wellington as a semi-official anthem at
the reopening of the Scottish Parliament in 1999, certain critical
attitudes were expressed by members of the landowning aristocracy.

[16] RA: The Royal Academy of Arts is an art institution based in
Burlington House, Piccadilly, London, founded by King George III in
1768 with the idea of establishing approved training, judgement and
expertise in the arts, and to arrange exhibitions of contemporary
works. Ideologically significant as a 'national' (British) establishment
legitimising fashionable establishment 'good taste', the painter Joshua
Reynolds (1723–92) was its first president.

[17] Dr John Moore (1729–1802), military physician, academic,
intellectual and author of books on medicine, culture and the *Journal
during a Residence in France* (1793), an eye-witness account of the
French Revolution, as well as a novel, *Zeluco* (1789). Moore read
Burns's *Poems* in the Kilmarnock Edition in 1786 and invited Burns to
write to him, which Burns was shy to do, but eventually responded
deferentially but with important autobiographical letters.

[18] Miguel de Unamuno (1864–1936), Spanish novelist, essayist, philosopher, poet and playwright, intellectual and modernist, whose political nationalism led him into confrontation with fascism towards the end of his life.

[19] *Apollo* is a monthly arts magazine founded in 1925, based in London.

[20] The Glasgow School usually refers to painter and glass artist Margaret MacDonald, her husband the architect Charles Rennie Mackintosh, her sister Frances and Herbert MacNair; there were also the Glasgow Girls, who, along with the MacDonald sisters, included Jessie M. King, Annie French and Jessie Wylie Newbery, Bessie MacNicol and Eleanor Allen Moore. However, Fergusson is here referring specifically to the group now more familiarly known as the Glasgow Boys, a loose collective term whose realist paintings depicted rural or Glasgow-based (though hardly ever working-class urban) scenes, their number including Joseph Crawhall (1861–1913), James Guthrie (1859–1930), George Henry (1858–1943), E.A. Hornel (1864–1933), E.A. Walton (1860–1922), David Gauld (1865–1936), William Kennedy (1859–1918), John Lavery (1856–1941), Harrington Mann (1864–1937), David Young Cameron (1865–1945), Alexander Ignatius Roche (1861–1923), Arthur Melville (1855–1904), John Quinton Pringle (1864–1925), James Paterson (1854–1932) and William York Macgregor (1855–1923).

[21] Fergusson draws attention especially to George Henry's *A Galloway Landscape* (1889), the collaborative work of Henry and Hornel such as *The Druids* (1887), Arthur Melville, James Guthrie's *The Garden Party* (1918) and James Lavery's *Miss Mary Burrel* (1894).

[22] Aitken Dott (1815–92) began the business in Edinburgh in 1842 and his son Peter McOmish Dott (1856–1934), set up 'The Scottish Gallery', displaying work by many Scottish painters, including the Scottish Colourists and Edinburgh School artists.

[23] Robert Burns, 'The Kirk of Scotland's Garland – a new song' (1789), Kinsley 264. It begins:

> Orthodox, Orthodox, who believe in John Knox,
> Let me sound an alarm to your conscience;
> A heretic blast has been blawn i' the West –
> That what is not Sense must be Nonsense, Orthodox,
> That what is not Sense must be nonsense.

[24] The Scottish Academy and the 'RA of Scotland': The Royal Scottish
     Academy (RSA) was founded in 1826 as the Scottish Academy
     (becoming the Royal Scottish Academy when granted a royal charter
     in 1838). It is not to be confused with the London Royal Academy.

[25] André Dunoyer de Segonzac (1884–1974) was a French painter and
     graphic artist, one of the modernists included in the Armory Show,
     New York (1913), whose first solo exhibition, at the Galerie Levesque
     in Paris, was in 1914, and whose experiences in the First World War
     led him to a produce a long series of etchings and drawings; Claude
     Monet (1840–1926) was the founder of French Impressionism, the
     term arising from the title of his painting, *Impression, Sunrise* (1872).

[26] David Martin, *The Glasgow School of Painting*, with an introduction
     by Francis H. Newbery (London: George Bell & Sons, 1897; reprinted
     Edinburgh: Paul Harris Publishing, 1976).

[27] Rembrandt van Rijn (1606–1669), Dutch artist and one of the
     greatest portraitists and self-portraitists; Jean-Auguste-Dominique
     Ingres (1780–1867), French painter of neoclassical historical scenes
     and portraits. Fergusson seems to be characterising Ingres as a
     conventional academic painter, as opposed to the rising Romanticism
     of Delacroix (1798–1863). Fergusson misses the radical aspect of
     Ingres, that he was the painter of some of the most erotic female
     nudes in the western tradition, and that he was a significant influence
     on Picasso, especially after the First World War.

[28] Jules Bastien-Lepage (1848–1884) and Pascal-Adolphe-Jean Dagnan-
     Bouveret (1852–1929), were both French naturalist painters.

[29] William-Adolphe Bougereau (1825–1905); Raphaël Collin (1850–
     1916); Gustave-Claude-Étienne Courtois (1852–1923); Jean-Paul
     Laurens (1838–1921); Jean-Léon Gérôme (1824–1904), were all
     French academic painters.

[30] Giorgione (*c.*1477–1510) Italian Renaissance painter; Diego
     Rodríguez de Silva y Velázquez (1599–1660), Spanish artist of the
     Golden Age of Spanish painting; Adolphe Joseph Thomas Monticelli
     (1824–1886) and Jean-Baptiste-Camille Corot (1796–1875) were both
     French artists whose work clearly anticipates Impressionism.

[31] *'pompier'* professors: *l'art pompier* signifies 'Fireman Art', a derisive
     late-19th-century term for large, academic paintings, usually of an

historical or allegorical type, in which characters were depicted with Greek-style helmets like those worn by contemporary French firemen; the term also suggests *pompeux* (pompous). Fergusson is evidently scornful of paintings by Bougereau, Collin, Courtois and Jean Paul Laurens, as officially-approved, insincere, over-inflated and bad art.

[32] The penultimate verse of 'Braid Claith' (1772), a satire on pretentiousness, by Robert Fergusson (1750–74), runs:

> Braid Claith lends fock an unco heese,
> Makes mony kail-worms butterflies,
> Gies mony a doctor his degrees
> > For little skaith:
> In short, you may be what you please
> > Wi' gude Braid Claith.

[33] William Kennedy (1859–1918), born in Glasgow, studied at Paisley School of Art before moving to the Académie Julian, and staying in Paris till 1885. He became president of the Glasgow Boys group in 1887, painting army life in the military camp near Stirling, before moving in 1912 to Tangier, Morocco.

[34] 'But tae oor tale': Burns, 'Tam o' Shanter', Kinsley 321, line 37.

[35] Robert Burns, '[To Dr Blacklock]', Kinsley 273B, lines 49–54:

> But to conclude my silly rhyme,
> (I'm scant o' verse and scant o' time,)
> To make a happy fireside clime
> > To weans and wife,
> That's the true *Pathos* and *Sublime*
> > Of Human life. –

[36] George Davison (1854–1930), an English 'impressionistic' and experimental photographer and civil servant, co-founder of the 'Linked Ring Brotherhood' of British artists. After early investment in Kodak, he became a director of Kodak UK and a millionaire. He was asked to resign his directorship of Kodak due to his sympathetic interests in social reform and anarchism.

[37] John Forbes White (1831–1904), director of the North of Scotland Bank and Aberdeen Jute Company, was a pioneer of amateur photography and a collector of innovative contemporary art.

[38] Jean-François Millet (1814–1875), French painter, famous for his

depictions of peasant working people, a founder of the Barbizon
school (typified by proto-Impressionist, rural scenes, named after the
village where its artist-members gathered). Millet was the great
painter of peasant naturalism whose art, in the aftermath of 1848,
became a rallying-point for aspirations towards social reform.
Jean-Baptiste-Camille Corot (1796–1875), French landscape painter
of the Barbizon school, anticipating Impressionism. Narcisse Virgilio
Díaz de la Peña (1807–1876), French painter of the Barbizon school.
Adolphe Joseph Thomas Monticelli (1824–1886), French painter of
the generation before the Impressionists. Johannes Bosboom (1817–
1891), Dutch painter in oil and watercolour of the Hague school.
Anthonij (Anton) Rudolf Mauve (1838–1888), Dutch realist painter
of the Hague school, early influence on his cousin-in-law, Vincent van
Gogh. Jacob Maris (1837–1899), Matthias Maris (1839–1917) and
Willem Maris (1844–1910) were Dutch painters of the Hague school.
Jozef Israëls (1824–1911), Dutch painter of the Hague school, whose
son Isaac Lazarus Israëls (1865–1934) was also a Dutch painter
closely associated with the Amsterdam Impressionists.

[39] John Forbes White of Aberdeen. See above, note 37.

[40] 'Flowers in the garden, meat in the hall, a butt of wine, and a spice of
wit': The first verse of the opening poem of *Underwoods* (1887), by
Robert Louis Stevenson (1850–94), runs:

> Go, little book, and wish to all
> Flowers in the garden, meat in the hall,
> A bin of wine, a spice of wit,
> A house with lawns enclosing it,
> A living river by the door,
> A nightingale in the sycamore!

[41] International Exhibitions: the Glasgow International Exhibition
(1901), the Scottish Exhibition of National History, Art and Industry
(1911), the Empire Exhibition (1938).

[42] James Abbott McNeill Whistler (1834–1903), American-born artist of
Scots descent, opposed to sentimentality and eager to engage in
controversy. Whistler's sister-in-law made a generous donation to the
Hunterian Art Gallery at the University of Glasgow, which has had a
lasting and profound influence on Glasgow artists from the 1890s
onwards. Walter Richard Sickert (1880–1942), born in Munich,

Germany, painter and an important influence on British avant-garde art in the period from Impressionism to Modernism. Ethel Walker (1861–1951), Edinburgh-born painter of portraits, still lifes and seascapes, influenced by Impressionism and Gaugain.

[43] James Ferrier Pryde (1866–1941), Scottish artist whose landscapes, cityscapes and theatre posters and designs often evoke monumentalism and human frailty. People in his work are 'transitory figures in a world of decay' and the light in his landscapes seems always to be a northern one. Where we do have an expanse of sky it is generally screened by clouds. *The Flying Dutchman* (c.1911) is being chased into harbour by an incoming storm, *The Deserted Garden* (c.1909) cast into shadows. Often the sky is only just glimpsed behind the looming focal structure, as in *The Red Ruin*. It's tempting to see the city of Pryde's birth in the high walls and obscured heavens. (See Louise Welsh, 'James Pryde: The Edgar Allan Poe of Painting', in *The Bottle Imp* (online magazine, issue 6, November 2009).

[44] William Sharp (1855–1905), from 1893, wrote under his own name but also that of Fiona MacLeod, deeply engaged in promoting the Celtic Twilight or 'Celtic Revival', a movement drawing on Celtic traditions in Ireland and Britain and most famous in the shape of the Irish Literary Revival, with writers such as W.B. Yeats, Lady Gregory and 'AE' (George Russell). Some critics and literary historians have seen this in opposition to Modernism while others have seen vital connections between the revitalising of ancient traditions and the engagement with modernity.

[45] Emile Zola (1840–1902), *The Masterpiece* (1886), a novel describing Zola's (fictional) friendship with Paul Cézanne and the Parisian art world in the mid-19th century.

[46] Charles Rennie Mackintosh (1868–1928), Scottish architect, artist and designer, influential in Europe, his masterpiece being the Glasgow School of Art. Mackintosh was married to Margaret MacDonald (1864–1933), artist and designer who defined the main features of the 'Glasgow Style' of the 1890s. Francis Henry Newbery or Fra Newbery (1855–1946), painter and art teacher, director of the Glasgow School of Art (1885–1917), when the School developed an international reputation. Newbery effectively commissioned Mackintosh to design the School and worked closely and encouragingly with him.

[47] Rudyard Kipling (1865–1936). These are lines 4–5 of 'McAndrew's Hymn' (1894). Kipling himself gives the phonetic roll to 'enorrmous'. The connection made here is between the reliable working of the engineer's mechanical design and the Calvinist doctrine of predestination. The irony lies in the fact that the former is desirable and of palpable human benefit, while the latter is repugnant and constrictive of humanity. From the epigraph on, in this chapter Fergusson's argument is sustained by subtlety and good humour.

[48] Stephen Phillips (1864–1915), English poet and dramatist, commissioned by the actor-manager Sir George Alexander, to write the play *Paolo and Francesca*, based on an episode in Dante's *Inferno*, and it was successfully produced in 1902.

[49] Bougereau, see above; Lord Leighton (1830–1896), English painter and sculptor, depicting historical, biblical and classical subjects. Sir Lawrence Alma-Tadema (1836–1912), Dutch painter. Marcus Stone (1840–1921), English painter. John MacWhirter (1839–1911), Scottish landscape painter. Benjamin Williams Leader (1831–1923), English landscape painter.

[50] Burns, 'Tam o' Shanter' again.

[51] William Blake (1757–1827), English poet and painter, generally unesteemed in his lifetime, and thought of as insane by some contemporaries. Openly hostile to Church of England orthodoxies and organised religion, he approved the revolutions in France and America and was a friend of Thomas Paine (1737–1809), author of *The Rights of Man* (1791). Holding Michelangelo and Raphael in high regard, he rejected the fashionable artists of the period, especially Joshua Reynolds, first president of London's Royal Academy.

[52] Louis Pasteur (1822–95), French chemist and microbiologist. The Curies: Polish-born Marie Skłodowska (1867–1934) met the French chemist Pierre Curie (1859–1906) and they married in 1895, devoting their careers to the study radioactivity (a term Marie coined), discovering the elements polonium and radium, and winning Nobel prizes in physics and chemistry. They lived in conditions of near poverty. John Logie Baird (1888–1946), Scottish scientist, engineer and inventor whose role in pioneering the technology of television has made him a figure of historical significance.

[53] Fergusson emphasises human value in a way that points forward to the American poet Edward Dorn's comments in an interview of 1991 reprinted in *Ed Dorn Live: Lectures, Interviews, and Outtakes*, edited by Joseph Richey (2007). Asked if he thought books were going to become obsolete, Dorn replied, 'Books are obsolete right now, and have been for a long, long time.' Asked then if that means poetry must be obsolete, his answer was this: 'There are a lot of great things that are obsolete. Kerosene lamps are obsolete, but there's no light like it in a cabin in northern Wisconsin. And maybe it's a good thing not to have electricity. Think of the best things in the world, actually, and they're all obsolete. Sure. But that's because a world that grows more and more venal and greedy and opportunistic makes things obsolete at a great rate, and what they replace it with is something pretty awful and foul and cheap and temporary and terrible. So poetry is real obsolete.' Fergusson's sense of human value, like Dorn's, distinguishes itself emphatically from blind adherence to scientific progress and reliance upon the machine. Fergusson, like Dorn, sees the intrinsic human value in the storyteller, the singer, the dancer and the artist. It's worth noting this affinity across vast differences of history and culture as it indicates the intrinsic humanity of the arts to which these men were committed.

[54] How prophetic is this!

[55] In *The Poems of William Dunbar*, edited by Priscilla Bawcutt (Glasgow: Association for Scottish Literary Studies, 2 volumes, 1998), lines 36–40 of poem 77, 'How Dunbar wes Desyrd to be ane Freir' are:

> In freiris weid full fairly haif I fleichit.
> In it haif in pulpet gon and preichit,
> In Derntoun kirk and eik in Canterberry,
> In it I past at Dover our the ferry
> Throw Piccardy, and thair the peple teachit.

Derntoun is Darlington, county Durham.

[56] The Scots College was part of the University of Paris, established in 1333. In 1793 the University was restructured along different lines. The Rue des Ecossais (Scotland Street) is in the Sorbonne district of Paris.

[57] Picasso was born in Spain but spent most of his life in France. Van
Gogh was born in the Netherlands but lived in England (on and off,
1873–77), Nuenen and Antwerp (1883–1886), Paris (1886–1888) and
Arles (1888–1889). Van Dongen (1877–1968), was also Dutch, but in
1906, he took up residence in Paris and was in the company of Picasso
and others, then from 1959, he was based in Monaco. Amedeo Clemente
Modigliani (1884–1920) was Italian, but worked mostly in France.

[58] Neil Munro, the third and final verse of 'The Heather at My Door',
published in *Blackwood's Magazine* (1896), runs:

> A hunter's fare is all I would be craving,
> A shepherd's plaiding and a beggar's pay,
> If I might earn them where the heather, waving,
> Gave fragrance all the day.
> The stars might see me, homeless one and weary,
> Without a roof to fend me from the dew,
> And still, content, I'd find a bedding cheery,
> Where'er the heather grew.

[59] Pablo Picasso (1881–1973), Spanish artist, co-founder with Georges
Braque (1882–1963), French artist, of the Cubist movement in
1909–10.

[60] John Ruskin (1819–1900), in *Modern Painters* (1843–60) argued in
support of the later work of J.M.W. Turner (1775–1851), and that
landscape painting should especially address the accurate depiction of
nature, beginning from its geological foundations.

[61] From Kipling, 'McAndrew's Hymn', but Fergusson makes the line more
Scots by changing the first phrase, the spelling of Burns's first name and
using the word 'sang'. In Kipling's poem, lines 148–55 run thus:

> Romance! Those first-class passengers they like it very well,
> Printed an' bound in little books; but why don't poets tell?
> I'm sick of all their quirks an' turns – the loves an' doves they
>   dream –
> Lord, send a man like Robbie Burns to sing the Song o' Steam!
> To match wi' Scotia's noblest speech yon orchestra sublime
> Whaurto – uplifted like the Just – the tail-rods mark the time.
> The Crank-throws give the double-bass; the feed-pump sobs an'
>   heaves:
> An' now the main eccentrics start their quarrel on the sheaves.

[62] John Milton (1608–74), *Comus* (1634), lines 476–80:

> How charming is divine philosophy!
> Not harsh and crabbed, as dull fools suppose,
> But musical as is Apollo's lute,
> And a perpetual feast of nectared sweets,
> Where no crude surfeit reigns.

[63] The word 'makar' refers to the older Scots poets, pre-eminently Robert Henryson (*c.*1460–1500), William Dunbar (*c.*1460-after 1513) and Gavin Douglas (*c.*1474–1522), known as the Scots Makars. In English literary critical history, these poets used to be referred to as the 'Scottish Chaucerians', suggesting a subordinate status. This term is no longer used. The word 'makar' was returned to common currency in the 21st century with the Scottish Government's appointment of Edwin Morgan to the role of 'Scots Makar' or 'National Poet', effectively the Poet Laureate of Scotland, in 2004, a post he held till his death in 2010, after which it was accepted by Liz Lochhead.

[64] The Prix de Rome was a scholarship awarded by the French government for young French artists to study at the Académie de France in Rome.

[65] An '*arrêt*': a stop, a sign of closure and fixity. Fergusson is saying that a 'finished' drawing or painting is determined to be completed not in an absolute, self-realised sense, but as a statement made in the context of dialogue with those who would see it or read it closely. All works of art take part in this living dialogue.

[66] An '*arreté*': something settled and fixed in order.

[67] The *métier*: the job, trade or expertise.

[68] 'The price of liberty is eternal vigilance' is usually attributed to Thomas Jefferson (1743–1826), but there seems to be no evidence for this.

[69] See note 12, above.

[70] 'Scots wha ha'e' are the opening words of Burns's song, 'Robert Bruce's March to Bannockburn – ' (1793), Kinsley 425:

> Scots wha ha'e wi' WALLACE bled,
> Scots, wham Bruce has aften led,
> Welcome to your gory bed, –
> Or to victorie. –

However, the patriotic fervour for freedom embodied in the song is easily quoted and too often superficially applied by pompous hypocrites, as Hugh MacDiarmid reminds us in his vitriolic diatribe against all those types of Scots he detests, in *Lucky Poet* (London: Methuen, 1943): 'the whole gang of high mucky-mucks, famous fatheads, old wives of both sexes, stuffed shirts, hollow men with head pieces stuffed with straw, bird-wits, lookers-under-beds, trained seals, creeping Jesuses, Scots Wha Ha'evers, village idiots…' Fergusson is emphasising that freedom, free thinking, the independence of informed critical judgement, applies just as much in art as in politics – in all thinking, in fact.

[71] Another striking similarity here with Ezra Pound, who, in his essay 'The Serious Artist' from *The Egoist* (1913), says this: 'The arts give us a great percentage of the lasting and unassailable data regarding the nature of man, of immaterial man, of man considered as a thinking and sentient creature. They begin where the science of medicine leaves off or rather they overlap that science. The borders of the two arts overcross.' Ezra Pound, 'The Serious Artist', in *How to Read* (London: Faber and Faber, 1954; reprinted 1974), pp.41–57 (p. 42).

[72] Formors: In Celtic mythology the Formors or Fomors are the beings who preceded the gods, as in Greek mythology the Titans preceded the Olympian gods. They embody chaos and the wild, whereas the Tuatha dé Danann are the gods of humanity.

[73] The sandblasting of the magnificent buildings of Glasgow in the 1980s did in fact make the dark, sooty and dirt-covered atmosphere of the city much brighter, so Fergusson is not being wishful here so much as prophetic.

[74] Stanza seven of Burns's 'Epistle to a Young Friend' (1786), Kinsley 105:

> To catch Dame Fortune's golden smile,
> Assiduous wait upon her;
> And gather gear by ev'ry wile,
> That 's justify'd by Honor:
> Not for to *hide* it in a *hedge*,
> Not for a *train-attendant*;
> But for the glorious priviledge
> Of being *independant*.

[75] Again, it is worth noting the similarity between the distinctions
Fergusson is making here and those made by Ezra Pound, noting the
six different types of important writer, in his *ABC of Reading* (1934),
Chapter Four, part two: the Inventors, the Masters, the Diluters, the
Good writers without salient qualities, the Writers of *belles-lettres* and
the Starters of crazes. Unless you can identify confidently writers in
the first two categories, Pound advises, you might know what you like
but you'll never be able to work out the value of one book in relation
to others. The same applies in all the arts.

[76] See note 31, above.

[77] Malcolm Arbuthnot (1877–1967), Alexander Jamieson (1873–1937),
Frank Dobson (1888–1963), Frank Rutter (1876–1937), Randolph
Schwabe (1885–1948), Charles Ginner (1878–1952), E. McKnight
Kauffer (1890–1954).

[78] In the summers of 1963, '64 and '65, John Bellany and Alexander
Moffat tied their work to railings outside the Scottish National Gallery
during the Edinburgh Festival. Bellany's 'Allegory' (an enormous 13 x
7 foot triptych), was among the works shown. In Moffat's words:
'That was the period when our generation did make a stand. There
was very little representation of Scottish art at the official Edinburgh
Festival, so we thought that if we can't get in the official festival, we'd
put it into the streets. Scottish art didn't really exist. It existed in the
studios of Edinburgh College of Art, but it didn't exist in the arts
establishment, which was completely Anglicised.' Once again, Fergusson
is making accurate prophetic speculations about art and society.

[79] Fergusson prefigures one of the central questions of modernism and
postmodernism here, in his pressing at the relation between content
and form, or the relation between depth of meaning and surface
appearance, that applies across the arts, not only in painting and
sculpture but also in architecture and poetry. One key summary is
arrived at in the correspondence of the American poets Charles Olson
and Robert Creeley, in Creeley's words: 'Form is never more than an
extension of content.' See letter of 5 June 1950, in Charles Olson and
Robert Creeley, *The Complete Correspondence*, volume I, edited by
George F. Butterick (Santa Rosa: Black Sparrow Press, 1980), p. 79.
(It occurs again in a letter of 1951, in volume VIII, p. 50.) Another is
a more proverbial adage: 'Content forms and form contents.'

[80] Arguably the most valuable discussion of this is the essay by John Berger, 'The Moment of Cubism', first published in *The New Left Review* in 1969 and widely anthologised. Berger's essential proposition was that Cubism 'changed the nature of the relationship between the painted image and reality' and therefore presented a new way of understanding the relationship between reality and humanity. The 'moment of Cubism' occurred 'when the promises of the future were more substantial than the present'. It is the moment of intimation of human potential, an understanding created particularly in works of art when the possibility of what might be becomes fully present. For Fergusson, this would be an affirmation of the most essential quality in art, politics, individual and social life: freedom, independence, Walt Whitman stepping out onto the open road.

[81] Walt Whitman (1819–93), the opening verse-paragraph of section five of 'Song of the Open Road' begins:

> From this hour I ordain myself loos'd of limits and imaginary
>   lines,
> Going where I list, my own master total and absolute,
> Listening to others, considering well what they say,
> Pausing, searching, receiving, contemplating,
> Gently, but with undeniable will, divesting myself of the holds
>   that would hold me.
> I inhale great draughts of space,
> The east and the west are mine, and the north and the south are
>   mine.

[82] The 'land o' the leal': the land of the loyal, heaven.

[83] Compare Hugh MacDiarmid, 'To R.M.B.', in *Stony Limits and Other Poems* (London: Gollancz, 1934):

> Nae man, nae spiritual force, can live
> In Scotland lang. For God's sake leave it tae
> Mak' a warld o' your ain like me, and if
> 'Idiot' or 'lunatic' the Scots folk say
> At least you'll ken – owre weel to argue back
> You'd be better that than lackin' a' they lack!

It is, of course, quite possible that Fergusson had read this book.

                    MODERN SCOTTISH PAINTING

[84] Robert Burns, 'To W. S*****n, Ochiltree' (1785) (William Simson),
      Kinsley 59, lines 19–24:

> O *Ferguson*! thy glorious *parts*,
> Ill-suited *law*'s dry, musty arts!
> My curse upon your whunstane hearts,
>   Ye Enbrugh Gentry!
> The tythe o' what ye waste at *cartes*
>   Wad stow'd his pantry!

[85] The Klondike, in the Yukon, in Canada, is famous because of the
      Gold Rush, which took place there from 1897 to 1899.

[86] Walter Emanuel (1869–1915) was a solicitor and author flourishing
      around the turn of the century in the short-lived satiric, humorous
      magazine *The Butterfly*. He also produced *One Hundred Years Hence:
      Being Some Extracts from the Hourly Mail of A.D. 2000* (1911), a
      newspaper satirising contemporary life.

[87] The Curies: see above, note 51. Édouard Eugène Désiré Branly
      (1844–1940), French physicist and inventor, involved in wireless
      telegraphy and physiotherapy and electrotherapy in medicine.

[88] The 1890s was known as the *fin de siècle*, the end of the era. Wilde
      published *The Picture of Dorian Grey* (1890) and *Salome* (1891),
      Conan Doyle the first Sherlock Holmes story (1891), Kipling *The
      Jungle Book* (1894), H.G. Wells *The Time Machine* (1895), Stoker
      Dracula (1897) and Joseph Conrad *Heart of Darkness* (1899–1900).
      The period saw the increasing importance of *Art Nouveau* as a style
      and a heady mix of political imperialist self-justification, imaginative
      fantasy, Gothic exoticism and so-called social and personal decadence
      and permissiveness. Wilde and Whistler were considered by the
      establishment to be at the forefront of the decadence, with Wilde's
      notorious court case stigmatising his homosexuality in 1895, after
      which he was imprisoned and died in poverty in Paris in 1900.
      Whistler's emphasis in his paintings on musical or atmospheric
      qualities (titles often used words like 'nocturne', 'symphony',
      'arrangement') affected a public critique of conventional narrative art
      and realistic depictions of sharply focused scenes. When John Ruskin
      condemned Whistler's painting *Nocturne in Black and Gold: The
      Falling Rocket* in 1877, the artist took him to court for libel, hoping

for recompense and the costs of his action. Fellow-artists backed away, worried about their reputations. The jury found in favour of Whistler, but awarded a farthing (one quarter of a penny) in damages. Whistler lost money and popularity because of the case. He published an account of the whole business with transcripts from the trial in *The Gentle Art of Making Enemies* (1890), as noted above.

[89] This is a key statement of Fergusson's commitment to 'the arts of peace'. He repudiates commercial and military priorities and instead he emphatically validates the purpose of the arts in the celebration, exploration and enactment of humanity. As a manifesto of decided purpose, as opposed to *laissez-faire* opportunism, surfing whatever waves come along in their economic peaks and troughs, this is a lasting challenge to everyone engaged in the arts in whatever capacity, and particularly to the leaders of the educational institutions as noted in this chapter's title.

[90] In the late autumn of 1931, The Society of Scottish Artists organised a small Edvard Munch exhibition in Edinburgh. This was the first time Munch's paintings had been seen in Scotland, or indeed in the UK. Rolf E. Stenersen recounts in his biography of the artist, *Edvard Munch: Close-Up of a Genius* first published in Sweden in 1944: 'In the 1930s, Munch selected 12 paintings to be crated and sent to Edinburgh for exhibition. After the crate had been nailed shut, however, he reopened it, removed one canvas and replaced it with two others. Later, learning that the Edinburgh exhibition included only 12 of his pictures, he paced the floor in great agitation as he commented to me on the news: "My best picture may have been stolen…" When the crate arrived back from Edinburgh, Munch insisted on opening it personally. As he pulled out the first canvas he remarked, "Aha, that one the thief didn't want. It'll be exciting to see what he has chosen. Who knows, it may have been a thief with good taste." There were thirteen canvases in the crate. The 13th, a reclining nude, the puritanical Scotsmen had withheld from the exhibition.'

This incident tells us a great deal about cultural life in Scotland in the 1930s. It certainly proves Fergusson's claim that the Scots were afraid to hang paintings of nudes on their walls and the hostile reception the exhibition received is symptomatic of a nation where, in Fergusson's words, 'the destructiveness of Calvinism' had crushed the imaginative lives of the people.

Robert Hurd (1905–63), an architect who specialised in conservation and President of the Saltire Society from 1943 to 1948, in a letter to *The Scotsman* (8 December 1931) begins by saying: 'The letters that have appeared in your columns, and the first article of your critic, reflect in the simplest manner the general reaction of the Scottish public that seems to have met (in Munch's paintings) extreme modernism face to face for the first time. Our ignorance of contemporary Continental art is revealed to the world at large with disarming frankness: and we seem almost proud of our ignorance. Continental ideas filter through to us so slowly that when by an amazing stroke of good luck an exhibition of really modern painting does occur in Scotland, we are discovered sitting in the dark, so to speak, and naturally resent the glaring light that makes us all blink so much that we can scarcely see sufficiently even to put our spluttering pens to paper to exclaim to the editor of *The Scotsman* that we hope (piously of course) that God will preserve us from any more of this modern "stuff".'

In a further letter to *The Scotsman* (18 December 1931) Hurd concludes: 'The critical opinion recently displayed has indeed brought to the surface an unconscious narrowness of vision that seems to increase within us alongside the growth of that provinciality which threatens to make Scotland in some ways the most backward and philistine country in Northern Europe.'

[91] William Dunbar, 'The Thistle and the Rose' (Bawcutt 52), lines 60–63:

> O luvaris fo, away thow dully nycht,
> And welcum day that confortis everywicht.
> Haill, May, haill, Flora, haill, Aurora schene!
> Haill, princes Natur, haill, Venus, luvis quene!'

[92] Robert Burns, 'To a Louse, On Seeing one on a Lady's Bonnet at Church' (1785), Kinsley 83, lines 43–48.

[93] Robert Burns, 'To the Rev. John M'Math, Inclosing a copy of *Holy Willie's Prayer*, which he had requested' (1785), Kinsley 68, lines 49–54.

[94]   As also was the great choral church music of Robert Carver
       (c.1485–c.1570), which went unperformed for centuries.

[95]   This continued until Allan Ramsay (1686–1758), in *The Ever Green,
       being a collection of Scots poems, wrote by the ingenious before
       1600* (1724), published an anthology of older Scottish poems
       including work by William Dunbar, anonymous traditional ballads
       and 'The Vision' by Ramsay himself. It had the effect of introducing
       the older Scots poetic tradition to its contemporary readers and
       helping to regenerate that tradition.

[96]   Attributed to George Bernard Shaw (1856–1950) is the line,
       'Alcohol is the anaesthesia by which we endure the operation of life.'
       However, it seems to have no definite source and is also attributed to
       Samuel Johnson (1709–84) in the *Life of Samuel Johnson* (1791) by
       James Boswell (1740–95).

[97]   Robert Burns, the third verse of 'The Answer' (1787), Kinsley, 147B,
       runs:

           Ev'n then a wish (I mind its power)
           A wish, that to my latest hour
               Shall strongly heave my breast;
           That I for poor auld Scotland's sake
           Some useful plan, or book could make,
               Or sing a sang at least.

[98]   *'nostalgie de la boue'*: a longing for the mud in the gutter, a desire
       for degradation or depravity; but Fergusson seems to adduce a
       further meaning here, a recognition of degradation as part of being
       human, a longing to recognise the earth itself as essential to
       humanity.

[99]   'Deirdre's Farewell to Scotland' is an ancient song, the text
       mediaeval, the story part of the ancient Celtic cycle of the tales of the
       Fianna. After nine years of happiness with her lover Naoise, they
       return to face their destiny in Ireland: tragic betrayal and death.
       Before leaving Scotland, Deirdre sings hauntingly of the valleys and
       mountains she loves and is about to leave. The song is discussed by
       John Purser in *Scotland's Music: A History of the Traditional and
       Classical Music of Scotland from Early Times to the Present Day*
       (Edinburgh: Mainstream, 1992; second edition, 2007) and can be

heard on *Scotland's Music* (double CD set, Linn Records CKD 008), where it is listed as 'Deirdre's Lament'. 'The Canadian Boat Song' is anonymous, first appearing in 1829 in *Blackwood's Magazine* and described as having been translated from the Gaelic of Canadian travellers of earlier times, though this has been considered as invention and more likely authorship possibly dated to the early 19th century. Neil Munro (1863–1930), novelist, poet, journalist, newspaper editor, author of the popular short stories about the small Clyde steam cargo vessel *The Vital Spark* and her skipper, Para Handy.

[100] Neil Munro, 'John o' Lorn', in *The Poetry of Neil Munro* (Edinburgh and London: Blackwood, 1931), lines 5–8:

> 'Twas for the sake o' glory, but oh! Wae upon the wars,
>   That brought my father's son to sic a day;
> I'd rather be a craven, wi' nor name, nor fame, nor scars.
>   Than turn a wanderer's heel on Moidart Bay.

[101] 'Blessing of the Road' is the first poem in Kenneth Macleod, *The Road to the Isles: Poetry, Lore, and Tradition of the Hebrides*, with an introduction by Marjory Kennedy-Fraser (Edinburgh: Robert Grant & Son, 1927), p. 23. In its entirety it runs:

> May the hills lie low,
> May the sloughs fill up
> In thy way.
>
> May all evil sleep,
> May all good awake,
> In thy way.

By closing his book with the opening poem from *The Road to the Isles*, Fergusson is perhaps signalling a continuity between the Celtic Revival of the 1890s, through the Second World War period to the future, implicitly looking forward to MacDiarmid's *In Memoriam James Joyce* (1955) and further. He is also connecting his own work to the contexts of Scotland's Celtic identity and of the radical transitional era of modernism, thereby rejecting the polarisation of sentimentalism and scientific objectivity and affirming the connectedness of 'independent art' and common humanity. This is the significance of the paradoxical proposition in the final part of his

last chapter: exile and return are both equally necessary. You see
Scotland new by leaving it and looking at it from a distance, then by
returning to live there, you can have a clearer idea of what must be
done. Fergusson's affirmation was founded upon his own experience.

J.D. Fergusson, 'The Artist's Intention' 1905

[This manifesto was published in the catalogue to Fergusson's first London exhibition. When he had his first one-man shows in Scotland, in Edinburgh and Glasgow, in 1923, it was published again as an introduction, Fergusson confirming that it 'still held good.']

As it is necessary to understand the artist's intention, in order to estimate his achievement:

He would explain –

That he is trying for truth, for reality, through light.

That to the realist in painting, light is the mystery; for form and colour which are the painter's only means of representing life, exist only on account of light.

That the only hope of giving the impression of reality is by truthful lighting.

That the painter having found the beauty of nature, ceases to be interested in the traditional beauty, the beauty of art.

Art being purely a matter of emotion, sincerity consists in being faithful to one's emotions.

As no emotion can be exactly repeated, it is hopeless to attempt to represent reality by piecing together different impressions.

To restrain an emotion is to kill it.

What may appear to be restraint may be the utmost limit of one's power.

What may appear to be the utmost limit of one's power may be restraint.

Brightness is not necessarily meretricious, nor dinginess meritorious.

It is absurd to suppose that everyone must be slow to understand – some have insight.

What is on the surface may explain everything to one with real insight.

That the artist is not attempting to compete with the completeness of the camera, nor with the accuracy of the anatomical diagram.

Genius is insight.

Responses to *Modern Scottish Painting* from Hugh MacDiarmid and Douglas Young 1944

Letter from C.M. Grieve (Hugh MacDiarmid) to J.D. Fergusson

[Hugh MacDiarmid (C.M. Grieve, 1892–1978), was a major 20th-century poet, a journalist, editor, cultural and political agitator and activist, a founding member of the National Party of Scotland in 1928, which became the Scottish National Party in 1934, and a member of the Communist Party of Great Britain. MacDiarmid was the author in the 1950s of an extended essay, *Aesthetics in Scotland*, not published fully until 1984, and the editor of *The Golden Treasury of Scottish Poetry* (1940), the first determinedly multi-lingual anthology of its kind.]

27 Arundel Drive, Battlefield, Glasgow S2

23 / 1 / 44

My dear J.D. Fergusson,

It is extremely good of you to send me this autographed copy of your book *via* our mutual friend MacLellan and I value it highly. I had already procured a copy and read it with great interest and appreciation. I hope it is going well. So far I have not seen any reviews of it.

And I hope you are going well yourself. It is too long since I've had any chance of seeing you or intervening in one of the refreshing discussions at the New Art Club. But I've been having – and am still in the throes of – a very hard time of long hours and overwork, and since the New Year I have hardly had a moment to myself at all. I can get no writing, and hardly any reading, done – nothing but my engineering work, racketting in trams there and back, eating and sleeping. What a life! And no end to it even in the most distant prospect yet!

I hope Miss Morris and yourself are not so beset by Philistia, but free to get on with creative work. Please accept, if belatedly, my best wishes to both of you for a happy and prosperous year. My wife joins me in these seasonable greetings and every good wish.

Again with my warmest thanks,

Yours,

C.M. Grieve

Letter from Douglas Young to J.D. Fergusson

[Douglas Young (1913–1973) was a poet, a classical Greek scholar and translator, leader of the Scottish National Party, 1942–1945, and famously refused conscription in the Second World War as a Scot to whom British military priorities were not, he argued, applicable. He was imprisoned and scorned. He later became Professor of Greek at the University of North Carolina, Chapel Hill, USA. The page references Young makes to the first edition have been amended here to refer to the present edition.]

Meikle Cloak, Lochwinnnoch, Renfrew county.
Tuesday 11th January 1944

Dear J.D. Fergusson,

Warmest thanks for your book on Modern Scottish Painting, which arrived here yesterday, after a cross-country run from Airdlogie. Already I have rushed through it once, and hasten to send my thanks, as a Scotsman and a freedom-wanting man, for this refreshing and stimulating expression of the Scottish view of painting, which moreover utterly corroborates the Nationalist position in all its aspects.

May I say also that, besides being based on the bedrock, it is written in a fully adequate way? Pedantic and censorious as I am I find no fault in it, although the printer might have done better.

For a running commentary I shall comment with page references. For a considered appreciation I wait till the March *Scots Independent*, February being filled up.[1]

Page 72. 'the spirit is the reality of a work of art, and ideal means not real.' For Plato, the first to boost the word Idea extensively (see J. Burnet, *Essays and Addresses*, and A.E. Taylor's paper on pre-Platonic uses), Ideas are the only true Realities, Plato would agree with your proposition, allowing for subsequent misuse of the vocabulary. I mention this point straightaway because you several times show a truly Greek attitude, e.g. p. 100 (and p. 72) in discussing what is truly a Question you are in step with Aristotle's insistence that one must καλῶς ἀπορεῖν [2] have a sense of fitness in raising problems.

p. 73 you have 'amplified and freed your idea by discussion'. Exactly the method of the Platonic διαλεκτική,[3] Dialectic.

p. 74 you never imagine you are capable of talking in absolutes. Just what Sokrates and Plato insisted on in their days.

p. 74 you are quite sure you know that people don't know about art. This goes beyond Sokrates. But Scotsmen are prone to guid conceits.

p. 75 your defiition of Snob is first-rate.

p. 75 You hint here that the notion of inevitable Progress is illusory. This point is expansible. See J.B. Bury, *History of the Idea of Progress*. And consider e.g. Scots history since 1320.

pp. 75–76 your tilting at 'skill in copying appearances' is exactly Plato's deprecation of Imitation, μίμησις.[4]

p. 77 Thank you for your emphasis on the Scottish character as permanent and inherent, This is 'la voix du sang'. I am against historical relativity, as Acton was, and wrote my 'Quislings' thus.[5]

pp. 78–79 Thank you for stating that the craze for authority is 'inexcusable in a Scot'. It is also dubiously Christian. Possibly it is mainly Jewish. The same fight went on in 'Classical' Greek days between Law and Nature, νόμος and φύσις.[6] Perhaps it is an eternal fight.

p. 80 you have exactly put the experts in their due place.

Thank you also for your counter-blast to 'Education'. Epicurus advised his pupils to hoist the main sail and flee from every form of 'Education'. Tom Johnston wants compulsory continuation classes.

p. 84 I dislike your word 'Modern', but think it helps to sell the book. However I approve your assertion of what 'progressive' should mean, 'liberating by the persistent attempt to find the fundamentals'. This is again Plato, e.g. the doctrines of Re-discovery ἀναμνήσις[7] in the 'Meno'.

pp. 85–86 Thank you once more for your expounding what is Scottish, 'expressing themselves freely, which in art means honestly', 'concerned with the quality and substance of things', having (p. 86) a 'feeling for the fullness of things'.

p. 87 your passing comments on 'the modern Athenianism of the East' rouses in me doubts (1) exactly what you refer to, (2) whether you are correct. I can however see a reference in which you are right, viz. The 'Greek Williams' influence in Edinburgh.

p. 88 The insistence on 'ambiance' could be developed.

p. 89 I don't entirely agree about the wrong tack being taken by the East Coasters specially. It is true that the division in Scotland is East-West, an atmospheric division caused by differences in rainfall, not the boosted Highland-Lowland, which is false from top to bottom. But Edinburgh is not the whole of the East. Forbes White was East Coast. Stewart Carmichael and David Foggie[8] could quarrel with you on this with chapter and verse. It interests me that in my own connection my great-granduncle Simpson had dozens of French Impressionists in his house at Broughty Ferry in the '70s and '80s, my step-granduncle Greig passed his time between Paris and Tayport and bought and practised Impressionism, and my second-cousin Louis Graux, grandson of my granduncle W.O.D.

MODERN SCOTTISH PAINTING

Young who went to Paris 100 years ago, carries on today in Paris a somewhat realist impressionism, which seems to me to combine his French background with old Scots East Coast traditions, seen e.g. in Allan Ramsay, Wilkie, Raeburn, and perhaps Jamieson. I think 18th-century Scots painting had far more of the Glasgow School qualities than is implied by your handling of it here, admittedly cursory. Fundamentally, however, I respect your point that Glasgow was realist, through its artisan background (p. 90 and p. 91), where the culturally dominant Edinburgh was imitative and academic. Dundee and Aberdeen were also artisan.

p. 89 You think of Picasso in connection with Forbes White anent 'the lens of an analytical mind'. Is it not true of Velasquez and his master Greco? Which again brings in the Greek connection.

p. 92 Your reference to Ethel Walker induces me to mention a Mr Dunn, who works near here. A Glasgow businessman till 40, he then developed a craze for painting, and started with the glaucous and subfusc tones of Corot. Today at over 80 nothing contents him but magenta and gamboge. He lives at a farmhouse three miles from Lochwinnoch, c/o Forrester, Conveth farm, Tandalmuir, by Lochwinnoch. If I am still here during the early summer I shall try and arrange for you to see him, as I am sure you would be intrigued. If not, perhaps you could remember him and where he is.

p. 94 Robert Hurd [written in margin: R. Hurd, 49 George Square, Edinburgh] and Catherine Carswell were or are collaborating in a book on C.R. Mackintosh, and you might get in touch with them. Patrick Geddes is similarly neglected here, but kenspeckle in USA e.g. with Lewis Mumford.[9]

p. 95 you cast aspersions on the pre-Calvinist sect, as 'lacking in the feeling of responsibility', and at pp. 108–9 doubt whether they were reliable. Now what about Louis XI, the canniest of French kings, taking them for his bodyguard? Have you read the Book of the Dean of Lismore? Or considered the Brehon Laws? Do they strike you as products of a society of irresponsible or unreliable men? Wm Wallace was punctilious enough, e.g. his safe-conduct to the monks of Hexham was valid for one year only, if I remember right. I still have to know that Calvinism did any good at all ever.

p. 96 your comment on 'trying to clear our heads, i.e. to be free and not slaves, Let's be Scots' all chimes in delightfully with a similar call of my own in another connection, e.g. in the article on conscription in the *S.I.* of March 1940, sub fin. (see the enclosed 'Scot's Free Fight', p.8). This is the sort of thing I mean, when I say your book corroborates the Nationalist position all over.

p. 98 you write 'The real artist is always a research man, and not an imitator of recognised forms.' This chimes in with Hugh MacDiarmid's *Lucky Poet* manifesto, and the infrequence with which he returns to traditional forms.

Very timeous also your statement that all real precision is human. Sophokles says the same in a chorus of the *Antigone*, πολλὰ τὰ δεινά, κοὐδὲν ἀνθρώπου δεινότερον πέλει, 'many are the marvels, but none more marvellous than man.'[10] Where the word for 'marvellous' also means 'clever, uncanny'.

p. 98 your distinction of 'practical experience' and 'imagination' is Plato's between the craftsman's knack τριβή and the artist's τέχνη creative imagination.[11]

p. 99 Kipling was half Scots.

p. 100 For Paris as 'simply a place of freedom' for ideas, cf Gibbon's account of Julian the Apostate at Lutetia Parisiorum. Or St Paul at Athens.

p. 104 your reference to Picasso's use of representational forms in non-plausible juxtapositions reminds me not only of Manet's picnic breakfast (with the irrelevantly nude lady), very 'épatant' in its day, but also of the Book of Kells, of Greek Geometric pots, and of a Chinese painting on silk I saw in Ferenc Hopp's villa in the Andrassy Utca at Budapest, where one saw at first glance a mere pattern, elegantly symmetrical, as in an oriental rug, and only gradually discovered it was an intricate combination of every kind of animal, portrayed in the most realist way, rolling about as if convulsed with laughter 'a perdre haleine'. But unplausible juxtaposition is unlikely to be fundamentally true. And truth is right with a kilt, but a lum-hat is not.

p.110 Thank you for your realisation that 'there is a power in love, in good will' etc. Dante 'amor che muove il sole ed altre stelle'. Scots Calvinism has lacked nothing so much as precisely this, the 'Charity' of I Corinthians xiii, as usually interpreted by Christians, whatever the Judaic background of it may be.

p. 126 'The artist is concerned with ultimate truth, not with final polish'. Again Plato's distinction, and also Greco's.

'The artist to live must go on'. This is the Greek idea of freedom too. Ἐλευθερία means 'up-and-coming-ness'.[12]

p. 126 Your thought on the 'courage of submitting to his emotions' chimes in amazingly with an important pronouncement of Hume's, the more notable that it was made in the 'Age of Reason', viz. 'Reason is the servant of the passions'. This shows again how you are on the bedrock of what is Scottish, permanently, inherently.

p. 127 The Dutch Calvinists starving Rembrandt. I shall put on your track Miss M.P. Ramsay, author of *Calvin and Art*. In fact you might get her to talk to the New Art Club, 11 Saxe-Coburg Place, Edinburgh.

English live and let live. Cf. William Johnstone *Creative Art in England*, who thinks it is Anglo-Saxon, when actually it is Celtic. Same mistake made by Gavin Bone in his 'Anglo-Saxon Poetry'. Both men Scots Celts, and true to the voice of their instinct in the recognition of kinship, but both hopelessly at sea historically, just as Burns was kept out of his cultural heritage, as you so well show, p. 142 Can you stir up the Saltire Society to put out, if need be subsidised, a proper anthology of Scots poetry in all our tongues, better than Grieve's *Golden Treasury*, instead of frittering away funds on expensive useless 3/6 pansy booklets, and the crowing fatuity of a 1/- chapbook with 4 poems?

Now we must hope that this book will be swiftly remaindered, so that young artists can afford to buy it and take it in. Till then we must wish that the better-supplied will absorb its doctrine and prepare themselves to shell out for the products of the young artists. But even if nobody reads or buys it, it is still there as a land-mark showing a new stage in the re-awakening of the Scots to fundamentals, a process which there is good prospect of this book and your other activities stimulating briskly along the right road.

My wife will be reading it soon. She has lately lost her mother, and been otherwise prevented from doing much with paint, but I am hopeful she will get going again before long, and quite think she may one day hit out on a trail of her own. On her behalf also I must thank you for the book and the good wishes with it.

I see little prospect meantime of coming to the New Art Club, indeed all my affairs are a bit unsettled, but I shall look forward very much to talk with you some day somewhere. Please give my kindest regards also to Margaret Morris.

Yours for Scotland

Douglas Young

Notes to Appendix 2

[1]   The *Scots Independent* is a monthly political newspaper founded in 1926, and claims to be the oldest political newspaper in Europe.

[2]   καλῶς ἀπορεῖν (kalos aporein), 'be in difficulties (or stuck) in a good way': i.e. more or less as Young glosses in the text.

[3]   διαλεκτική (dialektikē), 'dialectic': skill through or art of conversation; Young is talking about the Socratic method.

[4]   μίμησις (mimēsis), 'imitation': Plato's [negative] discussion of this is a major part of the *Republic*; poetry, and especially drama, is a major exponent of imitation, so these are bad things, for Plato.

[5]   Harold Acton (1904–94) was a poet, novelist, historian, well-known aesthete, dilettante and Sinophile, respected as a scholar of Italian history, who described his chief occupation as 'hunting the philistines'. In an article, 'Quislings in Scotland: A Review of the Fifth Column' in the *Scots Independent* (August, 1942), Young argued that anyone supporting the 1707 Act of Union and its legacy was by definition 'opposed to the freedom of the Scottish nation through democratic self-government'.

[6]   νόμος and φύσις (nomos and physis), law/convention and 'nature': this is a major opposition in 5th-century Greek thought, especially around the nature of society and justice: if society is a construct, what follows? Various answers to this are given by the Greek sophists, and Plato is responding to those, again particularly in the *Republic*, where discussion of a particularly nasty rendering of that opposition is the focus of book one.

[7]   Stewart Carmichael (1867–1950) and David Foggie (1878–1948) are discussed in Alexander Moffat and Alan Riach, *Arts of Resistance: Poets, Portraits and Landscapes of Modern Scotland* (Edinburgh: Luath Press, 2008), pp. 109–110.

[8]   ἀναμνήσις (anamnēsis), literally, 'remembering'.

[9]   Robert Hurd (1905–63, see Notes to *Modern Scottish Painting*, above, note 90; Catherine Carswell (1879–1946), Scottish novelist, journalist, critic, literary historian and biographer, author of *Open the Door!* (1920) and *Robert Burns* (1930); C.R. Mackintosh, see Notes to *Modern Scottish Painting*, note 46, above; Patrick Geddes (1854–

1932), pioneering biologist, sociologist and town planner; Lewis
Mumford (1895–1990), American historian, sociologist and literary
critic.

[10] πολλὰ τὰ δεινά, κοὐδὲν ἀνθρώπου δεινότερον πέλει (polla ta deina,
kouden anthrōpou deinoteron pelei) Sophocles, *Antigone*, 332–3 (first
stasimon). The translation is as given by Young, although it might be
more correct to say 'and none...' rather than 'but none...' This is the
beginning of a famous choral ode: it starts celebrating man's
achievement (as opposed to the conventional nature of society) but
ends on a somewhat more disturbing note (which is rather elided here,
as it often is).

[11] τριβή and the artist's τέχνη (tribē and tekhnē: the former suggests
something almost mechanically repetitive, the latter's basic sense is
art/craft/skill)

[12] Ἐλευθερία (eleutheria) 'freedom': the meaning 'up-and-comingness'
seems to be a reference to a connection with forms of the verb 'to go'
such as ἐλεύσομαι (future, 'I will go') and a rare causal verb ἐλεύθω
(I make go).

J.D. Fergusson,
'The Scotland I'd Like to See' 1946

[This essay was published in the periodical *The New Scot,* October 1946.]

The Scotland I'd like to see from the Art point of view. I'm not much interested in what is generally called Art. Except for myself, I don't know what *is* Art – or what isn't. I can't define Art or demonstrate what it is. What I am interested in, is *freedom*, but can I define freedom? No, but quite recent happenings in relation to Prestwick and porridge, should have proved even to the most stupid – that it is what Scotland hasn't got.

The Scotland I'd like to see would be a Scotland full of patriotic Scots – men and women – here the person with what's called the 'International' point of view, stops reading and says, 'Oh yes! Flag waving, tartan, kilts, Gaelic and broad Scots.'

We have been told that the Englishman's idea is to dress for dinner every evening, even in the jungle – in order to impress the Natives, it obviously has impressed the Natives of Scotland.

Would the Scotsman put on a kilt? – The mere idea makes him laugh, but why? Can any sane person believe that the starched shirt and black dress suit is a costume of more character or better looking? No, it is simply that it's 'not done' – not done by the British he means, that is by the British Empire, for he knows that anything that is British counts all over the British Empire, that the kilt is a fancy dress, for St Andrew's Day (unless regimental).

In my lifetime I have watched an influence *seeping* into Scotland, that has convinced the Scots that anything with bright colour is vulgar (why not black and grey flowers?), that tartan, Highland Costume and Bagpipes are absurd, except at Highland Games. That the black dress suit and the starched shirt is the only costume for a gentleman.

But to come back to the 'Scotland I'd like to see' full of patriotic Scots, kilts, tartan, bagpipes, etc, are certainly part of patriotic expression, and from my point of view a very interesting and valuable part.

But that's not what I'm thinking about when I talk of patriotism, by a patriotic Scotsman, I mean a Scotsman who loves his country, and I use the word 'love' as I would in relation to my Father and Mother, or a man's love for his wife and children which means to me a desire to do everything to make them happy, healthy and good looking. And to be willing to fight anyone that attempts in any way to interfere with their freedom to enjoy life in all its tremendous possibilities.

It is quite possible to turn Scotland into one of the most wonderful and vital countries in the world, but it has to be done by Scots.

The Scot has a country that should be his very own Motherland, he should govern it in a way that would preserve it as a part of the world for himself and his descendants for ever – he should be watching that nothing is done by the *quislings*, and the thoughtless to prevent it steadily becoming more beautiful and more worth living in, he should be terribly distressed to see the best men and women gladly leaving their country, which has been made uninhabitable for anyone with a desire to enjoy life, and produce new ideas and new things – he should find the reason for this and deal with the disease (which it is) as TB, typhoid, etc, should be dealt with – he should be ashamed of the slums, infuriated at needless poverty – he should refuse to allow anyone to destroy the natural beauty of his country, and should insist that everyone should have a chance to enjoy the natural beauty. He should defend his country to his last breath – when attacked, but not wait for a world war to show his patriotism – he should train himself to distinguish between people who are trying to do his country good, and those who are exploiting it for their own benefit. He should be International, and realise that he can't be International without being National in the real sense.

By International I mean, being willing to learn from any country which is quite different from imitating other countries – he should be able to take ideas from other countries, *digest* them, and convert them into Scottish energy suitable for his own land, and his own people, he should not try to nourish himself on stuff pre-digested and dumped on him – he should read the Arbroath Manifesto, in short he should be patriotic.

I admire tremendously the fierce patriotism of the French – I was

   MODERN SCOTTISH PAINTING

thrilled by their demonstration of it in the liberation film, *I'm International*, few Scots are more so, but I'm first a Scot then an International.

What has all this to do with Art? – with what is generally called Art – *nothing at all*, with the creation of a condition which might and should produce Art – *everything*.

Art, as I understand it, cannot be produced by a nation lacking the spirit of freedom, a servile nation produces servile Art, *in my opinion* Art is not a matter of skill, but entirely a matter of free expression. Let's have freedom in Scotland and Art *may appear*, I mean really Scottish Art, at present I think Scotland is producing *British Imperial Art*, that is, Art that is doing its best to fit in with the Imperial control.

It cannot be expected that people not concerned with Art, should be aware of the position of the artist in Scotland. One night at a lecture I gave, the chairman quite seriously said 'but surely Mr Fergusson the President of the Royal Academy is the highest authority on Art?'

That was a very honest and natural thing to say, like saying 'surely the Prime Minister of Britain is the greatest authority on government?' The first point is that Art to my chairman was British Art, and that's where the British people are in relation to Art – they of course haven't thought about it at all.

The position *is* that Art all over the British Empire, is controlled directly or indirectly by 'The Royal Academy', 'South Kensington School of Art' and 'The Royal Academy School'.

'The Royal Scottish Academy', the 'Glasgow Institute' and all other British Academies are stepping stones to the Royal Academy.

All Art education in the British Empire is dominated by 'South Kensington School', teachers have been sent to India to teach the 'poor Indian' Art, not to conform to the rules of these institutions is to be an outsider all over the British Empire – so naturally the Scottish artist if he wants money has to accept the Imperial control; he has to become British, which most of them are very glad to do. The tragedy of the 'Glasgow School' was that most of them did, perhaps not gladly, but in the hope of having more recognition. *On the Continent in Paris for example, British Imperial Art counts for nothing.* The Royal Academy is British, not English – the real English Artists founded the 'New English Art Club' in opposition to it. But this has I fear become another stepping stone to the Royal Academy.

The Imperial pressure is too great, most artists have given in. An Independent Art Society was started in London, but couldn't continue for want of a gallery. The present curator of the National Gallery, London, has an excellent article on the position of the artist in a recent *Listener*. 'A Square Deal for the Artist' by Phillip Hendy, *The Listener* (29 July 1946).

Glasgow, until the opening of 'The New Art Club' (six years ago) had no place where an independent artist without money could show his work. A dealer's gallery costs one pound a day, printing extra.

The New Art Club has a permanent exhibition changed each month, *no selecting committee*, any work by a member is hung – the subscription is one pound a year, and a shilling for each picture hung.

There is an exhibition of a selection of the Club's work called 'The New Scottish Group' at the McClure Gallery, Glasgow, for a month, every May. This is a step towards freedom.

The Scotland I'd like to see from the Art point of view, would be a Scotland liberated from the stranglehold of Academic Art, and where there was, if not a square deal, at least a fair fighting chance for the Independent Artist.

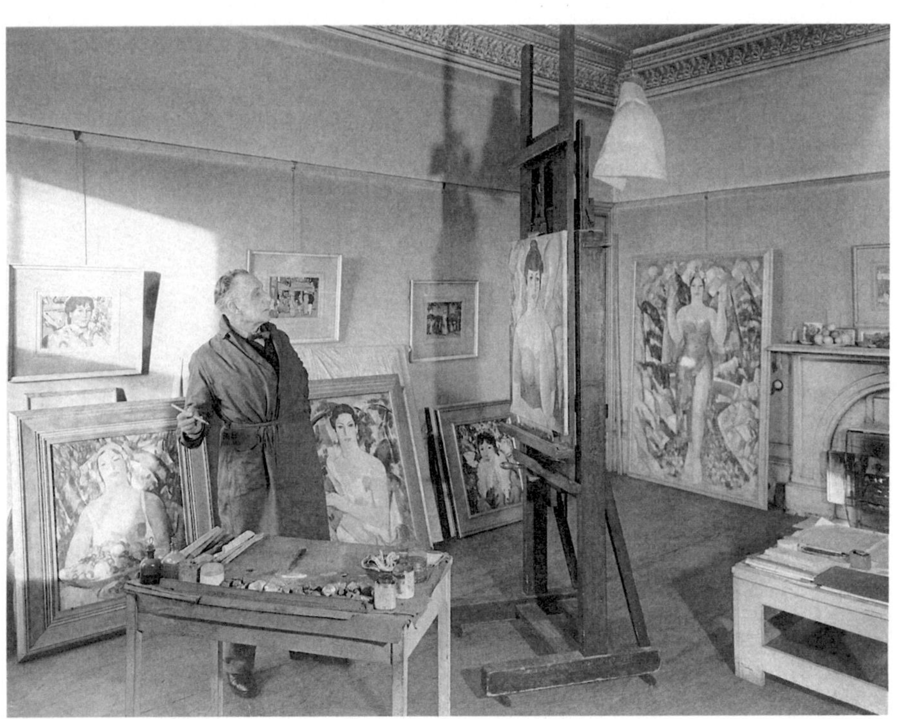

Davie, Alan 25, 44
Davison, George 88, 90, 155
Debussy, Claude 33
Degas, Edgar 27–28
Delacroix, Eugène 27, 154
Díaz, Narcisse Virgilio 88, 156
Dobson, Frank 163
Dorn, Edward 159
Dott, Aitken 153
Dott, Peter McOmish 83, 153
Douglas, Gavin 161
Dunbar, William 102–103, 113, 128,
    141–143, 159, 161, 167–168
Duncan, Isadora 33–34
Duncan, Raymond 33

Einstein, Albert 123
Eisler, Hanns 30
Elderfield, John 29
Eliot, T.S. 37, 47
Emanuel, Walter 133, 165
Epicurus 176

Faunce, Sarah 28
Fauré, Gabriel 25
Fergusson, Robert 113, 127–128, 142,
    146, 155
Finlay, Ian 53
Finlay, Ian Hamilton 50
Flam, Jack D. 15
Foggie, David 176, 181
Fox, Douglas 151
French, Annie 153
Freud, Lucian 54
Frobenius, Leo 74, 151
Fry, Michael 48

Galileo 96
Gauguin, Paul 27
Gauld, David 153
Geddes, Patrick 13, 35, 39, 51, 177,
    181–182
Géricault, Théodore 27
Gèrôme, Jean-Léon 21–22, 86–87, 89,
    116, 154
Gibbon, Edward 178
Gibbon, Lewis Grassic (James Leslie
    Mitchell) 36
Gillies, William 36, 44

Ginner, Charles 163
Giorgione 86, 154
Goodsir Smith, Sydney 12
Graham, W.S. 12
Graux, Louis 176
Gray, Alasdair 12
Greco 177
Gregory, Lady Augusta 157
Guthrie, Sir James 37, 81, 83, 86, 93, 153

Hardie, Gwen 54
Hardie, William 53
Harris, Frank 59–60
Harrower, I.W. 88, 90
Hay, George Campbell 12
Hendy, Phillip 186
Hendry, J.F. 12
Henry, George 37, 83, 153
Henryson, Robert 161
Hermann, Josef 24, 50
Hitler, Adolf 149
Hockney, David 54
Hopp, Ferenc 178
Hornel, E.A. 37, 83, 153
Hume, David 44, 179
Hunter, Leslie 81
Hurd, Robert 167, 177

Ingres, Jean-Auguste-Dominique 27, 86,
    154
Israëls, Isaac Lazarus 156
Israëls, Jozef 88, 156

Jamieson, Alexander 163, 177
Jefferson, Thomas 161
Johnson, Samuel 168
Johnston, Tom 176
Johnstone, William 36, 44–45, 179
Joyce, James 25, 37, 47, 52, 150
Jung, Carl 16

Kafka, Franz 47
Kandinsky, Wassily 15
Kauffer, E. McKnight 163
Kennedy, William 87, 90, 153, 155
Kennedy-Fraser, Marjory 150, 169
King, Jessie M. 153
Kipling, Rudyard 95, 99–100, 105, 150,
    158, 160, 165, 178

Luath Press Limited
committed to publishing well written books worth reading

LUATH PRESS takes its name from Robert Burns, whose little collie Luath (*Gael.*, swift or nimble) tripped up Jean Armour at a wedding and gave him the chance to speak to the woman who was to be his wife and the abiding love of his life. Burns called one of 'The Twa Dogs' Luath after Cuchullin's hunting dog in Ossian's *Fingal*. Luath Press was established in 1981 in the heart of Burns country, and now resides a few steps up the road from Burns' first lodgings on Edinburgh's Royal Mile.
Luath offers you distinctive writing with a hint of unexpected pleasures.

Most bookshops in the UK, the US, Canada, Australia, New Zealand and parts of Europe either carry our books in stock or can order them for you. To order direct from us, please send a £sterling cheque, postal order, international money order or your credit card details (number, address of cardholder and expiry date) to us at the address below. Please add post and packing as follows: UK – £1.00 per delivery address; overseas surface mail – £2.50 per delivery address; overseas airmail – £3.50 for the first book to each delivery address, plus £1.00 for each additional book by airmail to the same address. If your order is a gift, we will happily enclose your card or message at no extra charge.

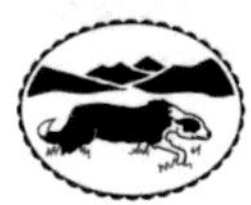

Luath Press Limited
543/2 Castlehill
The Royal Mile
Edinburgh EH1 2ND
Scotland

Telephone: 0131 225 4326 (24 hours)
email: sales@luath.co.uk
Website: www.luath.co.uk